MEN AT WAR 1914-1918

THE LEGACY OF THE GREAT WAR

A series sponsored by the Historial de la grande guerre, Péronne, Somme

General Editor
JAY WINTER

F o r t h c o m i n g

Antoine Prost
IN THE WAKE OF WAR
'Les Anciens Combattants' and French Society 1914-1939

Rosa Maria Bracco
MERCHANTS OF HOPE
British Middlebrow Writers and the First World War, 1919-1939

Patrick Fridenson
THE FRENCH HOME FRONT 1914-1918

Gerald Feldman
ARMY, INDUSTRY AND LABOR IN GERMANY 1914-1918

MEN AT WAR 1914-1918
National Sentiment and Trench Journalism in France
during the First World War

STÉPHANE AUDOIN–ROUZEAU

Translated by
HELEN McPHAIL

BERG
PROVIDENCE · OXFORD

English edition
first published in 1992 by
Berg Publishers Limited
Editorial offices:
165 Taber Avenue, Providence, RI 02906, USA
150 Cowley Road, Oxford, OX4 1JJ, UK

English edition © 1992
Originally published as *14–18 Les Combattants des tranchées*
Translated from the French by permission of the publishers
Armand Colin, Paris

Library of Congress Cataloging-in-Publication Data
Audoin-Rouzeau, Stéphane.
[14–18, les combattants des tranchées, English]
Men at war, 1914 – 1918: national sentiment and trench journalism in France during the
First World War / Stéphane Audoin–Rouzeau.
p. cm. – (The Legacy of the Great War)
Translation of : 14 – 18, les combattants des tranchées.
ISBN 0 –85496–673–0 / 0–85496-333–2 (pb)
1. World War, 1914–1918 – France. 2. World War, 1914 – 1918 – Psychological aspects.
3. Soldiers – France – Psychology. 4. World War, 1914–1918 – Journalism, Military –
France. I. Title. II. Series.
D548.A8313 1991
940.4' 1244 dc20 91–45272
CIP

British Library Cataloguing in Publication Data
Audoin–Rouzeau, Stéphane
Men at war 1914–1918: National sentiment and trench journalism in France during the
First World War. – (The legacy of the Great War)
I. Title II. Series
944.081

ISBN 0–85496–673–0
ISBN 0–85496–333–2 (pb)

Printed in Great Britain by
Billing & Sons Ltd, Worcester

C O N T E N T S

ILLUSTRATIONS

To
PIERRE BAZIN
2nd Lieutenant in the 336th French
Infantry Regiment in 1915

1890–1989

Translator's Note

Two words which appear repeatedly throughout this book have been left in French: *le poilu* is the universal word for the ordinary French soldier of the First World War, the equivalent of the British army's Tommy Atkins; *le cafard* is a deep melancholy, an over-whelming sense of depression and misery which has no precise linguistic equivalent in the English vocabulary of the Great War. Neither word can be translated into English without losing its specifically French connotations. The phrase *On les aura*! also remains untranslated: it indicates 'We'll get them!' conveying high determination and confidence, and is appropriate in both formal and informal contexts.

Helen McPhail

Foreword

One of the most distinctive features of French historical scholarship is its contribution to the study of *mentalité*, or the mental furniture of populations in the past. *'Mentalité'* in this discourse means visceral commitments rather than ideologies, unspoken assumptions rather than political or social programmes. When Stéphane Audoin-Rouzeau writes of 'national sentiment' as the tie which bound together French soldiers and civilians during the Great War, he means more than patriotism, and certainly more than the exaggerated swagger of propaganda. The solidarity of the French nation in the 1914–18 war bore no resemblance to the corrupt journalism, the *bourrage de crâne*, or eyewash of the day. Its sources lay elsewhere, above all in the *mentalité* of ordinary soldiers, the *poilus* of the Great War.

To find out why small groups of men in desolate pockets of resistance around Verdun held out, why the overwhelming mass of soldiers did not give up a belief in victory, despite anger at futile offensives and profound annoyance at civilian ignorance and privilege, Audoin-Rouzeau has turned to trench journalism. These small broadsheets and occasional publications constitute a set of contemporary sources of striking immediacy and authenticity. They appeared throughout the French army, just as they did in British and Dominion forces.[1] Their origins are unclear, but they certainly did not arise from the desire of High Command to provide information or amusement to the men in the ranks. These newspapers were the view from the bottom up, not from the top down. Their readership was ordinary soldiers, most of whom were farmers or farm labourers. The 'journalists' were front-line soldiers too, but it

---

1. On which see the outstanding study of John Fuller, *Troop Morale and Popular Culture in the British and Dominion Armies 1914–1918* (Oxford, Clarendon Press 1991).

is clear from their diction and the cadences of their prose that they were overwhelmingly middle-class and urban in origin.

Why should we accept the view, propounded by the author, that this middle-class journalism successfully spoke for the French nation in arms as a whole? This is the central problem in all histories of *mentalité*: what constitutes representative evidence? One reason for confidence is the striking consistency of the findings of this pioneering work with those of other studies, describing similar attitudes and responses for a wide range of soldiers. A valuable analysis of French postal censorship in 1916 confirms the picture presented by Audoin-Rouzeau, as do other accounts of the French nation at war.[2]

There were, to be sure, other languages and other voices heard in wartime France. Pacifism was neither invisible nor mute. But when set against the sheer weight of evidence provided by Audoin-Rouzeau in support of his thesis of *sentiment national* as an irreducible core of wartime commitment, we can understand better the isolation of the few pacifists with the courage to speak out against the continuation of the war.[3] We can also understand why the mutinies of 1917 after the disastrous Chemin des Dames offensives, did relatively little to undermine the commitment of ordinary French soldiers to see the war through to victory.

Much still needs to be done to explore the question as to the compatibility of what Audoin-Rouzeau refers to as 'national sentiment' with other identities, just as vigorous and valuable. Class-consciousness was not the antithesis of 'national sentiment'; indeed it is impossible to understand the tenacity of populations without recognising the compatibility of national and class awareness, both among soldiers and civilians. The social history of wartime is the negotiation and renegotiation of commitment to nation and commitment to local and sectional loyalties. Sometimes they conflicted; most of the time they overlapped. But when they collided on the home front, as in the strikes of 1917, 'national sentiment' did not

2. Annick Cochet, 'L'Opinion et le moral des soldats français en 1916 d'après les archives du contrôle postal', Thèse du troisième cycle, University of Paris X, 1986; see also her article, 'Les Paysans sur le front en 1916', *Bulletin du Centre d'Histoire de la France Contemporaine*, no. 3, (1982), pp. 37–48; Jean-Jacques Becker, *The Great War and the French People* (Leamington Spa, Berg, 1986); and David Englander, 'The French Soldier, 1914–18', *French History*, no.1 (1987).
3. See Thierry Bonzon and Jean-Louis Robert (eds), *Nous crions grâce. 154 lettres de pacifistes juin–novembre 1916* (Paris, Editions Ouvrières, 1989).

vanish. What was contested was the right of employers to determine what sacrifices had to be made for victory.

Such sacrifices paled into insignificance when placed against the crushing reality of trench warfare. Here Audoin-Rouzeau rightly emphasises the moral language of the front, the indictment of the *embusqués*, the shirkers, who complained about shortages while, 100 kilometres from Paris, thousands of men were being mutilated and maimed. And they were the lucky ones. Above all, Audoin-Rouzeau's book is a collage of the moral language of ordinary men in uniform, a language which expressed their anger at the unwillingness or incapacity of many civilians to understand their world. But their words also harboured a fascination with, indeed a love for, civilian life, a commitment to their villages and towns, their pastures and shops, and above all to their families. It was for them that they fought, and to them that they longed to return. It is Audoin-Rouzeau's achievement to bring us closer to their hopes, their fears, their humanity.

J.M. Winter
Pembroke College, Cambridge

Introduction

Is there anything new to be said about the French soldiers of 1914–18? Reading the hundreds of first-hand accounts written by the soldiers themselves, it is easy to feel that we know all about them: yet the soldiers of the Great War remain History's unknowns.

The bulk of the eight million men mobilised between 1914 and 1918 continue to elude us precisely because the veterans' own memoirs have provided a misleadingly exhaustive impression. The major drawback of accounts written after the war is the distortion of memory, and certain realities have been obscured because veterans have deliberately presented themselves as the only true historians of their war experiences. Much time passed before others dared approach such a subject.

Further, the Second World War overshadowed the war of 1914–18 just as the latter pushed the preceding ordeal, the 1870–1 war, into the background. Because the soldiers' written history of the Great War has not been reappraised as thoroughly as it deserves, many clichés still persist about the men who experienced trench warfare.

Some aspects of their experience are now emerging from these shadows, however. Troops from Languedoc, French units sent to the Far East or to Italy and colonial troops brought in to fight on French soil, have all been studied and written about in depth.[1] Certain periods of the war have been closely analysed, such as the disastrous weeks at the outbreak of war or the mutinies in 1917. Yet

1. Jules Maurin, *Armée–Guerre–Société. Soldats languedociens (1889–1919)*, Paris, Sorbonne, 1982; Marc Michel, 'Mythes et réalités du concours colonial: soldats et travailleurs d'Outre-mer dans la guerre française', in *Les Sociétés européennes et la guerre de 1914–1918*, ed. Jean-Jacques Becker and Stéphane Audoin-Rouzeau, Centre d'Histoire de la France Contemporaine, Université de Paris–Nanterre, 1990, pp.393–407; Patrick Facon, 'Les Soldats expatriés: Orient et Italie, 1915–1918', in Becker and Audoin-Rouzeau, *Les Sociétés européennes*, pp.385–92.

these have always been specific cases and exceptional circumstances. The ordinary French soldier and the banality of his daily war have remained out of reach: this is the individual we now seek out.

For many years the only veterans to write about their war experiences were men from prosperous or cultured backgrounds. Now we are turning to personal accounts of soldiers from the popular classes, both urban and rural, as interest shifts to these more numerous and less well-known categories of fighting men. The manifold individual destinies and the diversity of social, geographic and cultural origins are now less well concealed by the homogenising mould of the army. It remains true, however, that the universally shared body of soldiers' beliefs and instinctive reactions constituted a common ground for soldiers, unifying their individual attitudes and reactions. It is to this common intellectual and emotional property that we must look for the answer to a question which has never been answered satisfactorily: how to explain the French soldier's extraordinary tenacity for more than four years, in the face of a war the outcome of which was unclear until the summer of 1918, and despite the terrible physical and mental conditions of trench warfare. The key to this extraordinary endurance must be sought in their mentality, and its sources in the soldiers' psychological world. In what ways did they feel that they were part of the nation and their own community? What were the bonds linking them to those they were defending? What was their image of the enemy and what meaning did they attach to what they had to endure? Our understanding of the sources of the Allied victory of 1918 depends in part on the answers to these questions.

Nothing can be undertaken without a very thorough reappraisal of documentary sources. Primary sources must be traced: eyewitness accounts written on the spot and raw documentation. Trench newspapers, hitherto largely ignored, offer fresh perspectives. They were written there and then, and were unlikely to suffer from the distorting effects of recollection. True, they cannot constitute the sole source of information about the men of 1914–18; every source has its limitations, its gaps and its pitfalls, and the trench press is no exception. The trench newspapers should be compared with other written source material, but they offer several lines of immediate inquiry which throw new light on the soldiers of the Great War.

As we lose the last survivors, it is with this essential reappraisal of their history in mind, and in homage to what they accomplished, that this present work has been undertaken.

~1~

Trench Newspapers

Quantity and Range

The 'war of movement' came to an end on the western front towards the end of 1914 without achieving a decisive result. This was when the first soldiers' newspapers appeared. Their numbers grew as a great mass of men was henceforward bogged down in an interminable 'war of position'. The long-drawn-out ordeal, the combatants' isolation and the need to sustain their morale also brought newspapers to the surface. The 'front-line press' in both the Austrian and the German armies was primarily official in inspiration, generally edited by staff officers specifically detailed for the task. Each German army corps thus enjoyed a high-quality publication, often lavishly illustrated, corresponding to some extent to the French *Bulletin des Armées de la République*. The German troops' distance from home and the difficulties of distributing their national newspapers made this type of paper essential, but the Germans were not alone in having newspapers printed specifically for them. For similar reasons of distance the American troops and Russian units operating on the French front enjoyed the same service.

None the less, although newspapers prepared *by* the combatants themselves rather than *for* them were not totally unknown on the German front, they were much more characteristic of the Allied armies. Though few in number, the Belgian troops, totally cut off from their own German-occupied country, set up many publications of this type. English and Italian units also produced a considerable number, but the majority of the trench newspapers were of French origin. Papers were produced by prisoners, wounded men, troops operating on the eastern or Italian fronts, by sailors, airmen, the artillery, engineers, infantry, some for a handful of men and others for a whole division: the range is considerable.

Some titles were clearly produced by troops in the front line, while others appear to have been edited in much less dangerous conditions. The editorials themselves frequently agonised over this question of 'authenticity' and spent much time justifying their headline of 'front-line' paper:

Despite its assured appearance, *L'Echo de Tranchées-ville* is truly a paper of the front, which in places is no more than 10 or 15 metres from the enemy lines. (*L'Echo de Tranchées-ville*, 5 August 1915)

Contrary to what some others may think, *Le Ver luisant* is prepared exclusively by hand at the front, either in the trenches or 'at rest', during 'guard' duties or in the rare moments of leisure. (*Le Ver luisant*, July 1916)

This little front-line newspaper consists of strictly original material and has been entirely produced in the trenches. (*Les Echos du Plateau de Craonne*, 15 October 1916)

Other newspapers went further, not hesitating to claim a certain degree of privileged authenticity: '

Remember this! *Le Sourire de l'escouade*, the organ of the 1st Company of the 19th Infantry Regiment, is one of the rare trench papers printed *at the front* and written in the trenches ... with a circulation of three hundred copies. (*Le Sourire de l'escouade*, 5 October 1916)

Le Crocodile is the only paper to be written, laid out and produced at the front. It wishes, despite difficulties, to retain this badge of originality. This issue is printed in an underground shelter 1,400 metres from the Boches. (*Le Crocodile*, 10 and 25 August, 1917)

Such difficulties encouraged regular comment on editorial 'working conditions':

The proofs of this issue were corrected in the ruins of a henceforward famous village a few metres from the Boches and under heavy shelling. (*Le Poilu du 37*, April 1916)

1er année N° 1 — Le plus répandu dans tout le secteur — 5c — Mars 1915

L'ECHO DU RAVIN

Journal du 41e B.on de Chasseurs… Relié par fils barbelés avec les Boches.

À nos lecteurs

La Direction de ce Journal n'ayant pu réunir les fonds nécessaires au lancement d'un nouvel organe de presse, s'est vue obligée à ses lecteurs, de le leur présenter sous une forme à rudimentaire… Nous avons tenté de nous mettre en rapports avec une maison d'édition. Nos recherches n'ont point abouti. D'ailleurs, nous n'avons trouvé dans la région que des sapins, des routes, des tranchées… et des Boches !

Des fouilles minutieuses dans nos havresacs ne nous ont nullement révélé la présence de minerais ou de rotatives. Force nous est donc d'user de moyens de fortune.

Notre premier numéro paraît sur deux pages ; il manque d'intérêt mais les prochains seront plus amusants. Les collaborateurs de l'Écho du Ravin connaîtront la notoriété.

Et maintenant, amis lecteurs, préparez vos cinq centimes hebdomadaires pour que ne viennent pas s'appesantir sur nous les sombres horreurs de la faillite !

La Direction

Les Commandements du Poilu

Mon cher Poilu, tu trouveras Que c'est dur au commencement. Tout d'abord, tu t'habitueras A tirer vite et proprement. La baïonnette fourbiras Pour qu'elle pique hardiment. Terrassier, tirailleur seras, Tailleur, grenier pareillement. Les Boches dégringoleras Pour le plaisir, uniquement ! Certains jours, tu te serreras La ceinture complètement ! A ta peine, tu te livreras Plus mens deux fois seulement. Jamais tu ne te laisseras Aller au découragement. De temps en temps tu songeras Que ça se tire doucement. Et puis, s'il le faut tu mourras Pour la France, tout simplement !

Échos et Informations

En raison de la grande pénurie de métaux qui va s'accentuant de jour en jour, les Boches confectionnent des obus en fonte.

Comme ce dernier métal devient lui-même très rare, les usines d'Essen s'occupent de l'utilisation de la… fonte des neiges !

…

Nos braves Poilus ont pu constater de visu que les obus boches n'éclataient pas toujours.

Un de nos collaborateurs, se glissant avec audace dans les environs immédiats d'une batterie ennemie, a surpris la cause de cette non fructueuse pyrotechnie, qu'il nous dévoile en ces termes :

« Parfois, dit-il, un véritable obus est introduit dans la culasse, mais, le plus souvent les Boches usent de stratagème mes enfants ILS TIRENT A BLANC ! Et l'un des servants de la pièce, un général employé de cinéma qui, en temps de paix faisait les bruits dans la coulisse, tire un sifflet spécial de sa poche, et imite le sifflement caractéristique de l'obus dans les airs. Lorsqu'il estime que le projectile devrait avoir terminé sa trajectoire, il saisit un maillet placé à proximité et frappe un coup sonore sur le caisson.

• Ainsi sont sauvées les apparences ! ».

Etes-vous satisfaits de l'explication, ô Poilus, mes frères ?…

---

1 *L'Echo du Ravin*
   Front page of the first issue of *L'Echo du Ravin*, the roneoed paper of the 41st Battalion of Chasseurs, with a circulation of a few hundred copies, which appeared between March 1915 and June 1916.

Far from complaining, in fact, many of the papers openly congratulated themselves on the difficulties of all kinds which they might have had to deal with:

> Lacking in comforts but rich in ideals, it has never known the ease of some of its sister publications, developed in the luxury of quiet premises, sheltered from bad weather and from danger . . . Its home is more often a barn open to all weathers, as at Belrupt, an underground shelter such as the Mardi Gras post, or a ruined farm such as Vaux-les-Palameix, rendered untenable by enemy fire and under orders of evacuation. But, far from wishing for better things, it rejoices in these harsh conditions. (*Le Rire aux éclats*, July 1917)

The threshold of open polemic was occasionally crossed in certain articles, somewhat more virulent than others:

> I detest the front-line newspapers which have no other claim to fame than being 'adopted' by armchair patriots. Every week I hear false rumours . . . [which], if continued . . . would carry on the whole campaign without fear of shells. (*La Suippes à demain*, 10 November 1916)

Many other papers spoke ironically about certain of their 'colleagues' they considered a little too sheltered:

> We hope, moreover, that readers will understand 'the front' as the true front, the immediate front line, and that there will be a special classification for the category of sister publications written in staff quarters, comfortably established in villages from which they are hardly ever moved and ignorant of the discomfort of reliefs in advanced positions and distribution in communication trenches. (*Le Pépère*, 21 May 1916)

Sometimes there was prompt denunciation of certain scandals:

> An amusing mistake: in *Le Journal* Gustave Téry wrote recently about our humorous sister publication *Le Tête à queue*, published at divisional headquarters, with high praise for the contributors, those proud *poilus* who manage to retain their good humour under shelling in the *depths of damp trenches*!!! This is a good joke and we should congratulate the directors of *Le Tête à queue* on this witty tease! Let us hope with all our

hearts that the editors of this paper remain in their comfortable offices and never reach the trenches, for they would deprive the calm little town where they reside of unaccustomed bustle, smart uniforms in dazzling colours, and elegant cavalrymen dressed up with the most stylish care. Above all, they would deprive those bourgeois salons where they are received each week of tasteful musical entertainments given by veritable virtuoso performers, and would put an end to artistic ambitions hitherto totally unknown in B—. (*Marmita*, 30 May 1915)

The source of such acute sensitivity lay in the scorn felt by front-line combatant troops for those who remained a little too far from the line of fire. Some reproaches appear reasonably justified, and certainly some trench newspapers of high quality and reasonable authenticity contrast sharply with the pitiful news-sheets written far back behind the lines, sometimes at the instigation of a headquarters staff anxious to promote a wholehearted form of 'eye-wash'.

But between one paper whose contributors were decimated with regularity and another written by various clerks at headquarters there was room for a wide range of circumstances. Regimental histories show that all the units with a trench newspaper reached the front line at one time or another. Thus a newspaper of territorials long kept in reserve might suddenly become a paper for highly exposed fighting troops. *L'Echo de Tranchées-ville* is one example: distributed free throughout the 151st Brigade from July 1915 onwards, it displayed none of the signs of a paper for fighting men, looking instead like a publication inspired by higher command. A year after it first appeared, however, six members of the editorial team were dead or wounded in August 1916; the journal could not survive such a blood-letting and ceased publication a few months later. The progress of *Le 120 court* is somewhat similar: it was edited at the rear of the front lines by a clerk in the 120th Battalion of chasseurs; but he was promoted to sub-lieutenant and was killed in the front line in June 1918.

The contents of the newspapers might therefore vary considerably over a period of months: *Le Troglodyte*, which appeared in 1915 in a battery of the 44th artillery Regiment, was insipid at first but changed in tone and interest from 1916. *Le Crapouillot* represents the opposite case: created in 1915, it was for a long time a fascinating publication but did not survive the prolonged conflict and faded slowly during the final year of the war.

Circumstances were thus subject to change, evolving with the pattern of editorial deaths and replacements, the demands of censorship or of readers, and above all with the vagaries of war and the ordeals suffered by the troops. Varied as the war itself, sometimes elusive, always disturbing – such was the nature of the trench press. Hasty judgements are therefore inappropriate: nowadays a newspaper from soldiers in sheltered conditions appears less interesting than one produced by men constantly faced with death. It remains true, however, that whether or not they were placed in the front line, all were fully engaged in the turbulence of war, and all suffered its constraints and deprivation, in circumstances that were inevitably very precarious.

The newspapers produced by these men are not always easy to find. It is virtually impossible to determine precisely how many titles appeared during the war. Less than two hundred have survived for the whole of the French army, of which about 170 belonged to the land forces operating on the French front. Unfortunately the collections preserved are only the residue of an appreciably larger production, the precise total of which is almost impossible to assess. The degree of conservation of trench newspapers has varied according to two main criteria: their date of issue and their method of production. The earliest papers (late 1914 or early 1915) are those least likely to have survived. Some have vanished completely; in other cases the name is known, but no copies. It is for this reason that the number of papers preserved is greater for the later period of the war. Further, the simpler the production process and the smaller the circulation, the less likely that copies have survived to modern times. Papers printed at the rear in large numbers and therefore subject to official registration have survived better than the modest handwritten sheets with a circulation of a few dozen copies. Sadly, all these factors are cumulative in respect of the early days of the war, because the earliest front-line papers were mostly issued in this handmade way; few have therefore survived the tumult.

It is however probable that half the titles of front-line papers have survived, giving a total of approximately four hundred papers published in the French army between 1914 and 1918. Such a figure may appear substantial in view of production conditions at the front and the troops' daily life; but, disregarding technical skill and relating the entire circulation of the front-line press to the total number of soldiers, it becomes clear that the majority of the men would not have seen these news-sheets, or only very sporadically.

Editors and their Motives

Who were the men who launched and edited the front-line news-papers? The answer must rest on fragmentary indications. From a list of five hundred editors whose rank has been identified it has been established that the front-line press was not a product of the higher ranks. It was the soldiers in the ranks, non-commissioned officers and officers up to the rank of captain, who were behind the trench papers; higher-ranking officers and generals, none of whom managed a front-line paper in person, represent less than 2 per cent of the identified editorial staff. The very episodic contribution of officers of high rank to trench papers always appeared somewhat artificial: the editorial teams may have been coerced into having recourse to them from time to time, or perhaps they wanted to hide behind the protection of a superior officer.

The troops defending advanced positions, from rankers to sub-alterns, therefore created their own papers. Men in the ranks were in the minority among these journalists' of the front, however, form-ing approximately one-third of the total. Lower ranks such as corporals in the infantry or cavalry made up half the staff; the remainder were other non-commissioned officers and subalterns, each supplying a quarter of the editorial teams overall. The frontline press was therefore not a representative microcosm of the French army, and to a large degree this press stayed in the hands of people holding some degree of authority, however modest.

It is worth considering the range of circumstances. A paper such as *Le Diable au cor*, which appeared between 1915 and 1918, counted among its editors eight sub-lieutenants and lieutenants, two captains, and just one soldier in the ranks; this was clearly an officers' paper. *L'Echo de la mitraille*, on the other hand, was edited from 1916 to 1918 by two corporals, four sergeants and two sub-lieutenants, rather more of a paper for non-commissioned officers, while *l'Argonnaute* was brought out during the final two years of the war by five rankers and three corporals – essentially a paper for the men in the ranks. In other cases such barriers did not exist and the balance appears to have been better, as with *La Mitraille*, where the editorial team included six rankers, two corporals, four sergeants and three sub-lieutenants.

Virtually nothing is known of the social, geographical or cultural origins of these men. They refrained from publishing any informa-tion whatsoever about their employment prior to mobilisation: did it seem absurd to evoke civilian life in their soldiers' journals? Doubtless. However, such discretion may preferably be seen as a concern not to stand out from the anonymous mass. Silence regarding social origins was a tacitly observed obligation linked to a profound desire for the unanimity and dissolution of class barriers which were to remain vigorous until the inter-war years. Further, most of the mobilised men were young and some had not entered employment before joining the army.

The death or severe wounding of one of the editors sometimes lifted the curtain. His comrades would then agree to provide some information on the victim. Unfortunately a concern for respectability, to which we shall return later, often encouraged the survivors to emphasise the profession of the victims where it sounded impressive, and otherwise to 'forget' it. Thus it is that the sixty newspaper editors whose occupation is known included sixteen artists or writers, thirteen journalists, five lawyers, four teachers, two doctors, three *sous-préfets* or *préfets*, a ministerial civil servant, a *préfecture* general clerk, an advertising agent, a priest, an office manager, a clerk to a parliamentary deputy, a law student, a shop employee, a landlord, and eight with no active profession. A very incomplete survey, but adequate: the trench newspapers were the product of fighting men from the middle classes, of essentially urban origins. Reading their articles fully confirms this, with their style, references, themes and humour all reflecting the bourgeois culture nurtured by the classic humanities of the Third Republic available to a restricted number of pupils through secondary and higher education. It is therefore hardly surprising that officers and non-commissioned officers are found in large numbers in the front-line press: combatants of a high cultural standard supplied the French army with its greatest strength and were the best qualified to create newspapers and write for their columns.

Censorship and the atmosphere of the *Union sacrée* combined to create virtually total silence regarding their political, ideological or religious leanings. Some leanings, however, were not eliminated. The papers' attitude appears to have been on the conservative side, while still remaining in touch with the main themes of pre-war Republican ideology.

More is known about the losses suffered. Out of 602 editors whose war-time fate is known, 84 died and 104 were wounded, giving a death rate of 13.2 per cent, plus a further 17.2 per cent wounded. The first figure is relatively high, not far below the 16 per cent losses recorded for all land forces between 1914 and 1918. This contrasts with the proportion of wounded, clearly lower than the wartime average estimated very roughly at 40 per cent of all those engaged. Against this, many of the trench papers mentioned that their editors were wounded only when wounds exceeded a certain degree of severity. There is also a sharp disproportion between the rates of losses among men in the ranks and non-commissioned officers and for officers: for the former the rate was slightly over 11 per cent (5 per cent below the general average for the war), and for the officers slightly over 16 per cent (within three points of the 19 per cent rate of loss among officers between 1914 and 1918). Care must be taken with such figures: a substantial number of deaths and an even greater number of additional casualties have undoubtedly escaped our inquiries completely, whether because a paper made no mention of them, because they were mentioned without sufficient detail, or because the figure vanished when the 'journalists' were put out of action. Conversely, some papers mentioned their editors only when they were killed or wounded while others retained anonymity, a pattern which artificially swelled the percentage of victims.

How should we assess these losses now, and their divergence from military losses in general? Since the trench press did not really reach full production until 1915, deaths in 1914 do not form part of our calculations. Yet the military losses in 1914 were considerable, a total of 301,000 men dead:[1] had the trench newspapers begun appearing in August 1914, editorial losses would undoubtedly have been higher. A further explanation lies in the distribution of trench papers according to the type of unit. Those published by front-line troops constitute a clear majority and represent almost 58 per cent of the total, most of them infantry newspapers.

Even so, newspapers published by units more often in the second line still represent nearly 35 per cent of the total (mostly artillery and territorials, together with some engineers, cavalry and armoured units). Putting aside vague or undefined cases, it may be concluded that the papers published by units generally less exposed than the infantry of the line are over-represented among the bulk of newspapers preserved. The same applies to 'service' units and 'specialists' (storemen, stretcher-bearers, telephonists, postmen, cyclists, cooks, etc.), who made up 10 per cent of the editorial staff of

---

1. Deaths in 1914: 301,000 (60,000 per month); 1915: 349,000 (29,000 per month); 1916: 252,000 (21,000 per month); 1917: 164,000 (13,000 per month); 1918: 235,000 (23,800 per month).

these papers. Certainly the production of a newspaper was infinitely easier for troops slightly to the rear, with some freedom and relative 'comfort', than for soldiers constantly exposed, weighed down with duties and living in the mud. Further, the papers written by 'protected' units have survived better. Frequently produced on printing machines, in large numbers and more regularly, such collections have been better preserved.

Nonetheless we should be wary of any 'élitist' attitude to the front line, and any implicit value-judgement. Generally speaking, the life of a newspaper was as uncertain as that of its editors. *L'Argonnaute*, for example suffered two deaths and one man wounded in four years. *Le Bochofage* mourned four dead and one wounded during the Somme offensive late in 1916. *Le 120 court* recorded four deaths between 1916 and 1918, *Les Boyaux du 95e* three in 1918 alone; also in 1918, *Poil et plume* lost four of its editors, and *Le Mouchoir* six. The list is interminable, and marked by several sad incidents: at the end of 1916 the whole editorial staff of the *Sourire de l'escouade* was killed in the same shell-hole in front of the Fort de Vaux. As for *L'Echo du boqueteau*, it suffered thirteen dead and twenty-seven wounded in its ranks between 1915 and 1918, and survived such blood-letting only by a constant supply of fresh editors. There were frequently serious losses among infantry newspapermen, but it should not be thought that papers published in other branches of the forces went completely unscathed: although the list of their victims was less tragic, very few were totally unaffected. Death struck on all sides, if not uniformly, and most of those who wrote for the trench papers were fully experienced in the realities and dangers of war.

Given such conditions, why should they produce newspapers? This is more difficult to answer than may at first appear, for their stated objectives often concealed less public motives. The wish to entertain the fighting troops was very frequently put forward; papers such as *Allons-y gaiement*, *L'Anticafard*, *Gardons le sourire*, *La Musette*, *Notre rire*, *Le Quand même*, *Le Rire aux éclats* and *Le Sourire de l'escouade* proclaimed in their very titles their intention to sustain troop morale. Others made it clear in their first editorial:

> Our ambition is simply to entertain you for a moment, between two heavy mortar shells, or even between two fatigue-duties; and if we manage even for an instant to bring you pleasure, we will be only too happy to have achieved our aim. (*Le Poilu*, December 1914)

In your cellar or in your trench, when the hours drag, when the memory of your home or your dead friends becomes too sad, when depression breaks through, *Marmita* will be there to chase away *le cafard*. (*Marmita*, 10 January 1915)

L'Echo rit . . . dort hopes to distract you a little from the troubled times we are enduring and where morale needs so much support. (*L'Echo rit . . . dort*, 1 May 1915)

Our only aim is to cheer, to bring laughter to those who have suffered and – just sometimes – wept. (*Le Pou*, June 1915)

Such professions of faith, fairly typical of the early days of the war, became rare in subsequent years. Some, however, would pursue their aim to sustain drooping morale into 1917:

We hope to have the strength to fight the good fight against the dreaded *cafard*, the source of all misery, against the monstrous *cafard* which tortures us so terribly at times, seeking to ravage our ranks: to fight it and – we hardly dare add to conquer it – is the primary purpose of this paper. (*La Gazette du créneau*, 5 September 1917)

Were such words a response to the high command's hopes of the trench press? Impossible to be sure, such is the perceptible level of disillusionment. *Le Rire aux éclats*'s statement of its editorial attitude also sounds hollow:

In its cheerful pages designed to distract its companions under arms, to make them laugh or simply smile, *Rire aux éclats* seeks to avoid accounts that evoke too many unhappy memories: nights spent at the listening post in the frozen mud, bayonet charges, grenade fighting, eye-witness accounts of evacuating severely wounded men, etc. Its mission is to . . . recount . . . ordinary little anecdotes, to make the reader forget the sadness of the hour, not to remind him . . . of where he is now, in the midst of misery and of death. (*Le Rire aux éclats*, July 1917)

In June 1918 it was the turn of *L'Echo du boqueteau* to yield to spurious cheerfulness:

Addressing emotional memories to those who have shared this work before me and who are now dead or captured, I promise them to do my best to sustain camaraderie, cheerfulness and humour in our paper . . . we will do our best to bring new energy to our little newspaper . . . And so, long live cheerfulness, for ever and despite everything! (*L'Echo du bo-queteau*, June 1918)

Although they did not hesitate to stress the miseries of the troops, all these papers persisted in pursuing a certain form of escapism, in expressing their intention to get away from the atmosphere of distress and death. But, as the headline of *La Guerre joviale* suggested, are derision and cheerfulness anything but a simple façade?

Humour and death are simply the same. (*La Guerre joviale*)

The gaps between laughter and tears and between laughter and anger are equally slender, symbolised by a deliberate type-setting 'error' that in 1918 turned *Notre rire* (Our laughter) into *Notre ire* (Our rage).

Apart from sustaining morale, the trench press occasionally took on itself the task of stimulating *esprit de corps*, strengthening the ties of solidarity between the men within their unit:

The only purpose of this paper is to inform our friends about regimental life and to strengthen, to draw tighter still if possible, the ties of friendship which unite them. (*Le Poilu du 6–9*, 1 August 1916)

From there to a wish to maintain discipline and respect for the hierarchy was often only a short step:

Now here is the plan which we have drawn up for ourselves here at *L'Echo de tranchées-ville*: to amuse the *poilus* by maintaining their morale at a high pitch; to enhance their feelings of military duty and discipline; to sustain their *esprit de corps*. (*L'Echo de tranchées-villes*, 3 June 1916)

Such statements were infrequent, but indicate the concern of certain officers to use the trench newspapers to maintain order and discipline among their men. Most of the papers, however, had less purely military preoccupations. The earliest newspapers, which appeared at the end of 1914, were intended to inform the troops and to replace the regular papers which rarely reached the front lines. Such was the aim of *L'Echo de l'Argonne*, of which the first issue, barely larger than the palm of the hand, appeared on 26 November 1914. For some time this paper was distributed to the men of the 2nd Army Corps, appearing every two or three days:

> Since the friendly tourists who are currently taking the air in the Argonne have complained that the national newspapers are only obtainable some-what irregularly, it has been deemed essential to fill the gap with a newspaper in a format convenient for easy reading in the trench and easy transport in the cartridge belt. This particularly well-informed paper will supply daily the latest news of current events in Europe and the War. (*L'Echo de l'Argonne*, 26 October 1914)

As already stated, this concern to inform was linked to the con-tinuing absence of a well-organised postal service, and also to the persistent notion of a short war. Thus the *raison d'être* of this type of paper was completely negated by the definitive establishment of the war of position, and in a curious reversal of circumstances the front line press owed its expansion to a forceful rejection of civilian journalism:

> Why do we exist? . . . Quite simply because we, the men of 1914, 1915 and of the future, declare that the existing newspapers have irritated us from the day they reached us for the second time. (*La Guerre joviale*, August 1915)

It was in reaction to a civilian press which sickened them that the combatants created their own newspapers. The names of certain Paris papers were seized on and derided (*La Vie poilusienne*, *Le Bulletin désarmé*, *L'Indiscret des poilus*, *La Guerre joviale*, etc.). Even the headlines of the front-line papers enjoyed parodying the banners of the national press: one set itself up as 'literary, periodic-al, scientific, caustic and subject to censure', another pronounced itself 'resolutely periodical and even weekly'. As for *Le Crocodile*, it claimed to be 'the underground organ published at top speed'.

Certain trench papers also attempted to establish among their readers the feeling of the 'grandeur' of the task in hand. Patriotic factors would be asserted, and some papers adopted a chauvinistic triumphalism, even a bellicose Germanophobia – hence such titles as *Bellica, Le Bochofage, Le Cran, Le Cri de guerre, Face aux Boches, Jusqu'au bout, On les aura, On progresse, Le Vide-boche,* etc.[2] More explicitly, *Le Clairon territorial* wrote:

> We propose to offer you a patriotic undertaking, to sustain and stir courage, to emphasise the reasons for our bloody struggles, to prove the validity of our confidence in victory, to brace ourselves for the war, in fact to make ourselves more worthy of victory. It may be that some of the papers produced at the front are over-concerned to help pass the time agreeably . . . we wish above all to address the mind and the heart of the French soldier, to show him that his painful and dangerous role is noble and sublime, and that he should perform it with all his soul. We hope to make the soldier even more aware of the scale of his task. (*Le Clairon territorial,* June 1915)

Occasionally this didactic concern became distant from the actual war, even if it failed on the whole to disguise the paternalism of many of the non-commissioned officers or thinkers towards their troops:

> To distract and to amuse, as we have already stated – let us also add, to conclude this plan which is already extensive, *to instruct.* Why not? Why should the French soldier, the immortal *poilu*, be considered unworthy of occupying his mind usefully, and be treated as such? . . . For the moment, let us briefly consider life after the war, for that too is a sacred duty! . . . We must also work a little; *La Gazette* will do its best to help its readers by publishing scientific, historical and literary works in a form accessible to all. (*La Gazette du dauphin,* September 1917)

2. The majority of the trench newspaper collections (often very incomplete) can be consulted at the Bibliothèque Nationale, at the BDIC (Bibliothèque de Documentation Internationale Contemporaine) at Nanterre, or at SHAT (Service Historique de l'Armée de Terre) at Vincennes. The papers' titles reveal a variety of inspiration: there may be a reference to the part of the front line occupied at the time of the first edition (*L'Argonnaute, L'Echo de l'Argonne, L'Echo du Grand-Couronné, Les Echos du plateau de Craonne, La Suippes à demain*), to the type of armament or characteristic equipment (*Le 120 Court, Le Crapouillot, La Saucisse, Tacatacteufteuf, Télémail*) to a specific item of uniform (*La Bourguignotte* – the French helmet – *La Chéchia, La Fourragère*), or to the circumstances of daily life at the front, and its dangers (*Brise d'entonnoirs, Le Canard du boyau, L'Echo des guitounes, L'Echo des marmites, L'Echo de tranchées-ville, Le Filon, La Gazette du créneau, La Mitraille, La Musette, Le Pou, La Première ligne, Le Troglodyte, Le Tuyau de la roulante*). Other newspapers made use of slang expressions referring to the soldiers of 1914–18 (*L'Indiscret des poilus, Le Petit Pépère, Le Poilu*), sometimes including the

So many declarations of good intent can be explained by the constraints affecting the trench newspapers. In order to achieve publication, their first issues were generally thoroughly conventional;
subsequently, having proved their merit, they could loosen some of
the shackles.

Several papers, however, revealed distinctive concerns from their
inception, such as this wish to record all the ordeals inflicted on the
fighting men:

> These anecdotes recounted over and over again in dug-outs and during
> the tedious hours of rest in camp should be saved from oblivion . . . It is
> the duty of our comrades of all ranks to record their experiences for their
> brother soldiers and to history. (*Poil et plume*, May 1916)

Le Crapouillot undoubtedly displayed the greatest determination in
pursuing this line:

> Avoiding the complacent optimism and grandiloquent heroism of news-
> papers of the rear, and equally avoiding the perpetually jolly tone of
> certain papers along the front, *Le Crapouillot* seeks to depict the 'good
> fellow' loyally, just as he is, confirming his steady good humour yet
> without concealing his sufferings and distress. (*Le Crapouillot*, Septem-
> ber 1916)

A year later the same paper was to show even more forcefully its
wish to let the voice of all combatants be heard:

> *Le Crapouillot* was initially the humorous and satirical gazette of Paris
> soldiers determined 'not to worry' . . . The *poilus*' vocabulary has dried
> up. Trench humour eventually becomes boring . . . *Le Crapouillot* made

---

unit's number (*Le Poilu du 35*, *Les Poilus de la 9ème*) or the type of unit
('territorial' for example, as in *Le Plus que torial*, *Le Petit Echo du 18ème
territorial*). Others 'borrowed' titles, often with a parodying twist, from the
national press: *Le Bulletin désarmé* (from the *Bulletin des Armées*), *La Guerre
joviale* (from the *Guerre Sociale*), *La Revue poilusienne* (from the *Revue
Parisienne*), *Le Petit journal*, etc. Many titles simply reflected their intention to
sustain morale through entertainment (*L'Echo rit . . . dort*, *Notre rire*, *Le Rire
aux éclats*, *Le Sourire de l'escouade*, *Le Tord-boyau*), or proclaimed an element
of patriotism, sometimes heavily tinged with Germanophobia (*Le Bochofage*,
Face aux Boches, *Face à l'Est*, *On les aura*, *Le Vide boche*).

up its mind to give its readers a more accurate and more sincere view of the terrible conflict ... In its second year, expanding its plans, [it] accepted the impressions of combatants in all types of unit – something which no front-line paper had done – and tried to give a complete impression of modern battle. (*Le Crapouillot*, May 1917)

A record for others, civilian or soldier. A record for history, an indication that these men were well aware of living through something wholly exceptional. A record for themselves: to write, to publish a newspaper, to be read, meant regaining their dignity, rising above the anonymity, the levelling and the mediocrity of war as an everyday way of life:

The concept of this little sheet was born one day of the imperative need for a less exclusively materialistic life, and the necessity to seek distraction from the sombre preoccupation of comrades predisposed to the blackest gloom by six months of the campaign. (*Télémail*, 18 February 1915)

There was even greater frankness in *L'Echo des marmites'* announcement of the deepest motives of its editors:

Newspapers published at the front are increasing in number day by day, proof of their success. This success is due to several causes – first, the pleasure it gives their editors in relieving the monotony of trench life by taking up some of their rest hours spent in villages that are almost always evacuated, then the delight of being able to send their families a souvenir of the campaign, and finally, for those who return home, the joy of reading later, at rest, these pages full of memories. (*L'Echo des marmites*, 20 April 1915)

Two years later a similar testimony appeared elsewhere:

Killing time is not an aim. Yet this is our only *raison d'être*. Killing the long hours of inactivity at the front, killing the *cafard* and in addition killing the legend of the *poilu* who is interested in nothing but his 'grog' and his 'grub' and his cooties ... The soldier thinks, meditates, reads, writes, takes an interest in all aspects of life, to escape the daily constraints and distresses that come his way as part of the unending dangers of his life. (*Tacatacteufteuf*, 15 January 1917)

It is therefore scarcely surprising to learn that the editor of *L'Echo du boqueteau*, who was killed in 1917, dedicated a large proportion of his time and energy to enlivening his modest paper:

> The Director of *L'Echo*, Léon Rodier, killed in battle. He unceasingly dedicated to the paper the short intervals of rest allowed him by life in the trenches . . . The ingenious mechanism invented by Rodier to bring our presses to perfection and the impressive 'rotary' press made out of old curved umbrella handles that went as far as Champagne with us . . . Our paper's circulation . . . was a true passion for him. (*L'Echo du boqueteau*, 19 March 1917)

Distraction. Escape – but also to bring a little beauty to life in the ugliness of war . . . These papers worked at it with a highly significant attention to quality:

> Today *L'Echo des dunes* has reached its definitive form, i.e. it will adopt the style of a genuine front-line review, artistic, cheerful and factual, consisting of at least twelve pages with an optional supplement . . . Our aim henceforward is to present our friends with a paper which, if not the most interesting, will at least be the most handsome of the trench newspapers. (*L'Echo des dunes*, April 1917)

Such aesthetic concern impelled the front-line papers to ceaseless improvements in their printing methods, attempts to reproduce drawings or photographs, sometimes 'offprints', which may appear luxurious in view of the production conditions. Some even tried to use colour, despite a myriad of obstacles and results which were generally disappointing. Such efforts entailed setbacks: lacking professionalism, the front-line 'journalists' misused the titles of 'director', 'administrator', 'financial director' or 'editor in chief', even for a few dozen copies of handwritten sheets published once a month! Apart from its laughable aspect, such behaviour surely betrayed a deep wish to be recognised. Many of the front-line papers confirmed this in the proliferation of poems, sketches, or texts with 'literary' or 'artistic' pretensions in their columns. This was not far removed from élitism: some fell victim, happy to turn their modest newspaper into an emblem of cultural and social recognition, a means of recognition for those who shared a common background. As an indicator of the need for speech of a community deprived of opportunities for self-expression, the trench press finally established itself as the focal point of many and varied aspirations – the concern of senior officers to sustain morale, discipline, *esprit de corps* and respect for rank conflicting with the fighting troops' desire to rise above the daily misery of the war, to bear witness, and to regain some dignity through writing. The result was often an inextricable muddle of propaganda and personal testimony.

Publication and its Constraints

One of the main problems involved in a study of trench newspapers is that of censorship, the effects of which need to be understood. The task is made harder by our ignorance of the content of articles or sketches censored, and because the attitude of the military authorities was extremely variable at all levels of the hierarchy. Overall, the high command tended to encourage the growth of the front-line press; on 8 March 1916 Joffre addressed a circular to this effect to his generals:

> It has been brought to my notice that certain trench newspapers have been suppressed by order of staff officers in command of the corps publishing the papers. The aim of these papers is to divert and amuse the fighting men. At the same time they demonstrate to all that our men are full of confidence, cheerfulness and courage. The propaganda branch of the Ministry of Foreign Affairs uses the trench newspapers to demonstrate to the correspondents of foreign newspapers the excellent morale of our troops along the whole of the front. I consider that their publication should be viewed with goodwill as long as they do no harm to the army and on condition that their management is closely supervised, to avoid the publication of any article that does not fit in with the aim stated above. I would ask you to be so kind as to encourage the senior officers under your command to take heed of these considerations in relation to any trench newspapers which may be published by troops placed under your command.

General Joffre
Instruction no. 2287, 8 March 1916[3]

3. General Joffre, instruction no.2287, 8 March 1916, Service Historique de l'Armée de Terre (SHAT), Vincennes, 19N1198, 7th Army.

The high command was evidently aware of the advantages to be gained from the trench press, both for the army and abroad. Joffre also referred to the problem of the papers' contents, since no official censorship was in operation before this date and no proper policy had been established. The authorities' supervision at that time was intermittent, variable and pragmatic, which does not mean that it was restrained; the circular quoted above confirms that there had been straightforward suppression by commanding officers. In most cases, however, the higher command viewed the ranks' papers with a certain benevolence and sometimes helped to launch them, not without ulterior motives. This was the case with the *Canard poilu*, founded in February 1915 in circumstances recounted almost sixty years later by the designer (and cavalry corporal) Marcel Jeanjean.[4] His sketches, which were circulated among the 6th Hussars (a cavalry regiment which despite everything held the trenches in front of Verdun), reached the ranks of the commanding officers.

In January 1915 the Chief of Staff to the general of his army unit put him in charge of creating a paper designed to sustain the morale of the troops, who were flagging in these early days of trench warfare. Marcel Jeanjean was attached to the army corps head-quarters, assisted by a printer, a song-writer and a journalist, all similarly detached from their units. The production of the *Canard poilu* thus proved an excellent form of protection, and the paper's distinct mediocrity is hardly surprising. This was not the only paper to be encouraged or fostered by high-ranking officers:

Was I right or wrong to create *La Fourragère*? Now I can tell all. Like everyone with initiative, I was subjected to violent criticism and a degree of hostility . . . My gratitude must go first to Lieutenant-Colonel Teilhac . . . [He] showed an encouraging kindness which touched us deeply . . . [He] was protector and friend to *La Fourragère*; he was proud of our success, he was happy with its expanding distribution . . . He was determined, let it be understood, to use his high-ranking influence to give us moral support in difficult circumstances. (*La Fourragère*, August 1919)

This final ambiguous phrase seems to suggest that the military authorities were not always united over the paper. *La Gazette du créneau* proved more explicit:

4. Marcel Jeanjean, 'Les journaux du front de 1914–1918', *Revue historique de l'armée*, no.2, 1971, pp.110–20.

Greeted with enthusiasm by Lieutenant-Colonel Poupard, in command of the 134th at the time of its creation, this little news-sheet for the troops was somewhat roughly handled by his successor, Lieutenant-Colonel Clouscard, who in his various conversations with the editorial team of *La Gazette* revealed clearly all the narrow- mindedness of his liberality. Lieutenant-Colonel Sézille des Essarts, who succeeded him, followed Lieutenant-Colonel Poupard's example in showering the paper with his favour. (*La Gazette du créneau*, 1919)

This reveals the extent to which the pressure of censorship might vary. The lack of clarity in General Headquarters directives was partly responsible, as the initiative lay with the generals and their subalterns without any guide-lines being imposed. Pétain's arrival as Commander in Chief meant the end of this gap. In October 1917, disturbed by 'the dangers that might be presented by a lack of supervision in the editing of trench newspapers', he recommended that they should be censored at division level, and that a copy of each paper should be sent to the General Headquarters.[5] These instructions reveal a concern for close control combined with a wish for direct information on the troops' morale and state of mind. In theory the censorship was henceforward to be carried out by the divisional general, but in practice the work was delegated to one of his staff officers. Censorship continued to be extremely variable, depending on the individual officer's personality, and on the place and the conditions.

Such supervision was apparently perceived as very heavy and restrictive. There is no doubt, however, that many of the papers of very limited production and for groups of restricted size escaped the censor throughout their existence. A title such as *La Saucisse*, for example, edited by Corporal J.-F. Oswald from 1916 to 1918, consistently displayed an astonishing freedom of style. As many of the trench papers confirmed frankly, censorship was actually under-taken by an officer of the company or regiment; and although the censor sometimes suppressed a few papers, his efforts in general proved relatively ineffective and tolerant. The proof lies in the ultimately limited number of passages openly censored among the collections preserved, even though it was always possible to replace specific articles by others when something was banned. It would

5. Circular of the Grand Quartier Général (GQG), no.24962, 21 October 1917, SHAT, Vincennes, 19N1198, 7th Army.

obviously be of the greatest interest to know the content of the censored texts or sketches. Occasionally some indications survive, but they tend to be disappointing: here an article on soldiers' pay, there a feature denouncing the suggestion from a civilian journalist that American troops should be made welcome in French families; elsewhere a comment on the selfishness of civilians in 1918 in contrast to their generosity at the beginning of the war. Little enough, in fact, while seemingly much more virulent articles were published elsewhere without apparent difficulty.

Censorship proved to be relatively liberal, restricting itself to information of a military nature, political references, or the excessive sharpness of certain suggestions. If this had not been the case, the French army would never have sustained so many newspapers within its ranks. The high command understood that the survival of the trench press, which was considered desirable, imposed a measure of compromise over its contents without which, empty of substance, it would inevitably have collapsed. In any case, unbroken supervision on this scale of millions of men and in the living conditions which they endured remained difficult to exercise. Further, many of the junior officers were close to sharing their troops' state of mind, a factor which encouraged their indulgence. But although the front-line troops could be forgiven certain irregularities of language, civilian eyes should be spared: in May 1916 *La Guerre joviale* was forced to stop dispatching some of its copies back to the rear.

Self-censorship, on the other hand, formed a tougher screening process which spared the official censors the greater part of their work. *On les aura* explained to its readers in 1916:

> We cannot thank those who send us copy, nor explain why it will not be used. Our choice of articles is subject to complex and highly sensitive conditions that prevent us from criticising certain actions which must remain concealed from an organ edited by mobilised men, i.e. men subject to military discipline. (*On les aura*, 1 November 1916)

With a frankness bordering on naïveté, the process of self-censorship was occasionally described in all its details:

> Alas, all too often ... the editorial staff was forced to reject as 'inappropriate' articles which many reviews behind the lines would have

taken eagerly. In particular it was often necessary to refuse remarkable descriptions of the painful sensations which assail the wretched nervous system of the man hunted by death, experiences written with all the style of the naturalist school, very varied, very precise in the details, but from which one might draw conclusions of a discouraging nature. How often too it was necessary to reject the pleasure of including . . . delightful but rather indelicate stories . . . liable to disturb the civilian readership whose subsidies kept the paper alive.[6] Articles identifying officers were automatically excluded, even if complimentary, so as not to run the risk of appearing too flattering. Finally there were little cuts by the censor who, while showing us great goodwill, several times requested us to defer the insertion of articles including references that were too precise about military events in which we were concerned. (*La Mitraille*, January–February 1918)

It is clear that the official censor intervened as a last resort and somewhat marginally, supervision being carried out by the editors themselves in line with criteria described in turn by *Le Klaxon*:

The most pleasing moment is when one tells a few *poilu* friends . . . of a scoop among the articles. Their good sense is a valuable guide. Just like Madam Censor, we prune, we cut, we soften the sharp impact of inherently subversive articles. (*Le Klaxon*, December 1916)

Official censorship as a net with large mesh and little effectiveness? So it appears; but it must be feared that the mesh of self-censorship was much tighter, particularly as it is impossible to exclude the existence of an unconscious self-censorship intervening at an earlier stage and impossible to detect.

Three methods of production were available to the front-line press. Excluding the papers 'published' as a single handwritten copy and passed from hand to hand, the simplest were those produced by gelatine mix. This method, producing only very small numbers at the cost of substantial labour and a mediocre result, has left us with the most emotive documents. The process required the preparation of a handwritten matrix which was set in negative form on sheets of gelatine in a metal tray. Sheets of paper were then pressed onto the

6. Many of the trench newspapers appear to have been kept going, to an extent impossible to ascertain, through subsidies from personal civilian connections of the military editors. Civilian subscriptions were another form of home-front support for the front-line papers.

jelly, producing the pages one at a time. The operation might take six hours and then had to be repeated from the beginning for the subsequent pages. Newspapers of this type therefore rarely exceeded four pages and were necessarily produced during rest periods or in calm sectors, the articles themselves having been written in more active areas. Some fifty papers of this type have been preserved, each issue running to about a hundred copies on average.

Roneo printing, of which the same number of titles have been preserved, was already more sophisticated. Here too a handwritten matrix was the starting-point. The fairly cumbersome publishing equipment permitted larger print-runs, up to or exceeding a thousand copies.

Then there were the printed papers. The printing was done in towns at the rear of the lines or further away, the articles being sent to the printer who returned the printed copies to the front, not without serious delivery problems. Expenses, naturally, were high; although some papers originally written by hand advanced to printing, it was not unusual for printed papers to regress to less costly procedures, on a smaller scale. The printed paper had the advantage of satisfying the editors' or readers' taste for 'professionalism', and of reducing the work required, but the drawback – apart from the cost – was that it appeared less 'authentic'. Although it is dangerous to generalise, the printed titles are frequently those with the least obvious elements of interest and sincerity. Unfortunately these are also the best preserved, and in much more complete runs; seventy have survived, as a result of much better methods of conservation than that enjoyed by the hand-produced news-sheets – which were however infinitely more numerous on the battlefield.

Printing made much larger print-runs possible, extending to several thousand copies (although never more than ten thousand). This gave the printed papers a fairly substantial readership. However, it is not easy to ascertain the true influence of the trench papers at the level of the army taken as a whole. In the middle of 1916, at the time of front-line newspapers, the total printing may have been between 75,000 and 132,000 copies per month. Although scarcely negligible, such figures reveal that this was not a mass circulation press; only a minority of soldiers could have been reached by a front-line newspaper. The majority must never have held one in their hands, and there were very few who were privileged to be regular readers of a trench news-sheet. The trench press was a significant phenomenon; but probably no more than that. This would explain the overwhelming absence of veterans' reference to them.

Publishing a newspaper was expensive. André Charpentier, editor of *Le Bochofage*, estimated the sum required to launch a paper on the simplest lines at 15 francs, a sum representing sixty days' pay for a soldier in the ranks at the beginning of the war. For this reason many of the trench papers suffered financial difficulties, although others enjoyed the luxury of making no charge:

> *L'Echo de tranchées-ville* is a creative work which is not concerned with commerce. We are therefore not in a position to take the advice given us, to put a selling price on each copy. Everyone knows that the printing of this paper involves expense; everyone should therefore give of his charity, putting his contribution in the money-box close at hand when he collects his copy from our delivery point. The amount of the contribution is optional, and we feel sure that it will be in line with the means of the reader. (*Echo de tranchées-ville*, 23 September 1915)

Such optimism was soon disappointed, for a few months later the editors were forced to set a price of 10 centimes. Rates were always extremely variable: a paper could be bought one issue at a time, or by subscription (sometimes for the duration of the war!), prices varying according to the rank of the purchaser. The cheapest titles were sold at 5 centimes per issue, while the most expensive might be as much as 50 centimes. In general, the average price was between 10 and 25 centimes. Thus the purchase of a trench newspaper, generally of reduced size (21 × 27 cm) and rarely consisting of more than six pages, might well seem a thoroughly useless luxury to many soldiers. This difficulty was indeed clearly perceived by *Bellica*, a particularly highly priced paper:

> *Bellica* does not have a selling price. You may say that this is good, that many people and other papers might envy it for that reason. It is nonetheless true that it causes us considerable embarrassment. To be honest, at the front we have had only disappointments . . . our cyclists and agents have always lost or spoiled ten copies for each one sold, and although it may be magnificent to know that a 210 has wiped out a hundred copies, this is hardly lucrative. At the rear, the public ignores *Bellica*. Our subscribers . . . have helped us considerably, and we should

make it clear that we have survived until now only with their aid. (*Bellica,* April–May 1916)

Many of the papers survived only through their editors' utmost efforts and thanks to their personal resources. But there were always contrasts: copies of *La Gazette du dauphin* sold at 20 centimes with a loss of more than 8 centimes each. On the other hand *Le Diable au cor*, selling at 25 centimes, brought in a profit of more than 1,200 francs between May 1915 and September 1916. Such financial comfort was no doubt exceptional, although there were other successes: *La Fusée* made a profit of more than 800 francs between February 1916 and March 1917, *Le Poilu du 37* brought in profits of 480 francs between January 1915 and January 1918, and more than 3,000 francs in the last year of the war. In fact all depended on the gifts, subsidies and subscriptions at high rates available to certain trench newspapers. In October 1917, moreover, Pétain set a limit to such aid, requiring it to be passed through his office.[7]

Certain titles none the less made high claims for their total financial independence:

We have no income except the soldier's three sous, receiving no *official subsidies or hidden support*, or advertising; the hand we hold out to you is clean! (*Le Filon,* May–June 1918)

Others, it is true, proved less high-minded and accepted minor advertisements and all kinds of gifts from the rear, thanks to the editors' personal contacts. On the other hand, the trench newspapers never benefited from official subsidies. Despite very varied circumstances, the existence of these papers was frequently precarious, but financial reasons were never the primary cause for either breaks in production or definitive closure.

The budget of the trench papers varied considerably, depending on their frequency of issue. Some titles addressed vast groups of men, others more restricted circles. Papers aimed at the major units (brigades, divisions, army corps) make up less than 9 per cent of the total. Forty per cent were for average-size units (regiments or

---

7. Circular of the GQG, 21 October 1917, SHAT, Vincennes, 19N1198, 7th Army.

battalions), and 45 per cent were published at the level of small units (sections, companies, batteries and artillery squads). The front-line press thus acquired its truest significance only when it was published by and for small groups of men who knew each other well, who had shared in the same ordeals and lived together constantly. This attachment to a restricted group was claimed by many papers in their title: for example *Le Boyau de la 6e du 53e*, *L'Echo du groupe cycliste*, *Le Poilu du 6–9*, *Les Poilus de la 12*, *Les Poilus de la 9*, etc.

The appearance of such modest papers, produced on rudimentary equipment, was always uncertain. Some indeed laid heavy and frequent stress on the material difficulties which they had to overcome:

It was in this sector [the depressing sector 2] of Remières that the foundations for the establishment of the newspaper were laid, and where its first editorial committee was elected. This was not the calmest of areas. The trench itself, which lay in front of the French lines, was scarcely an ideal post. Isolated from the other trenches in the sector, it communicated with them . . . only on the maps of the General Staff. Finally, as a finishing touch to the amenities, it was enfiladed from an enemy trench. If this horrible cul-de-sac was already lacking in good points, the dug-out itself was even worse! . . . It was hollowed out of a trench parapet . . . in the midst of half-buried French corpses in a God-forsaken corner. The future director of *L'Echo* had to lodge with Sergeant Berody who was acting as aide-de-camp to his head of section. But the grotto could not hold both of them together, even curled up, so they decided to expand their site, digging out a narrow ledge at the back of the cavern . . . imagine their fright when the first blow with the spade unearthed a French officer, a strip of whose red trousers continued thereafter to hang dolefully at the back of the dug-out. No one managed to cover it with earth. (Memoirs narrated by A. Boudon, undated)[8]

Editing a newspaper in such surroundings understandably presented insurmountable obstacles. The interval between issues was often extended, then the final number broke off:

Le Poilu is essentially and primarily a trench newspaper, edited between one relief and another, and the moments of freedom allowed us by this

8. Handwritten memoirs transcribed by A. Boudon, preserved with the *Echo du boqueteau* collection, Bibliothèque Nationale.

mole existence that we are obliged to lead currently are not always adequate to ensure regular publication. (*Le Poilu*, 6 February 1915)

Eight months later it was the turn of *La Marmite des poilus* to give up:

For the time being it is impossible for us to continue publication of our humble news-sheet, 'Les Eparges' being a ... locality little famed for the bucolic calm so necessary to 'great writers' such as ourselves. Alas, we have other concerns! (Letter from Sergeant Riffe, director of *La Marmite des Poilus*, October 1915)

Frequently the paper never reappeared and ceased publication permanently. There were many reasons for such disappearances: it is idle to indicate the results of battle, with their series of deaths and woundings in each paper. On the other hand, the part played by incessant troop movements and the multiplicity of labours burdening the soldiers must be taken into account:

The reader in the rear does not know ... of all the difficulties which may be encountered at the front when distributing a newspaper. First there are the obstacles resulting from the war itself. These are purely material and secondary matters such as postings, shells, services, etc. (*Bellica*, February 1916)

Sometimes it was departure to the trenches that prevented the paper from appearing:

Following the departure to the front-line trenches of the principal editors and managers, the appearance of issue no.2 of our paper has been somewhat delayed. (*Face à l'est*, 8–15 August 1915)

The wisest therefore gave warning from the beginning that they preferred not to aim for regular publication:

The trenches where one can have fun are rare. In the trenches, the real ones, the trenches familiar to the 11th Division, there is not even enough leisure to produce a newspaper. This is why *Le Poilu déchaîné* cannot appear regularly, and declares modestly that it will be printed at the rear, when the Boches allow it enough time. (*Le Poilu déchaîné*, August–September 1915)

There were some who turned this situation to their advantage: when sudden departure into the trenches prevented cavalry corporal Guillaume Apollinaire from bringing out the issue of *Tranchman-Echo* dated 20 September 1915, he published two entirely blank pages with the heading 'subject to censorship'; an original response to a much less original set of circumstances.[9]

Trench newspapers did not in general last longer than two years, at the rate of an issue every month, attempts at more frequent publication being generally soon abandoned. Some titles managed to keep going throughout the war; others never got beyond the first or second issue. Longevity of publication should not, however, be misinterpreted: interruptions were normal, sometimes lasting more than a year. Some titles were even forced to stop nearly ten times between their first and their final issues. The trench press was thus intermittent and the impression of 'continuity' gained from the collections preserved is illusory: from the soldier's point of view a considerable lapse of time could intervene between one issue and the next.

The growing number of titles that appeared during the war is significant: the trench newspapers appeared by the end of 1914, the first no doubt after the battle of the Marne in September, at the turning-point between the end of the 'war of movement' and the beginning of the 'war of position'. The latter was to create material and psychological conditions favourable to the expansion of a front-line press. Development was spectacular in 1915, and the number of titles grew steadily until the middle of 1916 (sixty-one different titles have survived for the month of June alone). This strong growth appears to have been encouraged by the effect of imitation – even of competition – between the different units, with each front-line paper obviously aware of some of its 'sister' publications. This development also reveals the maintenance of reasonably sound morale linked to dogged confidence in the war's limited duration, even though it persisted in proving longer than anticipated. The notion of occupying the hours of idleness or boredom by creating a newspaper is proof of the existence of growing morale and a ca-

9. *Tranchman-Echo*, no.3, 20 September 1915, Bibliothèque Nationale.

pacity to resist steadily increasing adversity. The trench press began to decline after the middle of 1916. Although the early months of the battle of Verdun do not appear to have interrupted publication, the French counter-offensive on the Somme, in July–September 1916, combined with the counter-attack in front of Verdun in August–November 1916, did result in such a break. The number of papers being produced diminished in the first half of 1917, linked to preparations for the Nivelle offensive in April and its subsequent setback. Recovery appeared very cautious after this, as if the soldiers in full disarray henceforward lacked the resilience necessary to overcome their discouragement: for many of them, starting a newspaper no longer had any meaning.

The erosion continued throughout 1918, this time without remission: the final great German offensives of the first half of the year forced the French troops to change their positions and interrupted publication, while doubts gripped the army itself during this period. Then, after July 1918, came the opposite effect of the Allied troops' advance and the return to a war of movement that helped to reduce the number of newspapers. Surprisingly, there was no significant increase in November 1918 or succeeding months, when material conditions appeared ideal. Perhaps the joy was too great, morale too high? Boredom and defeat could, through reaction and on condition that they were not too crushing, give birth to the impulse to publish a newspaper. With victory, one decisive motivating factor had disappeared, and the editorial staff who felt the need to publish a final issue were rare. Nevertheless, some made the attempt, even if only to continue playing their liaison role a little longer:

L'Echo will continue to appear right up to the day of demobilisation . . . Our paper . . . has been above all a family bulletin, a notice-board for all our friends scattered over all the French fronts for four years, and over Belgium, Italy, and the East. This is not the moment, when many of our own men have been wounded, for us to cease publication of L'Echo which is now alone in being able to bring news to all friends and inform them of the fate of their wounded comrades. (L'Echo du boqueteau, 25 November 1918)

In the middle of the war some asserted that they would continue their work after demobilisation:

LE BOCHOFAGE

DIRECTION, RÉDACTION :	Organe Anticafardeux, Kaizericide et Embuscophobe	PRIX DU NUMÉRO .
68e Inf , 6e Cie, Secteur Postal 66	Rédacteur en chef : ANDRÉ CHARPENTIER	Pour les poilus ...... 0 fr. 00
Ce journal ne peut être crié		Pour les civils ...... 12 fr. 00
aux postes d'écoute	Marraine : Mme A. L. ROSSOLLIN	Pour les embusqués, 2.000 fr. en or

Deuxième Anniversaire

JUILLET 1916 — AOUT 1918

Nom d'une baïonnette rouillée ! Cuiller à pot et musette percée ! !... Si qu'qu'un nous avait dit en juillet 1916 que le Bochofage paraîtrait encore vingt-quatre mois plus tard et que la guerre suivrait toujours son sale petit bonhomme de chemin, nous vous fichons notre billet que, nonobstant nos manières courtoises et notre naturelle douceur, nous aurions appréhendé au col l'impudent et louche personnage propagateur de propos aussi défaitistes et, après lui avoir fait racler de ses deux fesses nues le fond du boyau, du P.P. 1 à la roulante, nous aurions hissé, tel un épouvantail, sa carcasse de faux témoin sur la selle du plus piquant cheval de frise du secteur !

Et nous ne connaissons pas un camarade, si débonnaire fut-il, qui n'eut agi à notre instar en telle occurence.

Et pourtant, nous v'voilà encore dans les tranchées; en dépit de Mme de Thèbes, de la voyante de Plougarec, du fakir Trajdekar, des sapins de Lorraine, de la receveuse de tramway de Cherbourg, et d'une foultitude d'autres prophéties de voyantes, de chiromanciennes, de cartomanciens, tous ultra-lucides, qui se sont fichus le doigt dans l'œil plus profondément que jamais baïonnette française n'entrât dans ventre boche.

Or donc, il y a deux ans et quinze jours, dans ce secteur de la Champagne pouilleuse qui fait face à Auberive, à quelques mètres des Boches (sans bourrage de crâne), le premier numéro du Bochofage était distribué aux poilus fis 6-8. Les anciens, et surtout ceux de la 6e compagnie, ne se rappelleront pas sans émotion ce fait de joyeuse mémoire.

C'est pour commémorer cet anniversaire, qui coïncide à quelques jours près avec notre entrée dans la cinquième année de guerre (aoi, papa ! aoi, maman !) que nous publions aujourd'hui ces quelques lignes et offrons à nos lecteurs, avec le portrait des principaux collaborateurs du « canard », la photographie de notre marraine.

En terminant, laissez-nous vous dire deux mots.

Premier mot : Sans vouloir vaticiner vainement, nous vous disons en toute sincérité que notre conviction bien arrêtée est que nous n'aurons pas à fêter un troisième anniversaire. La Victoire viendra avant. Les Yankees sont là, et les étoiles de leur bannière éclipseront bientôt l'astre, qui est comme la lune, des Hohenzollern.

Deuxième mot : Certains camarades pleins d'astuce, nous accusent de prolonger les hostilités dans le but de multiplier les occasions de faire paraître notre « canard ». Ce sont de fieffés calomniateurs ! Nous déclarons formellement que nous ne sommes pour rien dans la durée exagérée de la guerre.

La prise de Mêlé-Cass

Notre ami Boireau a fait un prisonnier. Il le conduit à l'arrière, et chemin faisant entame la conversation avec son boche.

Ce dernier ne tarissait pas d'éloges et d'admiration sur les Allemands et leurs hauts faits.

« Nous afons pris Paris, disait-il : nous afons pris Dijon... nous afons pris Bordeaux.

— Et avez-vous pris Mêlé-Cass ? interrompit notre camarade.

L'Allemand réfléchit un peu, puis : « Foui, nous afons pris Mêlé-Cass avec tous ses forts !

C'est ainsi que Boireau présenta à tout un état-major, l'homme qui avait pris Paris et Mêlé-Cass avec tous ses forts.

Et ce fut cinq minutes de fou rire.

« Nous avons quatre puissances comme ennemies et, sans compter la Russie, il y en a dix-neuf dans l'alliance formée contre l'Allemagne. La population des nations ennemies est de 143 millions d'habitants; celle des nations alliées s'élève à 1.250 millions, alors que la population mondiale n'est que de 1.685 millions »

Berliner Tag.

Le Bochofage, the paper of the 6th Company of the 68th Infantry Regiment, was printed in Paris. It lasted for 25 issues, between July 1916 and December 1918. Its editor in chief, André Charpentier, was a journalist in civilian life and in 1935 produced a unique book of record of the trench newspapers: Feuilles bleu horizon 1914–18.

When the happy day of Peace sends us all home to our peacetime occupations, L'Esprit du cor will remain as a link uniting all men who fought together under the colours of the Division. It will perpetuate the feelings of solidarity sealed with blood and facing the enemy. (*L'Esprit du cor*, 16 June 1917)

In the event *L'Esprit du cor* was not able to keep its word, and it disappeared like the others in 1919. Did demobilisation take away the trench press's deepest meaning?

> I was almost unable to publish this seventeenth and final issue of La *Fourragère*. It is no longer the same, you will understand, you my old friends from the front. Demobilisation, the return to civilian life, pre-occupation with other cares, with earning a living, with the joys and miseries of home life, mean that the state of mind required to create a front-line newspaper no longer exists . . . Briefly I dreamed vaguely of extending its life, of launching a paper for old comrades under another title, a vigorous platform where the spirit of the front could be maintained, where ideas born in the trenches could be given free rein. But why? All our fighting comrades have now dispersed. The demands of life have overtaken them again. A different atmosphere is appearing. All that belongs to the past is finished and over for good, for ever. Better resign oneself to say today – because some of my good friends are asking me for a final issue for their collection, so they say – Farewell all those who have followed and encouraged our modest efforts. (*La Fourragère*, August 1919)

The front–line press died with the victory. Even so, it died slowly: the temptation to prolong a particular state of mind, to create a press for 'veterans', was sufficiently strong to prolong the life of certain titles until September 1919. A few were to reappear after a long silence, during the 1920s, but in a format and in conditions that were naturally very different.

Trench Journalism and Attitudes

Although certain precautions are essential in making use of this unique press, it is worth emphasising at this point the power of the 'reaction effect' which characterises it. The editors were living in the midst of their readers and could not ignore their state of mind. They necessarily and very rapidly knew what their readers felt about their articles. For this reason most of the trench news-papers were increasingly authentic. Censorship and self-censorship could not prevent the trench papers from responding little by little to the concerns, interests, grievances and hopes of their readers, and echoing them. Any paper which persistently ignored this 'demand' would have condemned itself to failure.

The men who edited the papers did not reflect the composition of the army as a whole. We feel, however, that they knew how to capture its aspirations and how to speak in its name, for the war provoked a genuine osmosis between combatants from all backgrounds: a two-way blending of social categories, cultural levels, and even between soldiers in the ranks and junior officers, whose living conditions and state of mind could not be totally separated from those of their men. This osmosis obviously had its limits, but there is no doubt that it existed. It is a matter of what might be called 'a war culture': all these men shared a certain number of mental attitudes, of reflexes born of the harshness of their living conditions, of immersion in battle and confrontation with death. It is from this war culture that the army of 1914–18 drew some of its homogeneity. The trench newspapers, moreover, were aware of being the mouthpiece of this common culture:

> We certainly lack the temerity to claim that we are a coterie, a kind of clan, a form of State within the State, a sort of separate band in the domain which is our concern. Nor is it our purpose to put ourselves forward as the star, or to exploit our meagre knowledge in some way. On the contrary, and generally hiding behind a pseudonym, we shall do our best, in order to be perfectly understood, to remain in all things and everywhere in the realm of the ordinary, we shall write of the earth earthy ... The modest trench newspaper which we have been bold enough to establish is not the word of Holy Writ: it is the review of the 134th. (*La Gazette du créneau*, 5 September 1917)

> The editor on his own is nothing; for it is not his voice that speaks; he only translates ... the moments experienced with his comrades ... The task of the trench journalist does not exclude the demands of his service; it would be a grave misdemeanour on his part to neglect it, to sacrifice it to a fantasy which h᠊ has kindly been granted. It is a doubling of effort which, in assimilating him with his comrades, permits him to avoid coarsening his language and to evade falling inescapably into the commonplace 'eye-wash'. (*La Gazette du créneau*, 20 November 1917)

If these two quotations should not be taken absolutely literally, it remains true that the reality of the levelling among all these men appears irrefutable. It is for this reason that their newspapers, despite certain imperfections, were a reflection of the combatants' attitudes and way of thinking.

~ 2 ~

Everyday Life

Rigours of Life in the Front Line

The topic that occurs most frequently in the soldiers' newspapers, no doubt because of the relentless and unending sufferings it engendered, is the pattern of daily life. The proportion of column-inches devoted to this theme grew steadily from 1914 to 1918, so that extensive reading of the front-line press leaves an impression of increasing desperation as the war approached its end.

At first it might seem that descriptions of daily life in the trench press are no different from later histories of the war, written after the end of hostilities, but a closer look reveals that the tone is far from identical: perhaps because the ordeals endured were still at the forefront of the soldiers' minds when they wrote down their experiences immediately, but also because the memory of such events is particularly painful. In effect, the soldier's newspaper account of life as a combatant does not belong genuinely, or exclusively, to the past; in some respects the sufferings described are still to come.

Foremost in the ranks of these sufferings, and particularly dreaded, were the rain and the mud:

Here we are, caught in the rain. This simple word, the rain, is virtually meaningless for the townsman, the civilised man protected from bad weather by the roof he has built over his head, yet it is a word that contains all the horror of being a soldier on campaign. While at war, in short, I was never really unhapppy except on account of the rain. I can remember snowy mornings in the Argonne when I covered the sector as trench-major; sometimes a shell whistled past, but I told myself stories and whistled marches as I scrambled across the valleys. But rain, the eternal rain of the first winter in Artois, the sticky, runny mud, the broken roads in the Argonne where the mire came up over your knees . . . No, better think of something else. But what can you think about when it is raining? (*L'Horizon*, July 1918)

The reason why rain takes up so much space in the soldiers' papers is that it was impossible to be entirely protected from it:

I can hear it lashing down the sheet across the opening of the dug-out. It is dripping from sack to sack and running along the parapets to settle at the bottom of the trench. Sometimes it even gets through the dug-out entrance and creeps artfully under planks and blankets, the inhabitants' last refuge. At other times it scorns the trench, preferring to filter slowly through the soil and penetrate drop by drop into the saps, to remind the lads that we have had rain recently. (*La Bourguignotte*, 1916)

Naturally the rain was inseparable from that other scourge, the mud in the trenches:

The greasy tide, of alarming depth, awaits you and draws you in, duty pushes at your back. In one of those foolish decisions which throw you over the parapet on the morning of a big offensive, you take a chance and immerse yourself in the disgusting bath. The water penetrates into your shoes with the glugging noise of empty bottles, while the skirts of your cape swell out gracefully behind you like the light veil of a water-nymph. Sometimes the two lips of the trench come together yearningly and meet in an appalling kiss, the wattle sides collapsing in the embrace. Setting off fresh crumbling as you go, you must climb out and go round, unprotected. Luckily, there is a rain-truce. Boches and French, struggling hand-to-hand with the common enemy, the flooding waters, tolerate each other's excursions out on to level ground. A few lucky individuals with enormous trench boots to protect their legs try their skill in vain with mincing womanish strides, and, like horsemen on foot, look like Tom Thumb in the giant's boots. Then there are the detested digging fatigues for the reserve company, a real labour of Sisyphus, to fix to the parapet a clear runny brew which is determined to run down off it. The mud forms a camouflage from head to foot, burying beneath its sediment all distinguishing signs of age and physiognomy. (*Le Bulletin désarmé*, 1 March 1918)

First-hand descriptions of this torture by mud are innumerable and the front-line press devoted long passages to it throughout the war:

It has been raining all day, that cold, fine, relentless winter rain against which there is no protection. The front-line trench is a mud-coloured stream, but an unmoving stream where the current clings to the banks of its course. Water, mud. You go down into it, you slip in gently, drawn in by who knows what irresistible force. At first the molecules of this substance part, then you can feel them return together and hold on with a tenacity against which nothing can prevail. The parapet collapses in lumps. Twenty times over you have patched up this mass with wattles, yet it slides and drops down. Stakes bend and break, the earth slips down and into the water. Duckboards float, and then sink into the mire. Everything disappears into this ponderous liquid: men would disappear into it too if it were deeper. Some countries have an obsession with dust; here it is the mud which obsesses. It is everywhere, under your feet, under your hands, under your body when you lie down. It does not blow away with the wind, it sticks to your clothes, it gets right through to your skin, it soils anything immobile and everything that dies. By mysterious routes it finds its way into the saps and dug-outs. Formless and multiform, like everything fluid, water, dust, clouds, it is everywhere! (*L'Argonnaute*, 1 June 1916)

Mud like this is such a permanent presence in the soldier's life that it can attain the proportions of an evil beast:

At night, crouching in a shell-hole and filling it, the mud watches, like an enormous octopus. The victim arrives. It throws its poisonous slobber out at him, blinds him, closes round him, buries him. One more '*disparu*', one more man gone . . . For men die of mud, as they die from bullets, but more horribly. Mud is where men sink and – what is worse – where their soul sinks. But where are those hack journalists who turn out such heroic articles, when the mud is that deep? Mud hides the stripes of rank, there are only poor suffering beasts. Look, there, there are flecks of red on that pool of mud – blood from a wounded man. Hell is not fire, that would not be the ultimate in suffering. Hell is mud! (*Le Bochofage*, 26 March 1917)

The nights on guard duty are the most difficult times to endure the rain, the mud and all the rigours of the weather. Soldiers have some truly cruel memories of such moments:

One hour, two hours, three hours, the time crawls as if paralysed. This guard duty will never end. Weariness turns into stupor. The man who was determined not to sleep can feel his eyes about to close, but he will not sleep. He will feel the cold and the rain, he will slip occasionally into swift unconsciousness, but he will not escape completely into good deep animal sleep, dreamless and uninterrupted. There is always the rain, always the winter, always the shadows. The body vanishes, only the mind remains, watching and enduring; a little flame flickering in the shadows. So it will go on until dawn slowly casts its light through the rain onto these heroes, these pale faces and frozen bodies. (*L'Argonnaute*, 15 June 1916)

Cold was perhaps recalled less frequently than rain or mud, but that too was a severe ordeal:

Poor happy stay-at-home, you have never been cold. You need to have been here all this winter, in sectors where cross-fire prevented you from lighting braziers, sitting tight for six days and six nights, your stomach frozen, your arms clumsy, hands inert, feet without feeling; you need to have felt in despair that nothing in the world can warm you again, to have chewed the frozen ends of your moustache in rage, unable to sleep because of the pain of being cold. (*Le Crapouillot*, August 1917)

And yet, despite the arduousness of this trench life – or no doubt because of it – the front-line press could serve up a highly characteristic type of black humour:

Weather Report

Today, rain and wind. Height of water in the trenches: 0.25 m (they were cleaned out yesterday evening). (*Le Klaxon*, March 1916)

After bad weather of all kinds it was the physical effort demanded of the soldiers that occupied a significant part of the front-line newspapers, such as the marches, and above all the 'reliefs', which every time meant an apprehension of torture:

It is time to go. With tent canvas slung across our shoulders, haversacks at our sides, full waterbottles and our *cafard* drowned in cheap wine, we wait to set off when night has fully covered everything with its dark camouflage. After barely ten minutes' walking it begins to rain. This is when you must arm yourself with patience, determination and strength. (*Le 120 court*, January 1918)

This ordeal of 'the relief' made a deep impression on the troops, for it was both physically and psychologically merciless:

The dark, the mud, the rain – these three scourges together overwhelmed the men. They walked with their backs hunched beneath their kit, trudging through the water, their heels dragging in the mud, splashed with liquid earth, wet above and wet below, with a great noise like a scattered herd, dominated by the sharper noise of waterbottles and mess tins jangling together, shouts, orders from somewhere vague, muttered oaths from throats lacking even the strength to grumble or complain. Men walked bent beneath their kit and the weariness of hours of marching, their shoulders hunched, dragging along the pain of their wretched lives. They walked, seeing nothing, blinded by the downpour which made the darkness darker. They walked straight ahead, unseeing, the bulk following the leaders close behind the guide, bumping into each other as sudden movements rippled back along the column like a spark along a wire. They walked, not knowing where they were going. They certainly did not care. Out there was the trench, and all trenches are alike. It was just the war going on, that's all. War with its terrible shadow following behind: death. (*L'Argonnaute*, February 1917)

Desperately demanding, but also desperately dangerous, moving up to relieve the front line was an incommunicable experience:

Oh those reliefs, those fatigue-duties of working in the mud and the rain, on inky-black nights lit up only briefly by flares. Then, over everything, an occasional sharp whistle or a bee-humming reminder that not only is the march hard and wearisome, it is also full of danger. No, only those to whom it has been given to suffer thus can appreciate the strength of character needed to survive, the endurance that must be displayed to avoid falling into despair. Others may have read about it or have heard descriptions, but they can never understand fully and accurately what 'a relief' can be. (*Face aux Boches*, January 1916)

The terrible efforts demanded of the troops were sometimes described with a great wealth of detail, explaining to some extent the clarity of memories evoked:

We are suffocating, the straps of our haversacks cut in, drag and dig into our shoulders. They make our heads and necks thrust forward out of our clothes, and the shirt-folds dig into the bruised flesh. The straps of waterbottles and haversacks are like harness across our chests, crushing us and preventing us from breathing. We gasp, tortured by thirst, our waterbottles empty or holding nothing but tepid stale water tasting sickeningly of iron. The backs of our necks are terracotta-colour. Sweat trickles from under our *képis*, down over foreheads and cheeks and glistens along noses. It flows down bare necks into wide open shirt-collars. We can feel it breaking out in sharp prickles on our backs, under the baking square of our bags, and rippling down over our loins where it collects beneath the belt. It trickles down our arms, sticking our sleeves to the skin, and our fingers drip at the end of our hanging hands, red and enlarged, with the veins standing out. Our weak and weary legs feel soggy with damp and can barely carry us. Our swollen feet are stewing in their boots, bumping painfully against all the stones along the road. I listen to our dreary plodding, our lungs sounding harsh like hoarse whispers, dull sounds beneath the metallic ring of jolting bayonets bumping against the steel of rifles. The sharp little sound of jingling mess-tin chains rings in the ears gratingly, like everlasting cicadas. The monotony of such noises, always the same and endlessly repeated, acts like a lullaby, weighing down our sweltering brains. We end up marching half-asleep, unconscious, without order, unseeing and unthinking, like beasts. (*La Musette*, 24 February 1918)

'Beasts': the definitive term that throws light on the deep significance of these accounts of life in the front line. The brutality and barbarity of their existence seems to have marked the troops who list their innumerable bodily sufferings willingly, almost shamelessly. This profound need to bear witness, mingled perhaps with an attempt at exorcism, is surely unmistakable. These were certainly the men to express the inexpressible, for no one else was in a position to describe the reality of the front. Writing it down for others, for oneself – was this not a way of relieving the load, however slightly, of this crushing burden of terrible memories?

We should not however recall only the most dramatic moments of this front-line existence. In their papers the soldiers were equally articulate about daily concerns that were always very harsh but more banal. Here for example is an article on the combatants' night-life conditions:

A sap? . . . a sumptuous luxury only known in dead sectors . . . Elsewhere, you crouch down in a niche at the side of the trench, shrinking back ridiculously, wrapped up in tent canvas . . . to sleep . . . as for shell-holes, they solidify and stiffen the limbs, the shell-holes out under the stars – under the stars . . . when it's not flooded or under snow – shell-holes where your limbs shiver and . . . your heart too, where your feet are set firm in mud hardened by the sharp crackling frost . . . shell-holes where you fall asleep. (*Le Filon*, 1918)

There were other realities of daily life: dirty clothes, rats, lice and vermin of all kinds, the total lack of personal hygiene. Accounts written after the war remain fairly reticent on all these topics but they were often aired in the troops' newspapers:

I know that for a while it seemed very funny, particularly to people at the rear. Lice and rats were part of the décor, together with mud, rough beards and untidy appearance. This is *'poilu'* style, the blackest joke of modern times, the most improper witticism, making every soldier look as if he is enjoying himself amid the squalor and the dirt. Allow me, gentlemen, to tell you very timidly and very respectfully: we would very much like to be clean! We would be delighted to stop scratching. We would be thrilled not to find our bread contaminated by rats and our shirts invaded by vermin. When the time comes for us to move to a new sector, if someone says, 'the Boches are 20 metres away', we feel a chill; but if we are told: 'the dug-outs are full of lice' – that we find really disgusting! (*Le Pépère*, 21 April 1916)

It is clear that vermin and squalor were not welcome; and if perpetual dirtiness feels so distressing, it is because it is deeply humiliating:

You have to have undertaken, in this month of July, reliefs with 250 cartridges and two days' worth of rations on your back, your blanket and coat rolled across the top and your rifle on its sling, to know what being hot really means: instantly your shirt is wet, your trousers stick to your legs, your socks are damp, your eyes open wider, your tongue hangs out of your mouth, drops of sweat tickle your face and seem set on drowning it. After gathering above the eyebrows the sweat slides down your cheeks, gets lost in your open shirt-collar or rolls briskly down your nose, apparently reluctant to drop off the end, making unexpected excursions into nostrils, eyes and ears. You give up thinking, and your spirits are low because you smell bad. (*Le Crapouillot*, August 1917)

In consequence we should scarcely be surprised that, among other painful ordeals, one newspaper records as particularly striking the fact of

> not washing at all for a fortnight, not changing your clothes or shaving for thirty-five days. (*L'Echo des marmites*, 29 February 1916)

Food supplies are always the object of close attention in the combatants' newspapers. Naturally the times when there was no food to be had are the first to be described:

> On Christmas Day about twenty of us were crowded in a rotten sap captured from the Germans near Ablaincourt. We went in there twenty-four hours earlier, to organise that particular sector. Our men had covered nearly 40 kilometres on foot and had just spent four hours in the nauseating air of motor-buses. They had brought three days' supply of food with them which was supposed to last over Christmas night. For the evening meal, therefore, we ate what was left at the bottom of our bags . . . those bags which still had something in them. And in this area of the Somme – covered in mud – there was no water to be had. These two army corps – the relievers and the relieved – had a truly wretched Christmas night, distressing too . . . For this third Christmas of the war there were certainly – at the front – several other thousands of squads who had nothing but shells to help them celebrate Christmas. (*Les Echos du plateau de Craonne*, 1 January 1917)

The quality of food supplies was also frequently the target of sarcasm from the ranks:

> Coffee: a liquid, generally blackish, more or less clean depending on the water used. No sugar for a long time now, as a punishment, without ever knowing the reason. The cooks sometimes stir their consciences sufficiently to throw in grains of real coffee, though this is regarded as almost cheating. But they should try it sometimes, all the same. (*Poil de tranchée*, February 1916)

How should one react to such scorn? The high command persisted in regarding it as proof of the troops' good humour and steady morale. Certainly, sarcasm was one way to overcome the despondency and dreariness of daily life. But not entirely: it was not enough to stifle the resentment of the troops and frequently the spirit of revolt was not far away.

Everyday life was also, quite simply, idleness, boredom, the tedious drag of empty days of inactivity.

The morning was quiet. At about four in the afternoon the Boches responded a little to our batteries, which they were trying to pinpoint between two copses near Bouvigny Wood. The day is long, so long. Bored . . . Stiff from sitting or crouching on the ground all the time . . . we try and amuse ourselves . . . reading . . . playing cards . . . Soon give up! Try less wearisome positions . . . Stand up . . . Watch the aircraft and their manoeuvres through binoculars . . . Not much of a distraction! . . . Go back into the shelter . . . Bored as ever . . . write something . . . sleep. (*On progresse*, 1 September 1917)

Other newspapers provide confirmation:

Someone is writing on his knees, sitting on the edge of a berth while a candle splutters and drips down his back. Another chap, invisible, is eating; you can hear the bread crunching in his teeth. In a singsong voice a telephonist talks into his receiver to a distant friend. Weary men are snoring in a corner. What can you do in a sap when you don't want to eat or dream? Sleep is the best way to forget that this is a long war. And time passes, without you knowing how, measured miserably by a drip of water from the roof splashing into an empty tin . . . tzing!!! (*L'Argonnaute*, July 1917)

And so it has been going on for months, in this atmosphere where you can feel death always on the watch, disembodied, ungraspable, life goes on, monotonous and dreary, wearisome in its insipidity, in the quiet sector. (*La Mitraille*, January–February 1919)

One word is used more than any others in the soldiers' writings, for unaided it sums up the whole of their life: 'hardship', evoked again here:

The infantry is the queen of the battlefield, so it is said. The Queen! What a grand word to apply to continual, obscure, misunderstood and deplorable suffering. These lumpish fellows, muddy, dirty and dismal, their uniforms torn by the machine-guns, part of the trench where they live or the shell-hole which is their lodging and, alas, all too often their tomb – they receive no reward or attention. They are workmen for the roughest labour, and others will gather its fruits. The muddy coat that we trail along [is] the most vivid symbol of this existence of ours. (*Le Canard du boyau*, December 1916)

And, significantly, it is this word 'hardship' that one soldier chose to emphasise at the end of his article:

Fighting in a modern war means digging yourself into a hole full of water for ten days at a time without moving, it means watching, listening, gripping a grenade in your hand, it means eating cold food, sinking in the mud up to your knees, carrying your food through the black night, going round and round the same point for hours without ever finding it, it means being hit by shells come from Heaven knows where – *in a word, it means hardship.* (*Le Filon*, 1918)

There is the question of the significance of such descriptions of suffering and hardship, depicted here in only a few extracts. Its evocation brought nothing new to the men who were living through what they read about. What was its purpose? It seems probable that many of the soldiers felt great satisfaction at simply reading an accurate picture of their life as combatants. At last things were described accurately. It was only a description by soldiers and for them, true, but nonetheless a description, one which would, moreover, take on the significance of proof. Writing was thus a guarantee against oblivion. To this was added the secret hope that it would reach the non-combatants, the civilians who were so ignorant of life at the front. It was this wish to bear witness to a pitiless human trial and to preserve its memory that inspired all these texts and explains their quantity, their attention to detail. But this need to bear witness, however strong, is not the only explanation.

It is probable that material sufferings were not the most difficult to acknowledge. The evocation of everyday life could turn into an outlet for other sufferings – psychological ones, this time – that were infinitely more painful and more difficult to describe. The inexpressible could perhaps be expressed through this painful depiction of a pattern of everyday life that loomed ever larger as the war continued.

In addition, the townsmen who were the originators of the trench newspapers suffered more than the peasants from bad weather, from physical efforts of all kinds, from the lack of all ease, the dirt and the lack of food. For the former, and particularly for those from comfortable backgrounds, accustomed to the very sheltered – if indeed not wealthy – way of life of the early-twentieth-century middle classes, there is no doubt that life in the trenches was a terrible experience. This shock may also explain the abundance of descriptions.

Finally, perhaps these accounts also reveal a deep desire among the soldiers to recover their human dignity. This dignity was the first victim of the wretched trench life, and their articles are full of these outcast men's feeling of humiliation. To bear witness, to write – surely this was a specific attempt to recover their dignity, beaten down by daily degradation.

Brotherhood in the Trenches?

Faced with these trials of life in the front line, the daily mutual aid between soldiers was a survival reflex that enabled the veterans' movement to turn the 'fraternity of the trenches' into one of its points of reference after 1918. The motto of the Union Nationale des Combattants – 'Unis comme au front', 'Together as at the front' – is evidence of this.[1] And yet although mutual aid between soldiers was universal, the real brotherhood remained part of the privileged relationship between individuals, and the reality of its extension to all soldiers remains questionable.

Sometimes, it is true, bonds of astonishing strength developed:

Having shared the odd green apple gathered with difficulty during days of retreating without bread, having laboured together, marched together, suffered at the same places, having been buried by the same mine, stuck in the same mud; having bent their heads under the same rain, having suffered the blast from the same heavy shells, they have developed a deep friendship for each other. From their shared memories and pains has come an indestructible bond which keeps them always together. You can see them like this, in pairs, in the squads; two by two, as if friendship could not be extended to include more people without weakening, and

1. Antoine Prost, *Les Anciens Combattants et la société française 1914-1939*, Paris, Presses de la Fondation Nationale des Sciences Politiques, 1977, 3 vols.

would lose its intensity by being shared . . . You never see one without the other. Their look-out points are side by side in the trench, they march in the same rank and the more weary of the two hands his rifle over to the other; at dangerous points along the trenches they keep close together, helping each other along difficult stretches. On fatigue duties they carry the same bit of wood or hurdle, one shifts the earth dug out by the other. They practise the most brotherly communism and share their money; the contents of one bag belong equally to the other; they share parcels, drink from the same waterbottle and take it in turns to pay for their drinks. They read their letters to each other in the evenings in rest camps, before blowing out their candle, they chat very quietly to each other about their families, their affairs, and go to sleep exchanging plans for the future. They are known as *camarades*. Mutual friendship sustains them through their long and harsh labour; like oxen trained to the same yoke each feels the support of the other and suffers less because they know they are suffering together. It may happen that one of them is killed; but, between the two of them, they have made a sworn pact and they trust their word. If one is wounded, the other dresses his wound and revives him, carrying him if necessary for long distances, and if one is shot down by machine-gun fire in no-man's-land during an unsuccessful assault the other will crawl out as soon as darkness falls, through the terrible wire . . . He will search the body. And in order to send to the dead man's family some blood-stained letters and a few souvenirs he will risk being caught by a flare and may lose his own skin. They are known as *camarades*.[2] (*Le Périscope*, 1916)

Concern in everyday matters, trials endured together, fear faced together, promise of help in case of disaster, and even one life risked for the other: nothing is missing from this description of friendships forged at the front. But does the text perhaps hint that such closeness remained somewhat out of the ordinary?

In fact it was particularly when faced with being wounded or killed that the soldiers felt themselves swept up on extraordinary surges of friendship:

In a dressing-station a wounded man who was losing his strength fell on the first stretcher-bearer he met and whom he had never seen: 'Embrace me. I want to die with you.' (*Poil et Plume*, October 1916)

2. The word '*camarade*' usually indicates a relatively superficial relationship between individuals within a community. Its deliberate use here, to indicate the exceptionally powerful friendships that developed through front-line experience, emphasises the restraint of the soldiers' language and intensifies the emotive power of this extract.

Similarly, the distressed questioning of an evacuated soldier without news of his unit shows how much he values the bonds between him and his comrades still in the front line:

> What has happened to you? I heard that the regiment was in action and that there were serious losses. I've even heard that M. Foucheraud is dead. Is it true? . . . And my friend Prosper? and M. Rousseau? and all our friends? What has happened to them? (*L'Echo du boqueteau*, 23 May 1918)

As for the death of a close friend, it set off an outburst of despair, and the front-line press was often full of obituaries such as this:

> I have here in my note-book a few lines which he wrote for me while we were drinking our coffee together. He promised to finish them one day and said, 'If I don't come back, finish them yourself . . .' He did not come back, and I don't have the courage to touch even a comma, my hands are trembling as I turn over the pages he wrote . . . I can only think of him smiling, happy, his hand held out, his eyes bright . . . And I tell myself that all those dreams we shared will never come true, never, that I shall not see him again. (*Bellica*, March 1916)

Sometimes the soldiers' newspapers indicate the existence of certain friendships, hatched in the egalitarian atmosphere of trench life, that managed to cross the class barrier. But a rapprochement like this, between an intellectual and an uneducated working man, remained fairly unusual:

> Lively and willing, Gentil was born in Le Havre where he worked as a docker, or '*carabot*', as he called it. I met him when we were first mobilised, and we got on well straight away. At the corps depot chance – was it really chance? – put us in neighbouring beds . . . All our hardships, all our distresses, all our fears made us friends, like two brothers. And now that Gentil is dead, now that a stupid piece of shrapnel got him outside the sap, all on my own I am weeping for my brother! Memories, good and bad, are crowding in on top of each other, filling my memory. Gentil was talkative. His picturesque language, full of barbarisms, made his conversation interesting to listen to . . . This is the end of those talks in which Gentil made me his confidant and revealed his straightforward soul, his good rough heart . . . Farewell my good Gentil! You are now in the paradise of humble men. (*Bombardia*, 30 April 1918)

The text reveals the importance for the most cultivated and privileged members of the army of this *discovery*, in the true meaning of the term, of men born into other social circumstances. Its slightly dismissive condescension also stresses the limitations of equality and fraternity between combatants of very different backgrounds. This egalitarian theme was none the less a popular one:

The lesson to be learnt by us thinking men from this war is a lesson in humility. Our brethren in glory and pain are unsophisticated . . . Our comrades of the great war surround us with ignorance and intellectual tranquillity . . . Set in their midst, we have often admired and envied them. When our exhausted nerves and painful muscles let the pick fall, their strong arms continue to dig the trench with the same strong, regular rhythm; because our jerky efforts were slower and less skilled they had to do part of our work for us. Often during night fatigues they helped us carry the beam under which we would march at first, bending painfully down into the mud, and under which we soon staggered; they took our place and, still carrying their own burden, they helped us at the same time. It was they who pitied us, and our souls which were full of gratitude and prayer, humility and shame; for we were ashamed of our white hands and our feeble arms. And we were ashamed sometimes of our excessive sensitivity. On days when the prolonged and violent bombardment brought our poor nerves to their limit, their calm and balanced temperament endured without impatience, without restiveness, all the emotions of the pounding, of that waiting below ground, in the shadow where death hovers, in the face of the terrible unknown . . . When we had to brave the open ground swept by shot they faced the fire with a broader and stronger breast, with stronger arms, with more skilful movements, more simple and more sure. Better than us at labouring, they were often better at fighting too, better shots, better runners, more dextrous with their bayonets. At rest, they slept more easily than those of us whose brains persisted in thinking. They soon forgot their weariness. And, although sometimes they would admire us in turn when our knowledge was apparent, although we would then feel their slightly superstitious schoolboy respect for us as for a schoolmaster, we remained humble before them because we felt keenly how much we lacked their strength and physical skills, how much our over-sensitive nervous system was something inferior, almost a handicap. We understood that there is no need to be a philosopher to be great when faced with the greatest of all things, to face up to danger despite the shrinking back of the flesh, to understand and perform all one's duty, to approach death proudly, 'stoically' – that death before whom we are all equal and which lays side by side these bodies of ours, similar and equal in value when the unequal flame of intelligence leaves them. (*L'Horizon*, November 1917)

We can ignore the tone of false modesty which, however disagreeable, does not disguise the sincerity of the argument, for the value of the text lies elsewhere: it shows that on this particular theme an unconscious process of distortion of the truth comes into play very rapidly. Certainly life in the front line effected an undoubted levelling among individuals and their circumstances, but it never came close to establishing true equality between the combatants who, in uniform, remained tied to their origins and continued, materially and emotionally, to belong to them. Contrary to what they thought to prove, these two extracts demonstrate above all the persistence of social and cultural divisions.

The diversity of geographical origins also constituted a considerable obstacle to individual rapprochement, as seen in this embarrassed reaction at the discomfiture of Provençal men posted to a regiment of Bretons:

> We are with the 19th. This is a fact. It is not for us to discuss whether we would have preferred to join a regiment of men from Marseilles, or Limoges, or *'petit gars'* from the Nord. Whatever our personal preference, we are now Bretons . . . so let us live in harmony with the Bretons, who are good fellows and like us in more ways than one . . . But what if the Bretons' language is a complete mystery to us? . . . Is that their fault, should we blame them for it? . . . Just like Provençal, Breton is a venerable language which deserves to be preserved . . . Let us make the 19th welcome. (*L'Echo du boqueteau*, June 1918)

In the end, articles showing evidence of true fraternity are few in number – hardly more numerous than those which, conversely, reveal the individual's isolation and egotism; this overwhelming admission, after the death of a friend, is one such example:

> Morin must be with them. The victim had friends here. Morin? Not possible? The poor fellow was out of luck. We were school-friends. We went right through the campaign together. Beyond the memory of the dead man who was still warm, lying there in the upturned earth, my thoughts soon range further . . . The coffee is good this morning. I sip it and enjoy it, thinking that it is possible to be content at the front – for here I am, warm in my wire-draped bed while other poor fellows have suffered the misfortune of being wiped out in an ill-favoured hole. I have a very clear image of the five men heaped up in the clay, their limbs dislocated, their faces black and dreadful. I feel a surge of vague pity: no

doubt the self-centred agitation of someone who realises very clearly that the same thing can happen to him. And yet, after seeing so much, feelings are blunter and the heart less tender, luckily! (*L'Argonnaute*, 1 August 1916)

Indifference, in other words, the indifference which is no doubt born of the need not to let oneself be overwhelmed by emotion, failing which daily life would become even less bearable. Such indifference was certainly shaken by the sharp reminder of one's own death, though only briefly:

Danger, the waiting and the overpowering notion of death have hardened our spirits, and indifference is now the inhuman corset which protects us from all-too-human feelings. The less suffering the better. Is X dead? Poor devil! And after a minute or two no one thinks about him any more. The only shock is that death may, as with X, catch us unawares. And you grow accustomed even to that, like everything else. (*L'Argonnaute*, June 1918)

This ultimately reduced space for the theme of fraternity from soldiers' pens is the more significant in that military authority, anxious to strengthen cohesion within units, did its best to encourage every manifestation of solidarity. Thus the publication of a citation such as the following in a trench newspaper was certainly no mere chance:

Despite a lively fusillade he did not hesitate to leave the trench to help one of his friends who was seriously wounded, and brought him back to our lines. Congratulated on his courage by his friends, he said simply: 'I only did my duty'. (*L'Echo des guitounes*, 1 May 1915)

Here a few lines serve to summarise an additional ambiguity in comments on the 'fraternity of the front line', so easily distorted to support *esprit de corps*. For this reason a particularly articulate soldier was not mistaken when, at the time of the Armistice, he drew up this gloomy list of relationships formed at the front, and which would now dissolve:

In a few weeks, probably, we shall all part. We have lived together for

years, shared the same meagre pleasures, the same trials, experienced the
same dangers, sometimes without understanding each other, never without knowing each other. (*La Fourragère*, November 1918)

This indeed expresses the heart of the matter. Fraternity could be
made manifest in exceptional conditions, but it was not part of the
daily experience of war for most soldiers. If the contrary were true,
their newspapers would surely have left a stronger indication of it, a
sharper picture. This is not the case. Contrary to what some combatants in good faith urgently wanted to believe, contrary to the
memories that they clung to of their life at the front, the fraternity
of the trenches was largely illusory. This legend was born during the
war among soldiers of middle-class origins and grew to its full
extent after the end of the war, at the heart of the veterans' movement in which they occupied most of the leading places.[3]

Morale

As the war showed signs of lasting longer than anticipated, as the
troops on both sides became dug into their trenches, the problem of
the army's morale took on new significance. It received increasing
attention from the high command, who wished to weigh up their
troops' capacity for endurance and to assess their capacity for
'holding on'. The censors' reading of letters bears witness to this
concern, as does the duty – not always observed – of trench newspapers to send a copy of each issue, from 1917 on, to General
Headquarters.

The amount of space allotted to problems of morale in the front-
line press should not be overlooked, both because it admitted into
the columns the reality of moments of doubt or despair and because
it persisted on the other hand in minimising its gravity, even to the
extent of denying its existence. It cannot be denied that a small
number of papers – whose essential objective it was – attempted to
give credibility to the myth of an unshakeable high morale from the
beginning to the end of the war. The following extract indicates the
state of mind of the 120th infantry regiment 'revealed' in its paper,
Le 120 court:

3. Prost, *Les Anciens Combattants*.

Poilus who don't waver on marches even when the hourly break is omitted, whose feet are never cold, who enjoy the odd drink but who can also tighten their belts. *Poilus* who are steady, keen, habitually good-humoured, who don't jib at work, and who hardly complain even when the promised relief is late. Ordinary fellows, in fact, with stout hearts who only look for one thing: to satisfy their officers, to clean up for the last time, and go back home. (*Le 120 court*, 25 July 1916)

Here is an attempt to disguise the reality of the soldiers' disarray – a clumsy attempt, and with distinctly limited effect; the argument is generally more subtle, as in this extract from early in 1918, a time when doubt seemed to be growing:

It's understood . . . We all know it. Nothing is lacking to weaken the soldiers' morale, everything seems to operate together: true or false rumours, Russian anarchy, the eternal shirkers, the cold, the snow, mistakes, a thousand and one other factors. And then? Out of forty million Frenchmen it would be very surprising if there were not some who were stout-hearted . . . The Russian situation appears to put the Allies in a false light. Does it help our enemies? Not much, so far. Are there shirkers who will never be flushed out by the Mourier law?[4] It's possible; in any case they are rare, and it would be extraordinary if injustice ceased with the war. Is it a hard winter? Yes, but it is equally hard on the other side and their soldiers suffer as much as ours – more, because they are badly fed. Have our attacks sometimes failed to achieve their objective? True, but we cannot have a monopoly of leaders with genius. We can confirm, however, that on our front the enemy is piling up one setback after another. And so? Take courage. No more disparagement. No more criticism! We will weigh up responsibility later, this is not the time for it. First we must have victory . . . The hour is grave but not desperate. Take heart, we will be victorious to avenge our dead and not to let them down. (*La Musette*, 25 January 1918)

This more subtle approach acknowledges the causes of doubt, but does so in order to refute them and then to remind its readers that they should retain their sangfroid and resist any temptation to give up.

In the great majority of papers, on the other hand, *le cafard*

---

4. The Mourier Law was introduced to ensure greater effectiveness and fairness in recruitment. It was passed by the Chambre des Députés on 27 July and the Senate on 3 August 1917.

appeared as a familiar reality, an openly acknowledged element of everyday life; something to complain about, just like the food or the demands of reliefs.

First appearing in January 1915, this theme of *le cafard* remained prominent thereafter until the end of the war:

> All *poilus* have suffered from *le cafard*. It seizes you suddenly, you don't know why, and you start considering all the reasons for feeling depress-ed. It is a lowering of morale that takes hold of you. Everything looks black. You are tired of life itself. External matters lose all interest. (*L'Echo de tranchées-ville*, 10 February 1916)

Many soldiers tried to describe the feelings that assailed them in these moments of despair.

> There are days . . . when you feel invaded by a mysterious terror of the unknown. You see in your mind's eye your family, left behind at home, whom you may never see again, the life which used to promise so much after the war and which may be snatched away from you at any moment, and deep anguish grips you. (*Face aux Boches*, March 1917)

Intuition or fear of one's own death: therein lies the origin of *le cafard*. Such is the case with this young soldier when his section, to which he has just been attached and which was decimated in a recent action, is summoned:

> My section is billeted in a hay-loft: there are roof-tiles missing, the straw for sleeping on is wet with rain. We are cowed, awkward, a bit frightened by this wretchedness . . . Parcels are being distributed. The sergeant gets them out of a big bag: 'So-and-so!' – 'Dead!' is often the answer from the soldiers. Scarcely two or three packets reach their addressees. Deep in thought, we consider the pile of parcels addressed to dead men . . . Then the sergeant-major comes round to take our parents' addresses: 'You know why, you never know what's going to happen.' I don't know whether it was the effect of such disturbing phrases or the cold mist which still hung over the countryside, but I felt overwhelmed by a peculiar melancholy; a sadness in which men and things and thoughts all looked grey. I have never felt anything like it. I learnt later that it was a *poilu* speciality and was called '*le cafard*'. (*Sans tabac*, March 1917)

But the lowering of morale might be fed, if not provoked, by less tragic happenings. The return from leave, or contact with civilians behind the front lines, making the return to one's former way of life more desirable; anxiety over one's post-war future after such a long break from work; a simple delay in receiving letters; all were elements that could undermine morale.

Or it might be, as here, the return of the colder seasons:

Now it is autumn, soon it will be winter: for long days at a stretch the *poilu* will stay in the outposts, or in his billet, and the enemy to be repulsed will not be the Boche but *le cafard*. (*L'Echo du grand-couronné*, October 1915)

The onset of dusk had a similar effect:

You feel cut off from the rest of the world. This is when everyone turns in on himself; few words are exchanged; everyone looks into his own depths, seeking the mental strength to lift himself above this overwhelming atmosphere of death. (*La Fusée à retards*, May 1917)

This multiform, endemic and intangible *cafard* was a misfortune against which nothing could prevail:

Le cafard is caused by sufferings of indisputable precision, of the clearest possible desires and regrets, regret, nostalgia for everything – work, friendship, family – which together constitute the normal course of life. *Le cafard* is not the wish for a future love ... If there are thoughts of love within it, it is the thought of a very real love, waiting silently and far away. *Le cafard* proliferates in the mud, and the most stolid good fellow may fall victim ... Even in its revolts, *le cafard* is humble; it is born of the feeling that we are being crushed by events that are inimical but which lack any special distinction: we suffer like everyone else around us, and our sickness does not appear to prove that we are in any way extraordinary ... *Le cafard* is monstrous, without any redeeming feature: there is something deathly about it. It is as heavy to bear as a tomb-stone. Often you can laugh and be stirred in a moment of forgetfulness. Then *le cafard* returns, fiercely ... And you think of all those whom you love and who are dead ... and still you talk, and still you laugh, it's the tide of life driving us forward despite ourselves – and at the very moment that you are talking and laughing, the bitter thoughts are surging within you; and your mind is taken up with them alone. And at the very moment when you are joking, you have within you, in your heart and your eyes, only the memory of someone who is dead and whom you loved. (*Le Crapouillot*, September 1916)

Homesickness for family and for pre-war life, the daily harshness, the death of valued friends, the nightmare of one's own death and, dominating everything, this feeling of being crushed, the uselessness of any resistance; it is all here. How can one not be struck too by the ease of the argument, by this style of bringing moral distress down to the level of one more reality of war among others, affecting everyone?

Morale as seen in combatants' writings appears almost permanently mediocre from the beginning to the end of the war, with some strongly marked dips, as in 1917:

Having seized back a few square kilometres of land from the Boches last month, the 1st Zouaves have spent [August] fighting *le cafard* in the same way. That's their fate. (*Le Chéchia*, 1 August 1917)

Despite the reality of such particularly critical moments, the importance of this matter of morale should not be exaggerated, for it does not of itself sum up the whole of the soldiers' mental universe. Care should be taken to distinguish between morale and national feeling: although the moments when morale faltered were not without their effect on the soldiers' image of their 'duty', this link was neither constant nor automatic, and soldiers appear to have retained a genuine will to resist despite quite low morale during these four years of war.

Discipline, Claims and Revolt

It has been shown that in certain newspapers an intricate mixture of falsification and authenticity was by no means uncommon. The same applies to an obviously delicate matter, that of respect for discipline. The high command's objectives relating to the trench press and the rank of some of its editors largely explain the concern of many newspapers to sustain respect for command and military regulations. In general the front-line press sought to offer its readers an image of a military society free from tensions, focused round good relationships between superior and junior officers and obedience freely given. With a few exceptions, failures of discipline or respect for officers are never mentioned in this idealised picture.

That the reality was appreciably different is proved in this article by an officer who by 1915 thought it necessary to remind his soldiers of some of their duties:

> The soldier is not permitted to criticise his officers. First, with the little information he possesses, the soldier is not in a position to formulate a serious and definitive opinion. Yes, even when your criticisms make sense to you, keep quiet, it is in everybody's interest to do so. What may be the demoralising effect of sour words? Have you really thought about it? You would do better to trust your remarkable officers, not only because discipline is the strength of armies and because it is our duty, but out of affection, for love of your leaders. Duty done out of love is what will distinguish us – indeed it is what has always distinguished us, and still distinguishes us from the rough enemy whose obedience to his leaders is the result of the whip and the boot. (*Le Mouchoir*, 21 November 1915)

This is a frequent theme, that of deliberate attachment to the officers, of submission to military regulations accepted by all as necessary, and seen as proof of the French soldier-citizen's moral superiority. This acceptance also leads the non-commissioned officers to respect certain principles: the officer addressed by the trench press owes it to himself to win the confidence of his men, to arouse their respect and obedience, without recourse to constraint. Such demands may overflow into certain indirect criticisms of certain behaviour:

> A too frequent mistake is to take haughtiness and aloofness for dignity, brutality for firmness, a propensity to punish for professional zeal. Prestige, so essential to the officer, cannot be acquired in isolation. Live as much as possible with your men, share in their daily labours and dangers as much as possible. The men are neither inferior beings nor simple fighting machines. Our soldiers are not professional soldiers, they are citizen-soldiers . . . We must show the men that we feel their anxieties, that we sympathise with them, that we are aware of the enormity of their sacrifices. (*Le Crapouillot*, August 1917)

Discipline is thus not defended blindly, although this was not always the case and certain papers let themselves be dragged deep into realms of flattery: to such an extent that the *bourrage de crâne* which raged in the national press was sometimes outstripped:

> People speak [of the *poilus*], rightly, with the greatest praise, and it would be impossible to exaggerate their good qualities. However, there is a tendency to forget that their achievements would be nothing without the vigilance, the example and the steadfastness of the officers ... Thus, when at the right moment he leads his men forward to overcome the enemy, he should not be seen in the wrong light, as a herdsman leading his cattle to the butcher, but as a controller of movement whose aim is to spare us the maximum number of human lives while still attaining the goal ... In attack, then, you will see the French officer in front, at the head of his men, in danger from the enemy fire. Do you recognise in him the slave-driver of legend? Follow him along the trench, and observe his concern that his men are provided with what is essential and even what is useful, in the absence of what is comfortable ... The officers live together out of necessity and not out of scorn for their men, as there is a tendency to suppose ... This is not conspicuous pride but the need for frequent exchanges of opinion in the general interest and the maintenance of essential authority requiring the officers to remain apart. Respect, then, and admiration for our officers! (*L'Echo de tranchées-ville*, 9 September 1915)

We should not suppose that such ridiculously excessive arguments had any influence; but it is none the less significant that after the first two years of war there is virtually no trace of such articles. In fact the interest of their attempts at glorification lies in their revelation – while seeking to conceal it – of the full extent of frustration resulting from submission to military constraints.

More numerous and also more skilful are the papers which avoid all generalised eulogies of officers and the need for discipline, and restrict themselves to praising officers known personally to the men, often seen daily in their midst. This applies to the non-commissioned officers and subalterns who, in contrast to the superior officers, genuinely share the life of the men in the ranks and meet danger with them. It is the courage of these men which the trench newspapers highlight above all, aware that this criterion is decisive in the men's opinion of those who lead them:

> It is here that heroism and devotion abound. It is the company commander, followed by several men, who falls mortally wounded in the

assault on a casemate battery reconnoitred by him. Another, killed by two shots in the forehead as he was trying to ascertain the position of a machine-gun obstructing the regiment's advance ... Another again, whom we shall not name but who is known to all of us, who on the eve of battle, with cane in hand and pipe in mouth, boldly orders 'Charge' and at the head of his men runs magnificently into battle. (*Brise d'entonnoirs*, May–July 1917)

There should be no mistaking this: a proposition so generous to the officers, seeking to instil confidence into the men and to compel their respect, was not so unjustified as to be a legend without foundation. Even if some front-line newspapers used ridiculous language in their wish to arouse admiration for the officers, it is none the less true that certain acts of heroism are beyond doubt. We should remember that in the French army the death rate among officers was 19 per cent for the whole war and the six months following the armistice, against 16 per cent of men in the ranks. For the combatant troops of the land forces alone, 22 per cent of the officers were listed killed or missing, against 18 per cent of the rankers. Such figures plead eloquently in favour of the determination of the officers in the front line, and there is thus no exaggeration whatever in a description such as this:

The 15th were the first into the battle for 'Mont Tetu'. To give an idea of what this struggle was like, we can state that at the end of the day the 1st Battalion of this regiment was commanded by a sergeant-major, and when he was himself wounded during the night it was a sergeant who took command. Therefore in this battalion all the officers, all the officer cadets, all the warrant-officers and all the sergeant-majors had been killed or wounded. (*Bellica*, January 1916)

Even in their worst moments of doubt the critics almost always spared the officers who up to the rank of captain lived in the trenches with their men. However harsh their authority, it was no doubt easier to bear than was occasionally claimed by a certain tradition after the war in reaction against an idealisation based on equally little foundation.[5]

---

5. Louis Barthas, *Carnets de guerre de Louis Barthas, tonnelier (1914-1918)*, Paris, Maspero, 'La Mémoire du Peuple', 1978.

The everyday reality of relationships between officers and men in the ranks seems reasonably clear in this lieutenant's description:

> At 8.30 I went along my line for the last time, followed by my runner, reviewing my whole little world. Double rations of brandy had been distributed, and I feared that they wouldn't be calm enough. In these supreme moments one would like to make one's men feel . . . how close one is to them, how much one loves them, what gratitude one bears them in advance for the sublime obedience that will launch them forwards into the fearful and treacherous unknown. One would like to embrace them all, and can only find a few silly words: 'Well, old man? All right? – It looks as if it's nearly time? – Do you think we'll get them?' Heads are lifted, voices and the silhouettes on the parapet can be recognised . . . 'It's all right, lieutenant' – and that is the only demonstration of feeling from those who go into battle together. (*Le Voltigeur*, 21 July 1917)

Paternalism? Doubtless. Yet however disingenuous they may be, these few lines ring true and reveal all the ambiguity and all the complexity of rapport between men in the ranks and their superior officers.

But such insistence also makes it clear that respect for officers and discipline could not always be taken for granted, as proved by this brief explosion of anger:

> The rank stupidity of the army and the vastness of the sea are the only two things which can give an idea of infinity. (*On progresse*, 1 April 1917)

An isolated case, valid only for the spring of 1917? It is true that claims were more numerous and more bitter after that date, but from the first days of the war many soldiers voiced frequent criticisms whose content subsequently varied only slightly. The food, for example, was a constant topic of discontent:

> The basic meal . . . consists, morning and evening [of rice]. Our friends beg us to declare that a change would not displease them. (*La Saucisse*, August 1916)

Another criticism, with greater irony, a year later:

Food: it must be said that it is: nourishing, abundant and varied. All compliments to the postal service. (*Le Crapouillot*, November 1917)

One cannot imagine a more succinct insinuation that without the postal packages brought to the front from the rear the official rations would be wholly inadequate. On the other hand, this article on the distribution of tobacco gives free rein to a genuine exasperation:

The following confident statement can be read on the blocks of cigarette paper that are distributed free from time to time: 'Cigarette paper given by the government of the Republic to the valiant *poilus* at the front', or this, no less mirth-provoking: 'To its valiant defenders, the Nation offers our Z— Glorious soldiers: now and after the war, always ask for —' The *poilus* should be grateful to the government of the Republic, and to the whole Nation, for such considerate attention! But they would happily give up the free cigarette paper (and the free description of 'valiant' and 'glorious' too) if the commissariat would agree to allot them 100 grammes of tobacco instead of 100 grammes of rubbish every ten days. (*Le Périscope*, 1917)

The low rates of pay, particularly at the beginning of the war, were also severely criticised:

Do you know how much I am credited with for the first two months of the war? F 0.25. Exactly, five sous ... itemised no doubt as follows: Battle of Charleroi, F 0.05; Battle of Guise, F 0.05; Retreat, F 0.05; The Marne, F 0.10; Total, F 0.25. (*La Saucisse*, June 1917)

The poor standard of rest camps reserved for soldiers behind the lines also appeared unreasonable. By 1916 this question was heard from the ranks:

May one say that the unspeakable dumps where the troops are lodged before or after action are completely bare? (*Le Bochofage*, 21 October 1916)

And the following year, billets were stigmatised in greater detail:

The camp in the woods is a perfectly organised and self-sufficient unit. The Zouaves are cleverly lodged on berths which can also serve as company shop, saddlery, stores depot and sergeant-major's office . . . Drinking water is usually 500 metres from the camp and is easy to fetch – but without being unreasonable, for example between 5.15 and 6.22, and between 20.30 and midnight. It is very practical. The showers are in the next village. On the other hand, there is water everywhere on the ground. This is the only water supply of which the use is not strictly regulated . . . No war-profiteers visit the camp. It is not worth it, a general stores lorry comes on the 12th and 25th of each month, a little before pay-day. Apart from that, the *coopérative* is usually only 1 or 2 kilometres away . . . The camps in the woods are generally known as: rest camps. (*Le Chéchia*, 15 October 1917)

Here, as in the case of tobacco or pay, it is a feeling of degradation which nurtures exasperation. Yet again the soldiers' dignity is at stake.

Certain topics engendered even greater discontent, such as the use of rest periods for particularly wearisome fatigue duties, a practice denounced in 1915:

The day after your arrival you pick up any tool, a shovel or a pick, for example, and you go off to a point a few kilometres away in the middle of the countryside; there you set to work digging holes, stopping only for meals. At night you do the same, for nothing is so essential as variation in styles of rest, so as to render them effective. The only thing is, you make your holes in a different place from those you dug during the day. Next day, another change. You take a fairly bulky object, a rifle for example, and you go off again for a few kilometres. Once you are in the right place you wave the object or the rifle about in all directions, energetically. After two hours of this exercise you go back to your rest-place. You carry on with this treatment for about a week. Then your rest is complete. You are aware of a slight lassitude in your limbs, but your mind is calm and rested. And the mind, surely, is everything? (*La Guerre joviale*, August 1915)

The most sensitive topic, always, remained that of leave: too rare, too irregular, requiring interminable travel, leave nourished a permanent current of recrimination. In this case, it was clearly in 1917 that the critical point was reached, as can be seen in this list of demands concerning transport conditions:

A little greater speed in leave trains. A little less waiting in the stations. A little more comfort in the coaches. Slightly fewer draughts in the 'waiting rooms'. Slightly more accurate information on the part of the transport officers. If it were possible to achieve these improvements, which would aim at the most at not making the *poilu* on leave feel like a passive and hardy parcel, all would be for the best. (*Le 120 court*, February 1917)

That was the year when any delay in the rhythm of leave departures provoked a real crisis of morale, even in newspapers little given to subversion:

Here is darkness again. No one knows anything any more, or expects anything any more. As for our families, they are adrift, plunged back into the ignorance and uncertainty of former times ... [leave] once again appears as a favour: from the moment when the judiciously established rules were bent a little, it could never be a question of rights: the prodigious leverage of comfort and energy – and of discipline – is broken. And drearily bearing the immensity of his abandonment once more with fortitude, in the desolate abyss of his inward loneliness, the soldier waits. (*Le Tord-boyau*, July 1917)

Many topics were thus the focus of soldiers' exasperation. This might turn to individual protest when it seemed to them, rightly or wrongly, that officers' incompetence or negligence could be held responsible for needlessly inflicted sufferings, or when they thought that their fate could easily benefit from certain improvements. Accused of indifference or contempt, the commanding officer was thus directly challenged, sometimes over questions of apparently secondary importance, such as the inequality of material conditions:

Knowing the different rations to which officers and men have rights, what would be the portion due to each one at a table at which an entire beef carcase is served and at which come to be seated a general, a colonel, a quartermaster officer, a three-stripe interpreter, a lieutenant, a sergeant, a corporal and a *poilu*? (*Bellica*, 5 June 1916)

If the officers' privileges seemed so difficult to bear, it was scarcely a question of jealousy on the part of the men in the ranks; it was because such differences in treatment deeply offended their republican assumptions of absolute equality between citizen-soldiers united in defence of their country.

This was the reason for the particular detestation of the 'shirkers', the 'dodgers' and, supreme among their ranks, the staff officers:

> On my first leave I felt a certain surprise at seeing these people, all officers, in their smart uniforms. They gave as much care to their military clothing as to their pre-war outfits. Their faces had not changed: the fatigues and miseries of war had left no trace at all on their ever-impassive features. I was convinced immediately that they had never left Paris. I was filled with immense scorn for them and I summarised my impression by the only suitable expression 'shirkers' . . . But what I find terrible is that such men dare to put on the most glorious uniforms and wear decorations to which they certainly have no claim. The display of green, yellow or red *fourragère* ribbons on their uniforms, of *croix de guerre*, of military medals and of *Légions d'honneur*, is absolutely revolting. (*Le Mouchoir*, April 1918)

As for the High Command, they too were hardly spared. There was indignation, for example, over this foreign journalist's summary of his interviews with several French generals which a Paris newspaper was tactless enough to report:

> *Daily Telegraph*: 'The morale of French soldiers is magnificent. I was able to talk to four of their generals, whose calmness amazed me.' We have indeed every reason to believe that the morale of French generals is magnificent. (*Le Canard poilu*, October–November 1916)

Sometimes the resentment was more serious. Bitter accusations were made against the general staff and their daily communiqué describing the evolution of the front-line situation:

> Oh, that communiqué! What losses it has on its conscience. It is imperiously demanded in the name of public opinion, and to satisfy this opinion it must not dwell on a setback which is often apparent only to the yielding side. It is necessary to register a success from time to time. Thus it is that little local actions are undertaken, nibbling away at men and munitions, spreading despair among families a little bit at a time with no truly positive – let alone decisive – result. (*L'Echo de tranchées-ville*, 26 March 1916)

So the high command was openly accused of making light of spilt blood; and from this accusation of insensitivity to one of incompetence in the conduct of operations was only a step. This step was taken after the Nivelle offensive setback in the spring of 1917. Without being designated by name, the preparation for this attack is described here with a bitterness of tone unknown hitherto:

> These are the main conditions demanded by the preparation of any offensive: the *poilu* has his head closely shaved, he is taught the military salute, he is given no leave, he carries out about a dozen forced marches in the problematical search for a billet less bare than the others. There is nothing more to do except wait for a day of torrential rain on which to launch the troops on an assault. (*Le Bochofage*, 25 July 1917)

In another article the setback of April–May is openly broached:

> Two months have passed since our last issue, two very busy months. First, we concluded in March a series of manoeuvres in preparation for a major offensive, and manoeuvres, as everyone knows, are instructive. There were some fine themes of this kind: the cavalry would relieve a fictitious body of infantry who had just taken a fictitious fortified position . . . There were in addition some fine spectacles: we saw an officer from the General Staff go back up the column at high speed, asking at the top of his voice if anyone had seen the fictitious artillery. And there was the man who, to cross a 50-metre wood, solemnly took out his compass to guide himself . . . When you have seen that, nothing surprises you . . . After these amazing manoeuvres, and ripe for more arduous combat, we were directed to an offensive about which we will take care not to talk. That is moreover the best thing to do, and keeping silent can sometimes be an opinion. (*On progresse*, 1 July 1917)

Thus the trench press did not restrict itself to a poignant but neutral and resigned picture of the soldiers' life. Nor did not it hesitate to state their indignation or to claim a genuine right of protest:

> I understand that one does not permit civilians to complain. But we can, we have the right to complain: we get ourselves killed. It would be strange if they took this right away from us: sheep still bleat loudly at the door of the abattoir. Stop them from bleating at that particular moment, you who are so clever. (*Le Bochofage*, 25 June 1917)

Sheep. Abattoir . . . comparisons which bear witness to a new state of mind after three years of war, of a kind likely to undermine authority gravely.

For this reason the censor's apparent indulgence in such cases cannot fail to be surprising. Lack of effectiveness? Lack of will on the part of overworked or sympathetic officers, who simply prefer to let such rancour spill out freely, to some extent at least? Whatever the answer, the virulence of the criticisms tended to diminish after the middle of 1917, and the calmer mood extended into 1918. The appointment of Pétain as Commander in Chief, the abandonment of systematically offensive methods, the taking in hand again of troops, combining improvements in daily life with the re-establishment of discipline, all appear to have overcome indiscipline. This does not mean that the resentment died away, but it diminished in intensity while a henceforward stricter supervision of the soldiers' press further muted the expression of their discontent.

It still remains to appreciate fully the extent of this exasperation. Was it sufficiently serious to bring the army near to breaking-point? Even in 1917, when the anger was at its peak, this does not appear to have been the case. The cruelty of the interminable ordeal inflicted on the soldiers, despite their indignation, did not manage to crush their determination to persist in 'holding on'.

~ 3 ~

Ever-present Death

Battle

Once the war was over there were many who set about writing their memoirs. In their writings, however, the veterans reveal deliberate discretion or straightforward inaccuracy concerning battles in which they took part; only a very small minority conveyed a precise account of the assaults or bombardments which were a universal experience. Were such moments literally 'indescribable' for them? A few have confirmed that this was so – but the origin of the silence of some and the distortion of memory by others can more profitably be sought in the depths of terror which battle inspired among those who risked their lives. For most, reticence on the reality of these battles, concealment of this experience of fear and the attempt to forget such atrocities, were psychological necessities.

While the war was still in progress this need was felt so overwhelmingly that the majority of combatants avoided the subject in their letters and newspapers. The taboo was broken on occasions, however, and the trench press throws some light on the terrible tortures of waiting which preceded attacks:

At 1400 hours the third section of the fifth company will attack the barricade – this time the order seems definite, even though it was the third order to be issued: first 0800 hours, then 1000 hours and, twice over, having stocked up with courage as one takes a deep breath before diving, we had to relax our nerves, revert to being the peaceful soldier waiting in the trenches ... 'Is it true this time?' Corporal L. whispers in my ear ... He smiles, peaceful, not dreaming, one would say, of the danger ahead. I think too much about it, myself. I envy my friend's calmness, and to distract myself from such dangerous ideas I look at the flat land around ... I look at my watch again ... nearly 1400 hours.

Sergeant Lair, in charge of the small attack group, does the same. We are still watching . . . Five minutes, and a leap into the unknown. I think, despite myself, that in an hour from now I may no longer be in a position to philosophise. I shake myself . . .

The fifteen men of the assault group are all there in the trench, looking calm as they wait for the moment of action. Some are smoking, others are talking quietly, one man looks at himself surreptitiously in a small mirror. This strikes me as extraordinary. Would I have thought of doing that? . . . Yet I must look very odd. Only two or three men look edgy. They glance to right and left with a sort of animal nervousness, as if hoping that someone is about to say, 'It's over!' and they can stay where they are. But all of them, at the last moment, will rediscover their coolness, they, like all the others, will have got used to the notion of sacrifice. (*L'Argonnaute*, 15 April–1 May 1916)

Such detail was rare in 1916, although eye-witness descriptions later became the norm:

Columns of infantry went up the line one evening. Slowly, bent over their bags, dragged down by their haversacks, groaning beneath the weight of munitions and food supplies, silently they climbed up to their Calvary. Tomorrow, will they be coming back down this interminable trench lying on a stretcher? . . . Once there, they pile themselves up as best they can in the trench; the brisk chill keeps them awake and from time to time a light rain whips across their faces and washes away the black streaks of sweat. Tightly packed one against another, crouching in every corner, they are silent. An icy silence oppresses them. Each man is thinking of his family, his house settled for the night, the village asleep, his children . . . It is four o'clock, a liaison man goes through, upsetting everything as he goes. He whispers to one of his friends: 'It's for 4.15.' (*Le Filon*, April 1917)

This mental return to the beloved family is wholly characteristic of the moments immediately before an attack. There is confirmation elsewhere:

At last, only a minute more! . . . In a brief vision everyone thinks back to past contentment, family, loved ones still asleep while we go to fight: a moment of torture where purpose wavers beneath an excessive burden . . . the weight of memory! (*La Fourragère*, October 1918)

Many similar expressions were employed to evoke the moments before leaving the trenches: the interminable wait – which one would like to have extended indefinitely – the silent men with the stigmata of fear on their faces, movements betraying the depths of distress, the memory of his own people that besets a man at the critical moment.

Then, the attack. Here too there is a striking similarity of feelings and descriptions. Many soldiers describe the abrupt disappearance of fear, plunging the attacker into an apparently altered state of mind, giving his progress towards the enemy lines an almost unreal aspect:

Only a few moments ago, in the jumping-off trench, we were several hundred men who had seen plenty of other trenches. But we exchanged glances and quickly looked away, just enough to see the secret terror of 'in a few minutes'. And I could feel my thoughts going in the same direction . . . I was about to be afraid of the unknown, afraid of going out, afraid of fighting . . . And then I thought of nothing. I went over the top, I ran, I shouted, I hit, I can't remember where or who. I crossed the wire, jumped over holes, crawled through shell-craters still stinking of explosives, men were falling, shot in two as they ran; shouts and gasps were half muffled by the sweeping surge of gunfire. But it was like a nightmare mist all around me . . . Now my part in it is over for a few minutes . . . Something is red over there: something is burning. Something is red at my feet: blood. (*L'Argonnaute*, May 1917)

As proof of the very relative effectiveness of censorship, some papers deliberately described particularly bloody attacks driven back through lack of adequate preparation and uselessly murderous:

Through a little wood of fir trees which hid them from the enemy but gave no protection from gunfire, our leading patrols came close to the enemy trenches. They reached a line of wire; but beyond it lay two more. Stout barriers of tree-trunks lay piled up. We were facing a powerful defence system . . . Lieutenant Perrin realised at once that it was impossible to take the position today . . . At 1100 hours he decided that the action must be repeated the next day, when a stronger artillery preparation would have breached the enemy installations . . . [Next day] the 21st and 22nd once again took the lead and the 19th were in reserve, as on the previous day . . . At 1100 hours the 21st and 22nd reached the first line of

wire. This time the Boches were taken unawares by our attack [but] . . .
our losses were greater than on the day before . . . Captain Saudray, at
the head of his company, had realised the difficulty of the position. On a
scrap of paper, a few paces from the enemy trenches, he had time to write
hastily: 'Enemy defences intact. The enemy trenches are protected by
three rows of wire and felled trees. Impossible to hold on.' He had
scarcely written these words when he fell, shot once in the head and twice
in the chest . . . The order to withdraw reached us a few seconds later.
(*L'Echo des marmites*, 20 April 1915)

A double setback revealing perfectly the weakness of command in
these early days of the war: lack of knowledge of the terrain,
ignorance of the defensive strength of the barbed wire lines, a liking
for infantry attacks without adequate artillery preparation, stub-
bornness even in desperate circumstances. And yet this account
appears to reveal a surprising indifference; perhaps an assumed
indifference and detachment, but not an isolated example. Nor is
there any trace of indignation in this 1915 account, although there is
greater sadness:

At the prescribed hour the officers gave us the usual little pep-talk, with
last instructions, and then enquired if we were ready. At our response in
the affirmative, there was a moment's silence and contemplation, and
then suddenly the shout 'Advance'. We were in the second jumping-off
line. Without hesitation officers and men jumped up on to the parapet
and ran to the front line to take the place of friends who were already
close to the Boche lines. We hardly stopped before we heard the cry
again, 'Advance!' We scrambled over the next parapet and ran forward
after the first wave, shouting whatever came into our heads – Vive la
France! Get at them! Come on, boys! The guns were crackling away
ahead of us, the machine-guns spitting out their ribbons of death. Tack,
tack, tack, tack. We caught up with our friends but – to our horror – we
met a barbed wire barrier that was still intact and more than 30 metres
deep. And all this time the enemy machine guns went on, tack, tack, tack,
tack, while we could see our friends on our left, falling, covering the
ground with their blue uniforms, red with blood where they were hit.
Now the third and fourth waves arrived in their turn. Up ahead a few
men had managed to slip under the wire and reach the troublesome
trench. They jumped in, but sadly we did not see them again . . . There
were not enough of them. It was impossible to get across the wire en
masse anywhere else, and our position became more and more critical.
The shout went up, 'Tools!' We dug into the ground furiously and were

soon dug in right up against the Boche wire. Shots whistled over us and we hung on to the ground we had gained. This was what we achieved that day but . . . if the wire had been cut . . . while we were taking the position! . . . Good God! if only our artillery had managed to establish a breach! . . . And if we had not had the misfortune to lose our commanding officer, our captain, our lieutenant, and so many friends killed or wounded. (*L'Echo de tranchées-ville*, 28 October 1915)

This apparent resignation, perhaps linked to inexperience in the early days of the war, would not always be evident a little later. Thus it was in distinctly different tones that *L'Argonnaute* recorded the consequences of the effort for which the preparations are described above (p.68):

1400 hours . . . Sergeant Lair, with a more nervous gesture, looks at his watch again. He gives the signal . . . Advance! . . . It's funny, I'm not afraid any more. I feel that my mind is clear, my body relaxed. There is a sudden moment of calm and singular gentleness . . . It is so quiet that I can hear someone humming somewhere out on the level ground. My last glimpse is of a field of poppies, their scarlet petals rippling in front of me like a flame.

Resolutely Lair seizes the sandbags along our trench. He pushes them aside and goes through, followed by Lapernelle who is smiling sarcastically as usual. The others follow, frowning, with clenched jaws. How far away the enemy looks . . . A brief whistle, a Boche shot. Then seven or eight yellow box shapes fall on us like stones, no faster. They do not even seem threatening. It is only at the shattering explosion that I realise they are German bombs. Everything is confused, within me and all around . . . I see my friends falling like shadows or bent over . . . What is heartbreaking is the deep silence. How many seconds does it all take? I don't know . . . The wind blows away the fumes, bodies stand up again, dragging themselves back to the rear, to our own lines. Out of fifteen men twelve are wounded, and the barricade has not been taken. Lapernelle is crawling over the ground, red, one leg shattered. He clenches his jaws so as not to cry out . . . I seem to see blood everywhere. It's over . . . I feel a mixture of anger and grief. (*L'Argonnaute*, May 1916)

There is the same diffuse resentment, the same feeling of absurdity, after a failed assault early in the war:

We had advanced under machine-gun fire and were about to reach lines of wire when we realised that they had not been destroyed. We had to wait for three hours, without moving, without shelter, our heads behind little clumps of grass while the early dawn crept up. The German machine-gun kept firing all the time. When the gunner raised it a notch the burst landed in the ground beside my feet. For the rest of the time it fell 20 centimetres in front of me and covered me with liquid mud. (*Le Crocodile*, 10 July 1917)

Accounts of this type are fairly unusual, but they indicate very clearly a barely veiled challenge of the high command's systematically offensive methods up to 1917. Sometimes the criticism appears unintended, but in other cases genuine resentment is obvious – as in the mention of 'anger' in the *Argonnaute* extract quoted above. All this reveals much about the state of mind of many of the officers, no doubt as angry as their men for the same reasons, and disinclined to restrain or censor certain protestations.

There was none the less the matter of censorship. Seventy-five lines were cut from this account of a gas attack, no doubt because of the particularly demoralising effect of this type of weapon on the troops:

Gas: For Those who have Seen it

With the cloud, death enveloped us, impregnating our clothes and bedding, killing everything living around us, everything that breathed. Little birds fell into the trenches, cats and dogs, our companions in misfortune, lay down at our feet and did not awaken. Then we saw our battle companions going to the first-aid post and we waited long and anxiously for the enemy or for death. My friends, we spent there the most painful long hours of our lives as soldiers. We had seen everything: mines, shells, tear-gas, woodland demolished, the black tearing mines falling in fours, the most terrible wounds and the most murderous avalanches of metal – but nothing can compare with this fog which for hours that felt like centuries hid from our eyes the sunlight, the daylight, the clear whiteness of the snow. (*Le Filon*, 20 March 1917)

Although gas attacks were infrequent, almost all troops had to face shelling:

There is nothing worse in war than being bombarded. One man is there alone in his hole. He is not in the fire of battle. He thinks. His reasoning is extraordinarily clear. At first he talks to his neighbour in the next hole: he likes to feel someone near him, a comrade running the same risks. That's human nature. He tries to appear jaunty, forces himself to make jokes . . . But he is aware that his laughter sounds false, and suddenly he prefers to be honest with himself: there can be no doubt about it, this is a bombardment, a real one, one of those artillery preparations that precede attacks, when the ground to be taken must be completely churned up, where nothing can remain alive in the flattened trenches . . . he is not afraid of time-shells, the 30 or 40 centimetres of earth over his head are amply sufficient to absorb the blast. Percussion-fuse shells he cannot forgive, they mean certain death under the collapsing earth. He calculates, seeking the least unfavourable place, cowers down, puts his head near the opening of his dug-out so as to breathe more easily in case of a partial collapse . . . His ear notes each shot. He guesses the shell's trajectory, knows approximately where it will burst . . . If he realises that the shell will fall near him, he closes his eyes, makes himself as small as possible, instinctively puts his arm over his head for protection . . . Flame burns his eyelids, bitter fumes suffocate him . . . it's over for this time, he is not wounded. Soon the noise becomes hellish; several batteries thunder out together. Impossible to make out anything. Shells fall without interruption. He feels that his head is bursting, that his sanity is wavering. This is torture and he can see no end to it. He is suddenly afraid of being buried alive. He sees himself with his back broken, smothered, digging out the earth with his clenched hands. He imagines the terrible agony of death, wishes with all his strength that the shelling would end, that the attack would begin . . . What has happened to his friends? Have they gone? Are they dead? Is he the only one left alive in his hole? Then there is a sudden vision of those who are dear to him: his wife, his mother, his child . . . Without knowing why he sees again some minor detail at home . . . He wants his final thoughts to be of those he loves . . . He will say their names quietly, piously . . . Then he is in revolt, with a mad impulse to leap up. It's too stupid to stay there, waiting for death! Anything is better than that! Oh! To see danger face to face! To fight back!!! To act!!! The deluge continues. Blind force is unleashed. And the man remains in his hole, powerless, waiting, hoping for a miracle. (*La Saucisse*, April 1917)

This is a lengthy account, but deliberately so, for it was precisely the long duration of the ordeal which helped to make it even more unbearable. There is great similarity between the moments preceding an attack and the moments of waiting under bombardment; in each case the combatants are seized with the idea of their probable death while the faces of those whom they will probably never see again appear painfully before them. But although moving out of the trench snatches them abruptly from their distress, nothing can be done during a bombardment. Total inactivity and a sense of total powerlessness are thus added to their tortures.

The reasons which impelled certain soldiers to publish such accounts remain complex. The descriptions may be taken as a protest, more or less explicit, against the disregard in higher places for the life of an infantryman: yet such an interpretation is too superficial, for these texts also reveal the wish to describe an indescribable ordeal:

> When you hear, either direct from a soldier or by reading something, that men have launched a bayonet attack, can you understand fully the meaning of the words? We demand this understanding with all our hearts; we demand it because we are convinced that people do not fully comprehend what is meant by this well-worn formula, the heartbreak and the challenge. We demand it in the name of all those who are killed, every moment. Terrible words have become everyday, familiar . . . People are almost surprised that we no longer use this weapon much. The progress of the war is another reason for this ignorance and lack of respect . . . Try and imagine what it must be like to go into an attack with a naked blade. Picture to yourself the narrow pale steel blades at the end of tightly gripped rifles. And tell yourself that this fighting is the most terrible thing you can ask of our poor bodies, that are weak, trembling, and mortal. (*Le Périscope*, 1917)

Such extreme harshness towards civilians discloses fully one of the aims – unstated and perhaps unrecognised – of these accounts of attacks or bombardments: to spread awareness of the reality of war among those who cannot know it for themselves, who cannot even imagine it. It becomes a matter of establishing the truth, or re-establishing it.

Their accounts could not, however, reach those whom they were implicitly meant to reach, and the soldiers realised this. Some no doubt were aware that they were speaking to future generations, face to face with history, about the immensity of their sufferings: but for the time being their efforts were doomed to failure.

All such accounts have value as homage, as seen in one of their titles, quoted above: 'Gas, for those who have seen it'. They resound like a dedication, like the use of the expression 'my friends' in the lines that followed, for the account in this case was intended as a means of communication – or rather of communion – between men who felt that together they had lived through an exceptional experience and who thus exchanged a sign of recognition. But such cases are rare for, as noted above, this theme of combat occupies only very limited space in soldiers' writings.

Although much was allowed to pass, it can hardly be doubted that censorship was often exercised on over-vivid evocations unlikely to sustain military morale. Self-censorship, however, must have played an even greater part: to evoke the horror of attacks or shell bombardments, to plunge back into it the soldiers who would read accounts of them, to list in detail their anguish, their most personal and intimate attitudes when faced with the risk of death, demanded a very specific form of courage on the part of the newspaper editors. This degree of exorcism – for, again, this is clearly what it was – was not within the capacity of all. Beyond the powers of most, was it not also a singularly risky undertaking? Should one not fear that far from relieving the soldier of the weight of unbearable memories, excessive frankness would revive their suffering and demoralisation?

Men Wounded, Men Killed

Certain forms of anguish, however, compelled a means of expression. They achieved it through the ancillary path of a deep fascination with death. The pain of men's wounds, their death pangs, massacres of all kinds: such themes are extremely frequent in the trench newspapers from the beginning to the end of the war.

One's own death was the prime fear:

How quickly the rest-period has gone. The war that seemed so far away is gradually getting its claws into us again ... As we left the peaceful village more than one man was thinking, 'Shall I be back here next time?' He did not pursue his notion further, but behind the thinking there lay a blurred image of bodies lying out in the open and crosses tilting vaguely. The lottery was beginning again. Lucky for those who drew the winning numbers. (*L'Argonnaute*, 15 September 1917)

The fears of each individual faced with the possibility of his own death could, paradoxically, encourage a surprising and persistent cruelty:

A stray bullet: it was wasted, but you must not trust it! You don't know where it is coming from, but it knows where it is going. It is coming for you, implacable and accurate, a gold insect that hits the bull's-eye, perhaps your brain will be its chosen Terminus Hotel. (*Le 120 court*, 15 November 1917)

Each soldier feels threatened, targeted personally by death. And death is so constantly present that one could sometimes believe in its physical presence:

> Then all at once I saw, beside the straw,
> A ghostly being, who on battle mornings
> I thought to see bend over some among us.
> He passed on, watching men and wild
> With lightning flashing from mad eyes,
> At times he kissed the sleepers on the mouth!
> (*Le 120 court*, 10 June 1916)

Other examples prove the point: that, far from being an academic or artificial exercise, poetry was often used by the most cultivated soldiers to describe more fully the unbearable, to render more 'acceptable' the depiction of certain atrocities.

Macabre details were not always valued, however: thus the destruction of the 252nd infantry regiment was narrated with rare discretion:

> The poppy regiment, the 252nd, no longer exists! . . . A double disaster has befallen us. On 17 May a gas attack asphyxiated many of our comrades in their trenches and shelters, and caused many more to be evacuated. On 26 May, at 11.00 p.m., the 252nd was moved suddenly to the Chemin des Dames to face the first shock of the German offensive on the Aisne, where the 19th, the 62nd and the 118th had just been wiped out by an enemy twenty times their number . . . All parts of the regiment were in the front line in succession after the astonishing German advance, the first-line transport, the regimental supply train, the band, the divisional depot itself all . . . had a bone to pick with the Germans . . . All ranks of the corps had men killed, wounded or captured . . . And so when the order to retreat reached the 252nd's front-line units, there were few survivors able to rejoin their corps. (*L'Echo du boqueteau*, 9 June 1918)

Paradoxically, such extreme reserve probably adds to the impression of distress distilled in this account. But such restraint was not always the norm, and the trench newspapers did not hesitate to describe the wretched scenes after battles: the suffering of the wounded, the corpses strewn on the ground . . . To judge from the abundance of accounts, such visions constituted a core experience for all combatants.

The following example describes a soldier's last moments; significantly, the stress is on the extent of his sufferings:

> Our much-missed friend was killed on 27 February, hit by two shell bursts, in the head and on the right knee . . . He was immediately taken into the blockhouse and prepared for bandaging. But death had done its work . . . Rodier survived for only half an hour, suffering terribly and barely uttering a few monosyllables. (*L'Echo du boqueteau*, April 1917)

The ill-educated soldier whose article, below, appeared without any corrections of any kind, also thought it reasonable to emphasise the agonies of his friend's death:

> I only just knew that a sapper was wounded, I said I must go and see who that is and there as soon as I was back in the wood I saw the major looking after him and he told me to go and get the stretcher-bearers and that was no sooner said than done. Then I went near him and I saw that it was Bruguier. 'What a place this is!' I said to him, quietly. As soon as he heard my voice he recognised me and stretched out his arm to touch my hand: but poor man he felt death coming, I cheered him as best I could but it hurt my heart so much to see him smile and the last thing he said – 'My strength is going' – and all the time I encouraged him and all the time he asked for his bag to put under his head and so I put my cape over him because he was sweating: and then he died about 8 o'clock in the evening, and on his little cross we put 'Bruguier, François, first victim of the 18th infantry regiment'. (*Poil et plume*, May 1916)

As in the preceding quotation, the soldier seeks to depict a dignified death by deliberately leaving out certain macabre details. But this restraint, full of sadness and resignation, was not within the grasp of all and the realism and brutality described in many papers' sketches are astounding: medical orderlies clearing the battlefield with stretchers or tent-canvas with victims' arms and legs hanging over the side; trenches full of bodies after a bombardment; terrain after a battle, strewn with the bodies of soldiers killed or wounded; pictures of mass burials ... As for the texts, many revealed profound complacency in the face of the most terrible spectacles:

> The storm passed, we found nothing in the red tide but a head, a few remains of limbs at the bottom of the shell-hole and some unidentifiable fragments plastered over the parapet. That is all that remained here of our poor friend. (*Le Poilu du 37*, May 1916)

Another equally detailed account describes five soldiers shattered by a shell:

> I was walking along, happy despite everything because of the sunshine, when I stopped short at the edge of a shell-hole. At the bottom, in the freshly upturned earth, five bodies were spread out so symmetrically that you could see that the shell had burst right in the middle of a little group of men, sending each one flying in a different direction so that these poor bodies looked like the five arms of a macabre review. The force of the explosion had buried them in the earth, three were almost completely buried in the sides of the pit, like wisps of rag. The arm of one of these flattened bodies stuck straight out of the clay, the hand was intact with an aluminium ring still on one finger. (*L'Argonnaute*, 15 August 1916)

There is the same horrified fascination in another description:

> I can see those men who just now were two living beings and now, one is nothing but a mass of mud and blood, the other this long stiff body, with blackened face and three holes, in his face, his stomach and his thighs, and his two fists up in front of his face as defence, two fists demanding mercy and trying to ward off his death. The awfulness of this body! None of those who were his friends felt it was him any more, for human feelings no longer exist in the bodies which war has crushed. (*On progresse*, 1 July 1917)

Similarly, the trench newspapers also exploit the theme of bodies long abandoned, forgotten, and then suddenly uncovered:

> They were buried at the edge of a wood, in our lines, near some large trees shattered by gunfire. They had fallen all around; their remains were

gathered up hastily, by moonlight, in a canvas sheet; a hole was dug and in the evening we bade them farewell. For three years their scattered skulls grinned horribly through the young clover, and their bones, mixed with a few fragments of red capes and trousers, crumbled into dust near their rusty rifles. (*L'Echo du boqueteau*, 1 November 1917)

More painful perhaps, though more succinct, is this account of a night fatigue searching for soldiers lying between the lines, with the putrefying smell of bodies their only guide:

It was completely dark when we set out in a column by fours, silent as ghosts, equipped with stretchers and ladders ready to carry our funereal burdens ... After an hour we went through a village, or rather the remains of a poor village: a few bits of ruined wall. Rising from these ruins came a terrible smell, a dead smell which was unfamiliar to us ... Someone whispered near me: 'It smells like death here' ... Orders were given swiftly and quietly, and in groups of four we spread out over the ground and began our dismal labour ... The smell was our guide, the terrible smell experienced back there for the first time. (*La Bourguignotte*, 1916)

A further threshold is crossed with this brief list of some cries heard one evening after a battle:

'We'll all be staying here.'
'Mm— I've got something in my foot.'
'Mother! Mo—ther!'
'Poor boy! Throw his tent-canvas over him.' (*Le Bochofage*, 25 August 1917)

The most unbearable images, however, are found in certain poems:

> The sight of them haunts us
> Taut with supreme effort,
> A fearful grin stretches
> On dead men's dirty faces.
> Greenish pus-filled flesh,
> Hollow sockets, empty skulls
> Open stomachs where the rats gnaw,
> Bodies lying, rotting.

Vermin in the corpses
Daily fresh and wriggling.
Through the mist and drizzle
The rattle of death still sounds.
(*La Musette*, 1916)

Here the poetic form to some extent modifies the horror of what is described, and similarly in this evocation of the terror of soldiers as they feel themselves dying:

Some arms stretched up and others cut in two
Offered their scarlet stumps in hideous gesture.
The anguished silence filled with murmuring
And soon with cries and shrieks of horror,
'A drink . . . Maman . . . Maman! . . . A bullet in my heart'.
And there, right by my side, a monotone,
A childish cry that groans, intoning
'It hurts! Maman . . . Maman . . . Oh God I'm going to die!'
(*L'Echo du boqueteau*, 12 March 1917)

Next after human deaths the trench newspapers gave space to the death of animals, trees, fields and villages, of all the countryside laid waste by the war; all the depressing sights which distressed the combatants:

As a place for a rest, it was a bit depressing. The ruins of the village, completely devastated by the shelling, consisted of a few stretches of wall here and there, sinister and pale, from which emerged sad wrecks, the skeleton of a church, horribly gaunt, stripped bare, broken, jagged, a fountain and a cross remaining intact side by side in the middle of the dead hamlet. All round, dreadfully white, stones lay on the ground, scattered pell-mell, heaped up among the shell-holes, plaster and burned woodwork, and only a few hedges of brushwood showed black against this pale landscape. No one who has not seen this little place from the narrow road past the broken-down houses can imagine the intensity of feeling, the dark cold sadness, the unspeakable distress rising from this vision of desolation! . . . Here before our eyes is a sad harsh scene, in an austere and impressive setting. There we were living in the mud, seeing nothing but mud everywhere, and bodies, and more bodies! and more mud! and still more bodies! (*L'Echo du boqueteau*, 12 March 1917)

Note the key-words: skeleton, gaunt, bare, broken, jagged, dead, pale: this is surely a description of a human being, of a corpse of a village almost as upsetting as a human body. The result is a close connection, an osmosis between the death of men, of objects, of places.

It should be acknowledged that there is a certain unease in such an accumulation of morbid details which, in context, take on a somewhat unhealthy tone. Such fascination exercised by death, such acquiescence in the description of the most macabre details, such masochism as this in the trench newspapers – how is one to explain it? True, the atmosphere surrounding the soldiers, together with a sort of gradually acquired acclimatisation, made it possible to evoke certain realities without paying particular attention to the generally accepted rules of polite behaviour. But the explanation remains inadequate, for it recognises the weakening of certain taboos without saying why they have been transgressed in such morbid directions. In fact this omnipresent theme of death and the newspapers' curious acquiescence are evidence that the accounts were a channel through which the deep anguish of the soldiers forced its way. For the editors of the trench newspapers, such texts are valuable as a release and have the power of exorcism for at least part of an entire community placed under too great a tension.

The brutal evocation of death and suffering is an attempt at a measure of freedom from the fear that they inspire. Derision and sarcasm were powerful ways of achieving this, as in this announcement published after the armistice:

Joseph Camus regrets to announce the sad and cruel loss he has recently suffered, of his right trotter which was smashed by a German bullet in a battle near Craonne on 2 April 1918. Taken to Lyon where the pedal extremity was amputated swiftly and with the greatest possible care on 23 May of the same year. Born 3 February 1895, tipped down the drain on 24 May 1918. Sadly missed. (*Le Bulletin désarmé*, 1919)

There are many variations on this theme. This sample of 'bons mots', which were not lacking in the front-line press, is a good example:

The *poilu* dies extraordinarily easily: does he not have the deplorable habit of ingesting pieces of ironwork? On most occasions he dies of it, naturally. (*Le Bochofage*, 28 April 1917)

The unlucky *poilu* who is the last to be killed will regret it all his life. (*La Gazette du créneau*, 1 January 1918)

The *cafard* is not malignant except where it is complicated with shell explosions, which may cause death. (*L'Echo des marmites*, 10 March 1917)

> What's the point of scratching your head,
> A shell will do it very well.
> (*Le Cri de guerre*, 20 October 1916)

Tent canvas can be used for carrying food and materials. Is an improvement on a stretcher. The *poilu* is never separated from it, for he knows that it will provide his ultimate well-being . . . as his shroud in his grave. (*L'Echo des poilus*, October 1917)

Why do the post orderlies put on undelivered letters 'The addressee has not been traced' since in general it is, on the contrary, because he has been traced by a projectile that the addressee is not there? (*L'Echo des guitounes*, 10 November 1917)

Such scorn has little connection with healthy troop laughter, nor with any calm indifference in the face of death. It is primarily an attempt at reaction, a form of heroic and derisory struggle with fear.

The cult of the dead is the final aspect of this morbidity that characterises the trench newspapers. Having become a constant point of reference in the veterans' movement, it later gave meaning to the construction of war memorials and to 11 November ceremonies.[1] It found strength in a broad compassion for those who fell, and nothing reveals this more than the vocabulary of the soldiers' newspapers. The 'beloved dead' or the 'dear ones passed away' are evoked; sometimes there is a possessive: 'our dead', 'our beloved dead'; this respect for the dead, which was quick to appear, became a veritable cult at the end of the war or immediately after the armistice:

How many of our comrades remain there and will not return? Let us keep piously in our hearts the memory of these obscure heroes who fell

1. Annette Becker, *Les Monuments aux morts: mémoire de la Grande Guerre*, Paris, Errance, 1988.

facing the enemy in defence of the sacred French soil. No one will ever match the grandeur of their sacrifice. We who survive must perpetuate the memory of their heroic death and ensure that the benefits of their sacrifice are never lost. We who have been spared must now relieve the misery and suffering of all those broken by war, the disabled, the widows, the orphans. Brotherhood and gratitude must not be empty words! (*Le Ver luisant*, 1919)

Priests of this cult of the dead, the survivors also saw themselves as the trustees of an extremely demanding ethic:

How do you think, I ask of you, that after the war a smile can appear on the lips of those who have survived this world-wide drama? . . . The dead who fill our ground, the blood spilt out in floods . . . none of this, take note, will disappear at once! Time will not efface the pain and the sufferings endured, and nothing will take away from our sympathetic gaze the disabled who will be seen within our walls. They will reawaken the memories of those who would prefer to forget! (*La Mitraille*, October 1918)

Although it developed principally after the war, this funerary cult had a lengthy gestation:

You must realise that a terrible war which cut down without warning friends in a single rank, childhood friends, brothers, sharpens unbearably the love for the dead, to the point where you think of them as of living people, that they are more alive than ever. When you utter a name and someone replies: 'Killed at X—' there is no cold little silence, as you might expect. No. You recall memories, details, the death itself of which in most cases you were a witness . . . You invoke them, you see them, they are there, and you march on. (*La Marmite*, May 1916.)

Also from 1916 is this even more solemn homage:

Let us think of our dead! How could we forget them? They are part of the whole family. Those who left us suddenly and who lie beside our roads . . . They were struck down at our sides as we shared the same dangers and ran the same risks. The danger is still the same. We do not forget our dead! It is we who look after our dead, we live among the graves which we have piously adorned . . . We look after our dead!

Whether they sleep, these dear ones, at the foot of a calvary, at the bottom of a lane, whether their grave can be found at the roadside, cut into the grass, or whether it seems lost in one of those great cemeteries where the wooden crosses form a forest, we see them all in thought, they are here close beside us. We live with our dead! Indeed they still speak to us, our dead are not dead, they are only sleeping, their voices have not been silenced, they speak in our ear in the evening, as night approaches. (*Le Crocodile*, 25 October 1916)

This text is perhaps somewhat awkward. But it is this very shift of tone that offers a valuable insight: if the writer adopts a certain grandiloquence, it is because only a 'noble' tone – or what he sees as such – feels suitable when dealing with such a serious topic. Similarly, nothing could be more revealing than this issue of a front-line newspaper concerned only with soldiers of the 37th infantry Regiment overwhelmed in the battle of Verdun: here too the superficiality is only on the surface and such a feature is evidence of profound compassion for the dead. Further, it concerns the men of a single unit; more often this compassion remained independent of ties with those who had fallen. This is what is suggested by the feelings of this soldier at an isolated unidentified grave discovered by chance:

I had already encountered such solitary mounds lying faithfully beside our painful roads! But this one, so plain, so simple, the most humble and touching of all, the most heartbreaking! It bore no decoration except this clumsily outlined cross; and no name ... And it was hidden there in front of the trench, between the French and German lines ... I thought of the dead man ... I thought of his fate which perhaps would also be my fate. I thought of the long months of hardship which he had perhaps endured before he fell here, an obscure craftsman of a great work, a little ripple which spread out and died when it reached an empty shore ... And he was abandoned in the middle of the bare plain. One day unknown friends, led by chance, kicked their feet against him and, full of pity, buried him solemnly. Over his grave they set a little mound and outlined a white cross. No name appears on the grave, for they did not know the dead man's name. They did not add any ornamentation because they had no time. And they left, never to return ... A flare burst in the dark night ... I knelt quickly ... But I could not tell whether it was caution which threw me on the ground, or pity for this unknown brother, stretched out at my feet under this cross of white stones. (*Le Midi au front*, 25 May 1916)

There is evidence here of the close links between this profound solicitude for the dead and a morbidity which played a determinant role in combatants' minds and constituted a burden which might have felt more oppressive had it lacked expression.

Religious Sensibility

In this climate of permanent confrontation with death, it might seem natural for religious faith to offer a refuge or hope for many soldiers. Short of creating a true religious sensibility from everything, how could the constant presence of death not have revived a slumbering faith? Strangely this does not seem to have happened on a large scale. Certainly here and there a reasonable number of indications of a developing invasive superstition are apparent, as seen in the soldiers' taste for protective medals or good-luck charms of all kinds; but in their newspapers the affirmation of an authentic religious sentiment is largely absent.

It is however undoubtedly true that religious faith offered some combatants a shield against despair and against the feeling of absurdity born out of the sight of massacre:

I cannot believe, I shall always refuse to believe, that so much youth, so much ardour, so much strength cut down and broken, could be lost for ever and ever in space and time. (*L'Horizon*, July 1917)

'I cannot believe, I shall always refuse to believe' begins this writer with caution ... His Christian faith is beyond question, but it is expressed in very vague terms and in a purely negative way.

The very marked sensitivity regarding shattered churches, and the sight of Calvaries half-destroyed by shelling but still standing above the desolate landscape, also bear witness to a certain spiritual unease:

At the centre of the cemetery stands a large wooden figure of Christ. One arm has been broken by a shell and hangs sadly, held on to the cross by the nailed hand. And the face, dripping with rain, appears to reflect an infinity of suffering and sadness. (*La Saucisse*, June 1917)

Other eye-witness accounts have more precise significance. For example, they recall soldiers praying before an attack or under bombardment:

> Our little corner seems to be particularly picked on. Everything is shaking round us . . . Soon there will be fifty of us piled up in this hovel, packed in so tightly that we cannot move. I think with despair of the dreadful mess there would be if a shot brought down the roof; we would be in less danger in the trench! Everyone is certainly thinking the same as me; but no one thinks of leaving because here we have the advantage of not *seeing* the danger, and also because in a group we can all support one another. As the explosions of unparalleled violence shake our shelter, a few terrified men suggest that we pray together. (*Le Crapouillot*, January 1917)

This is clear proof of the existence of a deeply committed Christian faith in at least some soldiers. But the fact that religious feelings emerge in moments of danger is profoundly ambiguous: when faith is aroused at the instant of confrontation with death, it reveals its depth of conviction; but that it appears to die away once the danger has passed seems to indicate its relatively superficial nature.

It appears, however, that religious services celebrated behind the lines, in the open air or sometimes in damaged churches, drew in a certain number of men, as in this Christmas mass, where the priest was a soldier among soldiers:

> Pierre and I and some other friends went to the midnight Mass . . . Our good medical orderly L— had put on the lace alb and the gold chasuble. No one commented on his heavy nailed boots, reminders that the priest was a *poilu*. We knelt . . . and the mystery of Christmas, the mystery of love and of sacrifice, was reborn. (*Le Poilu marmité*, December 1916)

As for the Mass for the dead, it appears to have brought together the great majority of soldiers within the same regiment:

> Masses for the dead at the front were the most moving of all. Everyone was there. A coffin, banners and an altar – that's all there was; but the whole regiment took communion in the same distress. (*La Marmite*, May 1916)

Not a powerful indication; one may obviously question the

unanimity stated in this text but in any case, its significance should not be overestimated, for even non-believing soldiers could appreciate the moral support of taking part in a service of this kind.

Insights into soldiers' religious feeling in the front-line press are thus too slight and fragmentary to allow a precise assessment of this aspect of their thinking, still less to calculate the strength of Christian faith in the army as a whole. Such discretion in the soldiers' newspapers may have been encouraged by their 'apolitical' style which covered religious divisions: to talk about religion might, like 'talking politics', be taken as a failure to meet the demands of neutrality. In any case, their silence should rather be attributed to a phenomenon in line with what is known about the behaviour of most French people during the war: the outbreak of war brought many back to the Church, and the soldiers were not exempt from this.[2]

Later however, at the rear as well as at the front, this reawakened faith soon weakened. The theme of religion is thus more evident in the trench newspapers at the beginning of 1915 than during later months.

Life Goes On

This perpetual rubbing shoulders with death gave full weight to moments of relaxation and recovery, those moments when soldiers understand as never before what it means to enjoy life. Letters, parcels and leave could bring forgetfulness, for a few moments or a few days, of the existence of war. But when danger slackened, it did not need that contact with the rear to be aware of the full value of the simple pleasures of life.

They were the pleasures of day-to-day living, for the permanent presence of danger developed a very particular perception of time and left no room for looking ahead:

> For us, living an animal life where only primitive feelings existed, for us, . . . threatened with annihilation or the most terrible sufferings, this was the only way to be happy: not to think of the past, to enjoy the present moment intensely and uniquely. (*Le Crapouillot*, February 1917)

2. Jean-Jacques Becker, *Les Français dans la Grande Guerre*, Paris, Laffont, 1980; Jacques Fontana, *Les Catholiques français pendant la Grande Guerre*, Paris, Editions du Cerf, 1990.

Such pleasure was often that of the hours of rest, brief spaces where war seemed to withdraw:

> Sitting in a circle, on the ground or on their haversacks, the men brought out their tobacco pouches, lit their pipes or cigarettes, and exchanged views. This was mostly a good moment. Mug of coffee in hand, they recalled memories, told anecdotes and commented on the news. A mug of coffee . . . suddenly makes you forget everything: weariness, even the war itself . . . You don't think about it, perhaps you would not think about it any more if it were not for hearing, close by, the shells exploding, mines, and the tic-tac of machine-guns. (*L'Echo des tranchées*, 10 January 1917)

Thus it was that a somewhat unusual dinner, improvised in an abandoned house at the rear, took on the aspect of a true celebration, a celebration for a corps which was rarely fully fed and rarely sheltered:

> We settled down in the fine and scarcely spoilt dining room. We took the best crockery. Nothing seemed too good for us. There were pickles, ham, bottles of wine, champagne, sugar, jam, liqueurs, cassis. All this after two days of cold food. We felt a simple delight at such things, a satisfaction that would make one blush in normal circumstances. Alas, our minds are confused. Now we live only through our stomachs. (*L'Argonnaute*, July 1918)

Such moments of relaxation for body and mind were so important that only leave could match the value of rest periods with danger far away, for some weeks in the case of the '*grand repos*', extended rest, or just for the few days of acting as the second-line reserve:

> I can remember, last summer – they can remember it too in the 17th – a famous sector which we shall miss . . . What good times we had there! It was not just any trench, a wavering slit at the end of the communication trench, but a great fold of land, like the bottom of a bowl protected from the enemy by a fairly high bank from where the plain stretched away without features . . . Here we were not imprisoned between two earth walls. You could walk about freely and your view was not limited. We lived there 'in reserve' for two days, three days, sometimes more . . . We felt happy to be alive. Then cheerful faces and relaxed and rested bodies

appeared from all the dug-outs, where the excessively strong rays of the sun had driven our friends for the afternoon; the siesta had been a long one and everyone felt an urgent need to rush about and make a noise. But it was time for the evening soup; already sweating, their heads stretched forward, draped with cans, carrying bowls and stew-pots, the sacred troop of cooks advanced, imposing and serious. Ah! the table was soon laid. A few metres from the bank, on the grass which offered itself as a table-cloth, canteens were opened up in a second and everyone tasted the *plat du jour* . . . How far one felt from the war during these open-air dinners! Then out came the pipes from the pockets and the cooks distributed coffee. It was the finest hour, as dusk was falling, the time for contented digestion. (*Le Midi au front*, 25 May 1916)

The removal of the risk of death gave full value to such moments, as soldiers rediscovered a slice of freedom. It was a freedom sparingly granted, and valued accordingly:

After weeks of painful labour . . . you felt relief as soon as you arrived, you seemed to breathe more easily; you could see human beings who were not soldiers. This in itself was rest . . . No reveille, no fatigues, no assembling at fixed times, almost total freedom to come and go and fill your leisure time as you pleased. (*Le Crocodile*, 10 November 1916)

But such delight in physical freedom did not require being at rest in conditions more agreeable than those of the front line. Pleasure was never so intense as immediately after danger, when death had passed close by:

After terrible anguish, this was wonderful relaxation; we had 'come through' once more, we friends! Life was good! In this existence of perpetual contrasts, after waiting in despair for death or mutilation, what inexpressible satisfaction to realise that you can go and eat, drink, sleep peacefully . . . and live, in fact! I have never felt such physical pleasure, such burgeoning delight, as when we returned from those terrible trenches at Souchez. (*Le Crapouillot*, January 1917)

The simple awareness of being alive and unharmed was sufficient to bring this deep and sudden *joie de vivre* flooding in. And yet it did not always manage immediately to obliterate the sense of death once the danger had passed:

~ 89 ~

The smoke of our cigars made a halo round the intense *joie de vivre* that we felt at getting away from the grip of Death, whose icy embrace we had felt so terribly up there, so much so that our clothes still held that stale smell of corpses with which they had been impregnated for five terrible days. (*Le Voltigeur*, 21 July 1917)

It is hardly surprising that soldiers were convinced that they emerged profoundly changed by these ordeals endured. Henceforward almost all considered that they understood better the true value of life. Such certainty was shown in a violent appetite for life revealed in the sincerity and naïveté of some readers' answers to an inquiry in October 1918 in the newspaper *La Mitraille*, concerning life after the war:

I left school in 1916. I joined the war without having lived . . . If I get out alive I promise you that I shall live. I knew nothing of the pleasures of life . . . I shall go [to Paris] and live there, I shall enjoy myself and pass the time agreeably. I shall live with all the ardour of my youth . . . Then, *après moi*, after all, *le déluge*!

The *poilu* . . . will have only one idea left: that of living in peace, quietly at home, surrounded by those who are dear to him and loved by his own family . . . He will know the value of life and will enjoy the rest of his days appreciating the true happiness of gentle peace.

[The soldier] will stay at home, in his own house, with his own family. He will work for himself and his family . . . He will become a true egotist. He will be indifferent to the clamour of the outside world; whatever may happen, sad or cheerful, will not affect him . . . Other people's lives are no longer of interest to us. We will live for ourselves and for our own people, that's all.

I am not one of the most senior combatants, I would like, if I am lucky enough to come out of this war alive, to learn what it is to live, for I can certainly confirm one thing, which is that the day I was called up to join the regiment, I knew very little of life. (*La Mitraille*, October 1918)

This taste for freedom, this determination to appreciate life on their return to freedom, shows that soldiers saw themselves as convicts condemned to wait for death or mutilation in the prison of the trenches. Their fascination with the macabre, their tendency to treat tragedy with derision, mixed with respect for those cut down by death, the value attached to the simplest pleasures of an existence taken one day at a time – all of this can be explained only by the need to escape, if only briefly, from the tortures inflicted on the soldiers by their confrontation with death.

~ 4 ~

The Hated Home Front

Hatred of 'Eye-wash'

'The rear' formed a large part of the soldiers' preoccupations, but although the space devoted by their newspapers to the civilian population increased steadily between 1914 and 1918, the attention focused on those continuing a virtually 'normal' life far from the front remained full of ambiguity. It included a definite feeling of rupture between the rear and the front, and this breach was so painful to the fighting troops that it threatened the cohesion of French society faced with the four-year ordeal of war.

To the soldiers, the image of the civilian population was closely connected to that of the Paris national press, reflecting the rear's perception of the realities of life at the front and also civilian behaviour in wartime. Since the press was so comprehensively discredited in the eyes of the soldiers, the men's notion of the rest of the population suffered a similar reaction, and the way in which news was framed and disseminated helped to enlarge the gap separating the rear from its front-line defenders.

The press was not judged in equally severe terms throughout the whole of the war. In 1915 favourable opinions or a degree of indifference balanced critical views. In was in 1916 that the latter began to outweigh the former, introducing in consequence a steady lowering of the combatants' image of news.

What became universally known as 'eye-wash' ('*bourrage de crâne*') became the focus for much of their resentment: they suffered great despair at seeing nothing described or understood as they would have liked, seeing their life, their thoughts and their activities so thoroughly travestied. Inevitably the soldiers felt that every passing day reduced their chances of bringing home to the civilian population any understanding of the extent of their distress and their hardships, or of bridging the gap separating the rear from the front. This 'eye-wash', including censorship of news as well as propaganda literature, created a heavily opaque screen between civilians and troops and was the less pardonable by the latter because, in the isolation of their trenches, they remained deeply attached to the maintenance of links between the two worlds separated by war.

Denunciation of 'eye-wash' took a variety of forms, but pastiche and scorn often appeared in the trench newspapers in efforts to re-establish the truth. This 'account' of an attack is a characteristic example:

The men were there by dawn. They waited impatiently for the order to attack, which should arrive at any minute. They had not slept all night, full of joy at the approaching onslaught on the Boche. They were ready, fierce and proud. Not a man wanted his coffee, however much appreciated in normal times, not one asked for it, for this would mean a fatigue squad leaving the ranks which would then not be available. So they would go without their coffee. Several went without bread, having claimed the honour of replacing their day's ration with two grenades . . . There were already some victims, however. A major bent over the wounded men, who suffered in silence. One of them, a mature man with a broken leg, begged the doctor not to evacuate him. The doctor refused his plea, and the heroic wounded man wept to think that that night he would lie in a sound bed while his comrades remained bound to the demands of glory.

7.30 A brief command was heard: fix bayonets. The steel gleamed, and the men set out on the finest hours of their lives . . . The charge sounded. The waves of men leapt forward with smiles on their lips . . . The Boches, taken by surprise, offered only slight resistance; they threw down their rifles, jettisoned their equipment and fell on their knees, crying '*Kamarad!*' They were completely demoralised and had not eaten for a week . . . The trumpeter sounded the charge again. A machine-gun bullet broke his jaw, but he continued to sound his trumpet, holding his instrument with one hand and his jaw with the other . . . Their relief arrived: the brave *poilus* refused it. What heroes! (*Le 120 court*, 25 October 1916)

Delight in attack, heroism during the assault, superhuman courage when wounded, enemy cowardice: every journalistic stereotype put into a single text, the better to offer a target for effective ridicule. Yet it was even easier to quote directly certain items picked out of the national press:

It is indeed true that as we passed through a ruined village we saw and heard a shell a few metres away. *But no one takes any notice.* It is true that in the trenches one can hear the rattle of *the odd rare rifle shot* and the whistle of *the odd rare shell* but the sides are so high and the shells so distant that one is not in the least afraid. (Quoted in *Le 120 court*, 5 July 1916)

Immediately below this *Le 120 court* added a commentary of its own:

The public religion is explained: our struggles are fables for nursery schools, our sufferings and our deaths are fine affectation served up for the benefit of idle bystanders. Still, we take pity on pilgrims, who must have been led astray by a bad joke in a basic instruction camp . . . Let them spend just twenty-four hours in a corner of the real front where we currently have the honour to be operating . . . Perhaps they could have themselves photographed as they leave the spectacle, severely wounded! (*Le 120 court*, 5 July 1916)

Articles in the Paris newspapers were not the only cause of contention: the pictures of the war which they offered their readers also provoked anger among many combatants, as in this case of a photograph of a shell explosion, taken, according to the caption, from very near where it fell:

Shell explosion taken at less than twenty metres from the photographer. I have never seen such photographers, and I very much doubt I ever shall.
What I have seen, however, is the extreme speed with which everyone takes shelter as best he can when a heavy shell falls nearby, since the shell usually explodes over a radius of 200 metres. (*La Saucisse*, April 1916)

Cinema 'news' was equally unpopular, with the soldiers on leave unfailingly commenting that they were obviously filmed at a considerable distance from the front lines:

[There are] innumerable patriotic films in which squads of discharged actors take the bastions of Vincennes by assault with extraordinary panache, leaping intrepidly over inoffensive fire-crackers and, lifting their arms to the heavens, die happily with a smile on their lips while the orchestra plays a jaunty little tune. (*Le Crapouillot*, May 1917)

According to the soldiers, certain topics and even the application of certain words were consistently wrongly used. One such was the name 'Rosalie', much appreciated at the rear as a term for the bayonet but thoroughly disliked by the troops:

> [The *poilu*] does not call [his bayonet] Rosalie. The bayonet is only called Rosalie in a song by Théodore Botrel, which nobody sings, and in the *Bulletin des Armées de la République*, which nobody reads. (*Le Poilu*, 30 April 1915)

Even less bearable for the soldiers were ill-informed statements about the enemy; systematic underestimation of their opponents was unacceptable:

> The credo of the civilian in the street-corner bar: I believe that the Boches have been eating bread made of sawdust since 1 January 1915. I believe that they have had no ammunition for twenty-seven months and that since September 1914 all their shells have been duds. I believe that their officers are totally ignorant about waging war, that their airmen never fly, that their zeppelins are harmless, that their men shout '*Kamarad*' from morning till night. (*Le Diable au cor*, 20 December 1916)

This last point was particularly sensitive. More even than doubt over the German capacity for sustaining a lengthy war effort, it was the questioning of their determination in the front line that struck the French troops as intolerable:

> *Le Matin* published a photograph on 18 July of which we would not want to question either the origin or the accuracy of reproduction and interpretation (although it is wholly imaginary). This is the well-known refrain designed to give an accurate notion of the value of German soldiers: 'Look how they surrender! Deserters! Haggard faces! Terrified eyes! Hands up! *Kamarad*! etc.' What wretched opponents we are faced with here, and what paltry praise is offered to the victors on the Somme! (*Le Troglodyte*, 20 July 1916)

To present the Germans as cowards was thus not only a travesty of the truth, it offended the French troops and denigrated their courage.

Nor was the falsified presentation of military operations any more acceptable. By 1915 the way in which the press described operations on the Russian front – of which at first there had been great hopes – stimulated indignation in the front-line papers:

> All our grand sister publications spend their time telling the most improbable stories. From the moment they made up the notion that the Boche was destined for a speedy end through inactivity, they have put out a sequence of the most extraordinary fantasy ideas and, except to us, Frenchmen, the most unlikely . . . The latest discovery is, alas, known to everyone. We are shown the Russian retreat as a strategic operation of the highest value. The loss of Przemysl – oh, unimportant . . . the fall of Lemberg! – oh, what a marvel! (*Boum! Voilà!*, 26 June 1915)

This climate of disillusioned scepticism explains why the military commentators attached to the main Paris newspapers became the object of such bitter criticism. The trench press focused unfailingly and pitilessly on all the journalistic tricks used to enrich the tone of the daily General Staff communiqué, without adding any further information whatever:

> I challenge anyone to say he has learnt from military commentators any bit of news whatsoever that was not already in the communiqué. Our parlour strategists know no more secrets than you or I. They embroider the official account, sometimes stupidly: when we have lost ground they cry, 'Our reserves have arrived'. When we advance: 'Our glorious troops'. Impressive! When the Boches are pushed back: 'Their terrible losses' . . . Our soldiers have been so misled that they are convinced that what they read is false, in principle, even when it is true. (*Le Filon*, 1918)

Journalists were therefore thoroughly unpopular in the trenches. At best their incompetence and ignorance were stressed; more often their professional integrity was questioned, and they were accused of venality and bad faith. Even when some of them tried to get near the front to learn more directly about life in the front lines, they were reproached:

> Gradually the civilian has come to think of the front as a place for an excursion. Duly equipped with a valid pass he sets off, helmeted and gaitered, astonished at everything, noting – 40 kilometres from the front line – the violent shelling, the steady rumbling of motor lorries, the

mud-covered relieving troops, the excellent morale. His feelings over-
whelm him, sobs stifle him as with feverish hand he writes the opening
lines of his article: honour ... nation ... they shall not pass! Such
outpourings from civilian warriors sick with patriotism will add nothing
to the glory of the Republic's armies, and will always distract those at the
front. (*Bombardia*, 30 September 1917)

This reveals clearly the soldiers' hostility towards the arrival at the
front of any non-combatant, whether he be journalist, politician,
well-known personality, staff officer, or service unit soldier. Between combatants and civilians there could be no intermediate
category deputed to 'conduct visits' among the troops; such concern would appear unseemly – once more, it was a question of
dignity.

Apart from the 'eye-wash' itself, however, the overall press view
of the war was cause for reproach – its selection of news to print and
the hierarchy of events it created. Did it not give too much space to
news affecting only the civilian population, to the detriment of news
from the front?

The death of a civilian from Boche barbarity, certainly highly regrettable,
leads to endless follow-ups, while it needs a wholesale loss of *poilus* to
gain a mention in one of the national daily papers ... On the pretext that
people go without meat for one meal, that they lack a bit of coal, that
there is a tax on useless objects, that they cannot go to the theatre or the
cinema because they are closed, the papers write endless rambling pieces
with headlines in type as big as signboards. (*La Gazette du créneau*,
April 1918)

So there were two scales of value, with the press finally treating
the war simply as one source of news among others, instead of
giving absolute priority to the events at the front – the only events
of importance in the eyes of the soldiers. Consequently, the soldiers
were inclined to think that their sacrifices were neither recognised
nor properly valued. This was the most serious mistake, for in this
way the press undermined army morale and the achievements of the
troops:

No depiction of life at the front ever made a *poilu* depressed, he is only
too happy to be understood at last ... It is the intensive propaganda that

eats away at his morale, chucks him into *le cafard* and plunges certain men, exhausted with effort and revolted by the continual lies, into a sort of nihilism which must at all costs be eradicated. To sustain morale at the front, to restore *poilus* and civilians, nothing is better than *the truth* . . . Surely this is the time to throw out all the paraphernalia of false news, all the hollow and useless phrase-making, all the sickening literature, all the lying products of these propagandists whose only achievement has been a brief interruption in the communion of ideas between those who are dying at the front and those who are living at the rear. (*Le Crapouillot*, July 1917)

Occasionally it was the light-heartedness with which the press presented certain items of news that contributed to this process of demoralisation:

Since our good friends the Russians have discovered the road to 'progress' – which consists precisely of not 'making progress' against the Boches – most of the newspapers at the rear boast to us with great emphasis about everything they do, say and think. The censorship which is elsewhere so strict finds it entirely reasonable that the recital should be published everywhere, with high praise, of deplorable deeds . . . which get us into trouble! The slightest words of the leaders of the mess in the Caucasus are faithfully reported back to us – like oracles – by all the press in the rear. The French press seems to us to have a strange attitude. (*L'Echo du boqueteau*, 24 August 1917)

Note that this article complains that the papers are not keeping silent about the Russian defeat, while elsewhere the trench newspapers complain that they are doing everything in their power to hide the truth from their readers.

What the soldiers resented most deeply about the 'eye-wash', however, was the distortion of their image, both in the present and for the future. In confusing fashion their papers attempt to express the men's distress in the face of this veritable enterprise of 'false witness':

These amiable narrators know how to describe the charms of our troglodyte life in a very particular way. Nothing escapes them. You would think they had lived through those hours themselves when, well sheltered in their 'covered trenches', our soldiers laugh at the enemy machine-gun fire . . . You would think, indeed that they had spent those long winter evenings, when the well wrapped up *poilu* mounts guard, next to a hot brazier. (*Brise d'entonnoirs*, December 1916)

Here again it is a matter of lies concerned only with the soldiers' daily life. But the 'false witness' was even less bearable when it dealt with attacks, bombardments, or the fighting men's state of mind:

The humorous papers perpetuate the legend of the laughing *poilu* and are dead set against the cowardly Boches who only stop cutting off the hands of little girls to raise their own in the air. As for the big 'news'papers (so-called no doubt because they inform us of the revolution in Constantinople, Cossacks five days' march from Berlin, Wilhelm's cancer and corpse-factories) and those stupid *bons mots* of *poilus* made up wholesale by specialists . . . But what disconcerts the soldiers most is to see that the intellectual elite has proved incapable of rising higher than cinema newsreel patriotism, and joins in the chorus with the vile purveyors of eyewash. Heroic old men (who swear periodically to hang on to the end, without anyone laughing in their faces) have no hesitation in describing life at the front because they were once led along a seventh-line communication trench, get worked up narrating improbable battles, and explain the psychology of the fighting man coolly to their sympathetic readers. One . . . routinely delivers up a glorious burial permit to some poor devil lying torn to pieces in a shell-hole, and assumes the right to speak in the name of the dead (who, obviously, will not contradict him). Another narrates in heroic style the terrible struggles he underwent in a general staff headquarters behind the lines, while another chews over in his own particular way the letters addressed by humble *poilus* to their own families and not for clamorous publicity. To all, the war, which has brought them glory and profit without causing them any suffering, appears wholly admirable. They shout in chorus, perpetually, that 'it's all going well' and unwearyingly sing the praises of our 'heroic' deeds, the joy of dying, the exquisite intoxication of hand-to-hand fighting, and the innumerable benefits of the regenerating war! (*Le Crapouillot*, June 1917)

In short, if exasperation is so marked in the face of propaganda, it is because the soldiers saw it as an insult: an insult to their experience of war, an insult to their everyday hardship, an insult to their courage.

The style in which this eye-wash was presented did not, however, remain identical from 1914 until 1918, for propaganda evolved throughout the war. It was at its most outrageous at the beginning;

thanks to the 'soldiers' letters', carefully selected, cut, or made up from a variety of sources, the Paris press asserted unhesitatingly that life in the front line was still easily bearable:

Letter from a Telegraphist

The only difference between you and me is . . . that you sleep in a bed and I sleep on straw. But you don't have the pleasure of going to sleep to the sound of the cannon and machine-guns. I have that advantage over you. Here life is very cheerful and everyone appears to forget that family and friends are waiting anxiously. They should be allowed to see what happens all around us. It would console them thoroughly. I have the opportunity to talk to soldiers every day as they return from the trenches, or go back there. They are unanimous in declaring that life in the firing-line is very bearable and they know how to pass the time. When they are sent to the rear to rest the only advantage they observe is that they can change their linen and have a wash. In the hospitals, the stoicism with which the severely wounded men bear their sufferings is admirable . . . Apart from this, everyone waits very patiently and serenely for the deeds that will bring us victory. (*Le Petit parisien*, 6 January 1915)

The light-heartedness of the men in the front line, cheerfulness, indifference in the face of danger, superhuman courage in suffering, imperturbable confidence in victory: all were frequent untruths. Yet *Le Petit parisien* seemed undisturbed that this 'eye-witness account' was in no way the product of a soldier in a combatant unit – a fact which considerably reduces its significance. As for the particular procedure that consisted in offering 'realism' by quoting the words of fighting men, it clearly aroused the latter's indignation. Maurice Barrès, the most famous of the writers who offered their services to the writing of propaganda, built up a pattern of this use of personal letters and 'real-life' anecdotes:

I hope I'm not boring you, talking to you about our young soldiers? Here is just one anecdote out of thousands, an ordinary incident and thus all the better for helping you understand them, and I offer it to you as an example of this unexpected insight into the army and the family I was talking about just now. A college student of 18, mobilised on 2 August 1914, went into the firing line on 25 August, was wounded in his leg on 2 September, and returned again on 13 October. On 24 October his mother received a letter from his captain: 'Madame, your son has been slightly wounded for the second time. He acted like a hero and has been put forward for a decoration, which he certainly deserves . . .' The youth's letter followed soon after. He wrote cheerfully. You could imagine that you were listening to a young voice, out of breath from having run too fast, to announce the good news more quickly . . . His father, who went to see him in hospital, asked him one day if in risking his life he had not also thought of his mother and his sisters. 'Oh, yes Papa, but I also thought that if I succeeded we could go on to take the trench and that would be 300 metres gained!'

Can you hear the silver voice, the crystal tone, the pure sound of youth? Such heroism gleams with the illusions of childhood. Oh why must it be the old people who stay at home while those who march out to the sacrifice are children capable of inaugurating the finest period in France's history! (*L'Echo de Paris*, 11 December 1914)

The precision over dates and the didactic style of the piece are designed to reinforce its credibility. The final phrase alone, however, is sufficient to explain Maurice Barrès's unpopularity in the trenches: surely it is indecent to praise the combatants' spirit of sacrifice while simultaneously regretting one's own sheltered position? As for genuine military operations, the press presented them in such a way that the reader cannot doubt that the war is turning in France's favour:

In this area (the right bank of the River Aisne) we are meeting with repeated success and have for a long time been advancing daily. We take trenches, and thus win ground. The enemy launches offensives in return; he is driven back, and we benefit by seizing new lengths of trench. It is always the same action, repeated at every opportunity offered by offensive enemy movement. Sometimes, however, we take the offensive and attack, and it can be noted in these as in the other circumstances we very rarely lose what we have won. As for the superiority of our heavy artillery over the enemy's, as with our assault cannon, it is now an established and accepted fact. (*Le Petit journal*, 13 January 1915)

The deliberately sustained blurring of events is inescapable, epitomised in the tautology of 'We take trenches, and thus win ground . . .' It is also noticeable that enemy offensives very mysteriously turn into a gaining of terrain for the French, while setbacks are systematically minimised: 'We very rarely lose what we have won . . .' The final sentence contains the most flagrant untruth, for although it was true that the French 75 mm cannon had clearly proved its effectiveness, the German heavy artillery benefited from a crushing superiority.

As for the enemy troops, were they not depicted as physically and mentally exhausted from the very beginning of the war?

Their Enormous Losses

German prisoners taken on Christmas Eve near L— state that they had been in the same trenches since 12 September, i.e. for more than three and a half months, and that during that time the manpower of certain companies had been renewed either two or three times ... Such figures are ample proof of the enormous losses suffered by the enemy. The men are forbidden, on pain of the most severe punishment, to mention the losses suffered in their letters home. They are ordered to write: 'We are always victorious but as a result of the bad weather we are unable to advance very quickly.' The men know very well what is happening, and many of them can read French and manage to get hold of French newspapers from time to time ... They also know that the famous complete defeat and destruction of the whole Russian army is a gross lie. In short, their soldiers are no longer duped by the fantastic inventions of the General Headquarters, and as they have also learned that prisoners are treated with the greatest kindness by the French authorities, desertions are becoming increasingly numerous. (*Le Petit journal*, 1 January 1915)

But these troops without resilience and ready to give up remain no less barbarous:

The Germanic nation, the nation of Schiller and Goethe, of Leibniz and Schubert, was transformed forty years ago into a mass of fierce and revolting brutes, destroying, raping, pillaging, massacring and torturing in the same way as the Turks – their allies today – three hundred years ago. And yet I err. Mahomet II's followers were superior to Wilhelm's men in being sober. They did not demand spirits to stimulate their rage and barbarity, while the Teutons, no doubt fearing to be insufficiently odious when fasting, seek out the most degrading drunkenness as reinforcement for their savagery and brutality. These disgusting creatures are drunken, thieving satyrs and assassins. The worst of it is, that this monstrous violation of human law is raised by them to the level of a system. The officers themselves lead the dance ... for they are nothing but torturers and murderers. They light the torches carried by their soldiers into the methodically sacked houses and preside, a cigar on their lips, over the dreadful executions that betray their passing with a long trail of blood ... The united Germans have become indistinguishable from savages, whether they call themselves Baden men, Bavarians, or Württembergers. So much so that among the ranks that Wilhelm II is leading to universal devastation, at the heart of a procession of enslaved petty kings, there are almost as many common-law criminals as there are soldiers. We must remember this when the time comes for the settling of accounts, when the Allied legions, finally victorious, crush the cursed soil where for nearly half a century these gangs of brigands have proliferated. (*Le Petit Parisien*, 8 January 1915)

This text sums up the accumulated complaints brought against the enemy at the beginning of the war, and at that time was by no means an isolated piece. But it would be unjust to reduce the journalistic 'eye-wash' to the level of such rudimentary propaganda for, from the beginning of the war, the press knew how to re-echo certain anxieties:

It is understood that, for us and for our allies, 1915 will be the year of Victory. We all say it and we do not doubt it . . . But in order to achieve victory, there must be the means, and to bring it as close as possible the cost must be recognised. The heroism of our troops and of the allied armies is not enough; nor is our patience enough . . . The trench war, as it is being waged, is clearly not the war which, according to our generals' thinking, will free us of our enemy. It can only end in exhaustion, that is over a long period of uncertain duration . . . I know it is said that Germany cannot long continue its economic survival, its nourishment and essential war supplies. Famous economists confirm this . . . But I am less optimistic than these ingenious and wise experts . . . It would be unwise to trust to the decisive effectiveness of a blockade which is not without its inconveniences and gaps. We should not therefore count absolutely and unquestioningly on the enemy's economic exhaustion . . . We know that it will not be long before we find ourselves faced with a considerable increase in German numbers. We will ourselves have fresh troops, both French and English. Will they be sufficient to meet – and surpass, for that is what is needed – those who face us? Let the high command of our armies reply . . . It is only through substantial numbers, superior to those of the Germans, supplied with weapons and abundant munitions, well instructed and trained, that we will end this terrible war that is ruining Europe and decimating our young generations. (*Le Petit journal*, 4 January 1915)

Although the writer further asserts his confidence in an approaching French victory, this is in order to express more fully the extent of his doubts as to its rapidity. Various certainties relating to the enemy's economic and human exhaustion – although widespread in general opinion – are clearly questioned. Such realism was no doubt still the exception at this early stage of the war, but this text reveals that even then propaganda was sometimes more subtle than is generally realised. Even Maurice Barrès occasionally allowed himself the luxury of misconstruing the more simplistic assertions of the Paris press:

Cheerfulness reigns in the trenches! You know that from the papers and from the letters of your sons, husbands or brothers. But one must not exaggerate; they should not be believed too literally, these brave fellows; one must not think that they are out there in these long rainy nights as if in a restaurant for a celebration. Doubtless the men exercise their ingenuity to conquer boredom. And I know of an area where in the 8-kilometre labyrinth carved out over the last month, there are well-kept tracks grandly marked avenue des Champs-Elysées or rue Monsieur-le-Prince. I know of an officer's hut with an armchair of crimson velvet, a table with a bunch of Christmas roses and plates of old Strasbourg porcelain. What does this prove? It is proof of the moral courage and state of mind in our army. In a shelled and abandoned village these men found some furniture among the ruins which the owners will rediscover later in the trenches. In fact the day is won through the power of gallantry and good humour. Friends, you may well not understand, but you will never stop us sympathising with you and admiring you. (*L'Echo de Paris*, 17 December 1914)

Here is *bourrage de crâne* of a more measured, insidious and doubtless more effective nature. In this respect it prefigures a form of propaganda which was to expand in subsequent years.

The tone of newspapers from the end of the war is indeed very different from that of 1914 or 1915. Total concealment of the distress among the troops had become impossible:

The *poilus* feel cold. The trenches do not provide adequate shelter.
I will repeat what I have already said: the *poilus* feel cold. I have described the sad, cold and gloomy camps where, lacking heat or light, the men stretch out on the straw as soon as night falls and shiver until dawn. Here are born the despair, the resentment, the unfocused hatred, the rage and the discouragement which obscure the image of duty. The *poilus* feel cold. To prevent these dreadful moments we must hasten – if

there is still time – to give them rest periods and care . . . I did not reveal everything in my previous article. I spoke only of the rest camps; they are not all that worries me . . . To the question of rest billets is linked that of battle shelters, meaning all the arrangements in the front lines, the reserve battalions' camps, shelter in the trenches . . . Are those at the rear fully aware of the true state of the front line trenches where shells and bullets whistle past? Are they aware of the advance guards' listening posts, the condition of the bombardment shelters and the saps, the communication trenches and the reserve battalion shelters a few hundred metres from the enemy? Are all these reserve battalions safe beneath stout roofs? Has care been taken everywhere to create . . . stronger and safer shelters, deeper and warmer, where the men can wait without undue suffering and in relative safety for the moment of guard duty and the day of attack? Have deep saps been dug where the men can circulate with the minimum of danger, sheltered from bursts of firing? Have communication trenches been dug everywhere along the front so that munitions and troops can be moved without excessive losses? Can we be certain that access ways have been created wherever possible, right up to the front lines, giving the reliefs shelter from bullets? (*Le Matin*, 9 January 1918)

This article does more than draw attention to the poor quality of troop living conditions. It insinuates politely that the men are not adequately protected and that not everything has been done to protect their lives. Was this not an indirect challenge to military authority?

The gravity of the situation became equally difficult to conceal totally at the time of the final German offensives in the first half of 1918:

We Must Hold on and Wait for the Americans

Events now are the direct and inevitable consequence of the Russian defection. We are living through the worst days of the war; the Russian army no longer exists and the American army is not yet capable of giving its maximum effort, which will soon be very considerable . . . It is we who must hold on in the field of battle against the speedy arrival of their great numbers. We will achieve this; the latest communications are confident of it, but the struggle is very hard . . . For the last two days the enemy has indeed been held. But we would be wrong to expect immediate stabilisation and that nothing remains for us but wait for the anticipated moment of victory, that is when we have sufficient allied forces with us to move resolutely on to the offensive. The enemy divisions are being worn down, but they have reserves . . . These reserves are centrally placed and can be sent by the shortest route to whichever point of attack the enemy may select . . . Meanwhile, we must defend ourselves, and strengthen ourselves to do so by counter-attacking locally when possible, and above all kill as many Germans as possible. Will we retreat again? No one can say; no one can foresee the outcome of battles. But our primary duty is to hold our lines firmly on the ground so as to restrict any possible retreats to the minimum. In this respect the enemy has given us numerous examples since the beginning of the war, since their retreat from the Marne. We have only to follow them. (*Le Petit journal*, 6 June 1918)

The triumphalism of the early days of the war has given way to doubt and anxiety. Moreover the writer of this article admits that further French reverses may follow the first defeats, and he defends in advance a strategy of purely defensive retreat.

The 'eye-wash' thus did not remain unaltered in style between 1914 and 1918, but it is true that the soldiers were scarcely aware of its evolution. It was the most obvious excesses of propaganda that they first noted, particularly at the beginning of the war. Doubtless this is why only a tiny minority of soldiers admitted the need for news control and direction:

This is certainly not the time to blame stubborn optimism. It is well understood that a good newspaper strategy is definitely not to explain in measured tones the phases of the battle . . . but that its role is to 'sustain morale' by emphasising success and playing down setbacks. And it is essential that this modest adaptation of accuracy should be carried out tactfully! . . . Steering public opinion is acceptable, but do not offer only deception. It is to be feared that in offering only ridiculous exaggerations, such stratagems may achieve the opposite effect to that intended. (*Le Crapouillot*, June 1918)

Corporal Jean Galtier-Boissière pleads for more skilful and credible propaganda, for in his opinion it was its form that was wrong and not its existence. Set in context, such arguments are proof of the author's rare intellectual courage: it was not often that a soldier admitted openly that some form of censorship and propaganda was inevitable in the setting of the war effort demanded of the whole nation. If a concession on this scale remains the exception, it is none the less true that the attitude of soldiers faced with 'eye-wash' was not wholly summed up in the disgust expressed in their newspapers. It is surely striking to note that while the trench newspapers rejected journalistic heroism, they themselves did not always escape the temptation to produce some *bourrage de crâne* in their own columns.

> Attack! . . . under the unleashed barrage of fire we advanced, out there, towards the liberation of the territory, while many of our own men already slept their last sleep on the recaptured ground, made heroes and great men by the most noble sacrifice of all. Nothing could be more poignant than the death-agony of these men, seeming to demand a last reviving caress from the warm spring sunshine, to see ahead, to see at last the destiny of eternal France realised . . . There were so many quietly smoking their pipe or puffing quickly on their cigarettes as they advanced, as if it was only a matter this time of a simple manoeuvre. How philosophical they were in their unconcern! What grandeur there was in their fine style. And how true that word, that cry of admiration from someone's heart: 'The *poilus*! It's enough to make you kneel at their feet!' . . . The sun, which seemed to be hiding at the beginning of the attack, now shone down on the field of battle, making the steel of the bayonets sparkle in the fire of its burning rays. Hope grew in the hearts of all these brave men whose calm courage and determined sangfroid never faltered for an instant. (*Brise d'entonnoirs*, May–July 1917)

Many of the usual propaganda themes come together in this uplifting text, from the joy of doing one's duty and attacking to stoicism in the face of wounds and suffering, via the acceptance of death for one's country. And yet the newspaper from which this article was taken lost most of its editorial staff in this attack, proof that it was produced by soldiers who were highly exposed and usually disinclined to mislead their readers. Does this betray the hand of higher command? It is undoubtedly true that many of the papers were occasionally forced to publish articles written or inspired by higher authorities and which contrasted with their usual content. But above all one must remember that many trench newspaper editors were naturally susceptible to the note of heroism, which explains why very few titles entirely escaped it.

The deep ambiguity of this attitude is perfectly revealed by comparing the two extracts from *Le 120 court* below with the article from the same paper shown at the beginning of this chapter (see pp.93–4):

> At about 1000 hours we received the order to attack. The young men,

impatient and nervous, happy to be facing a serious challenge, went without their breakfast . . . A captain fell mortally wounded, a smile on his lips . . . The Boches, taken by surprise by the suddenness and audacity of the attack, were unable to resist. Begging hands could be seen going up . . . the men were exhausted but their faces lit up with joy as they realised the significance of their gains and captures. Already their hardships were forgotten. (*Le 120 court*, 1 October 1915)

Everyone's energy became frenzied, the exhausted chasseurs refused to be relieved because they were afraid . . . that the Germans might return to the attack! At the first-aid post the wounded made no sound except cries that were cries of triumph. Kind Doctor Dubief joked with them . . . Machine-gunner Burtin is wounded in the face . . . [he] seized his rifle and, marching towards the enemy, he fired and struck with his deadly flame. The grey horde ebbed back before the grim reaper . . . At the heart of the action light-infantryman Champdavoine calmly declared: 'I've got a four-leaf clover, like I had at Verdun, it will bring me luck, I shall see Hortense again!' And he went on firing his machine-gun. (*Le 120 court*, 10 August 1917)

These two articles would do no discredit to the most traditional forms of 'eye-wash', while the former, in a pamphlet, outshone the articles of Paris journalists. The juxtaposition is striking, for the themes are the same in each of the three accounts. While the latter two state with all seriousness that the men are happy to attack, that they casually went without their morning meal, that the enemy capitulated without resistance, that there was no feeling of fatigue, that the wounded did not complain, that the soldiers joked under machine-gun fire and were unconcerned about the bullets reaching them, the pastiche presented earlier deliberately mistook all these untruths, denouncing a series of lies of which *Le 120 court* was guilty elsewhere. And even supposing that the latter had evolved between 1915 and 1916, the final account, which dates from 1917, contradicts the theory of a change in content.

The key to this mystery lies in the difference seen by soldiers between heroism of external origin and heroism for internal consumption. What they detested was the false rapture of the Paris journalists who, safe from danger, were totally ignorant of the realities of war. This does not, however, mean that a heroic style of language would be automatically rejected if it came from combatants genuinely exposed to shot and shell. It is this deep ambivalence that the following text of June 1917 tries to express:

Do you suppose that out there we charged with a flower held between our lips, that we leapt over the top singing of romance, that we died asking for news of the battle, and that the survivors only left the trenches regretfully and asking for more? . . . The *poilus* do more than utter expressions of patriotism, they live it – indeed, they die of it. They are true patriotism, patriotism incarnate, the patriotism that suffers, bleeds, dies . . . To be of merit here a patriotic article should be written at one of the picket positions. Then we would see . . . We cannot turn up our noses at certain great preachers of patriotism. We tell ourselves one thing: since these fellows keep on saying that to die for one's country is the finest possible fate, why do they not come and share it with us, this most enviable fate? There is still room for them here . . . We take lessons in patriotism only from our leaders who, over the top and at our head, show us the enemy trench with bared swords. (*Le Bochofage*, 25 June 1917)

The purely verbal heroism of those who run no risk whatever was thus rejected forcefully. As for the very real heroism of the fighting troops, it can only be praised legitimately by those who risk their own lives, and by them alone. Fighting heroism is theirs alone: civilians must keep quiet and refrain from exploiting the courage of others for propaganda purposes. From this courage the soldiers drew a purely personal pride, while wanting their merits to be recognised: but their ceaseless confrontation with death gives them alone the privilege of speaking of it.

Civilian Mediocrity

During the opening months of the war the image of civilians in the trench newspapers was on the whole positive; then, from the beginning of 1915, harshness took over from indulgence, and the rear grew steadily more unpopular until 1918. Although there was no lack of complaints against the French who remained in the rear, it was their light-heartedness that was most often held against them:

The nation's economic life must go on, that's obvious . . . But all the same, does it not go on a bit too much, and not altogether in the way discussed in speeches? Look at the cafés! . . . the cafés are full; if business is picking up, it is above all the business of bistros, breweries and the makers of apéritifs for drinking at 70° in the shade. Look at the theatres! They offer just now an incalculable number of reviews where scantily clad little women sing in succession – but all as out of tune as each other –

of Allied glories. And look at the streets! . . . the pavements are black with people; and for a disabled man to be noticed, he must be terribly disabled. Ah well! People get used to war . . . it is just that the rear has quietly got used to the idea that people are dying about 100 kilometres from Paris. (*Le Pépère*, 15 June 1915)

To this indifference at the rear can be added its irresponsibility and egotism:

One fact strikes the man on leave: the inertia of the public, its indifference, its lack of discipline. It is a dead weight dragging behind the front like a ball and chain restricting his freedom of movement. The education of the civilians is still to be achieved . . . At the rear there is the most scandalous waste, the most appalling muddle. Threatened by the lack of livestock the government ordained two days without meat. That was sensible. Immediately the large food suppliers began to get together, trying to demolish the measure proposed, as if a few private interests should take priority over the interests of the nation! As for the public, they were worse: they rushed to the butchers and bought provisions in such quantity that they were able to get round the law, and had enough meat to eat even on the two days when they were supposed to go without. . . . People, the public, we must say it openly, these are our own parents, our families, our friends back there at the rear. We cannot count on the press to make them understand the gravity of their wrong-doing, for the press is chiefly responsible for the state of mind clearly revealed in those two civilian remarks: '*On les aura*' and 'Everything is all right', implying, there is no problem, we can carry on life without worrying. So it's up to us . . . to try . . . and prevail against this wretched attitude. In our letters, in our conversations on leave, we must make them understand, those who still value us and have some regard for our lives, that their stupid negligence threatens to destroy the gains of our three years of resistance and sacrifice. We must tell them straight out that they are shooting us in the back. (*Tacatacteufteuf*, 1 June 1917)

The fighting troops were convinced that the behaviour of almost all the French at the rear was motivated solely by concern for their own personal interests. This was a firmly entrenched conviction, allowing them to heap up all kinds of reproaches on civilian heads. Were they not profiting from their absence to take over the combatants' jobs? Did they not refuse to help soldiers on leave, or even to travel with them in the trains? And what should they think of those who felt themselves absolved from their debt of recognition by sending a wretched bit of aid to the front, and even that increasingly rarely? This deliberate denigration did not spare even those French citizens who each year subscribed to National Defence loans. Were not such investments financially advantageous?

> The civilian takes his money to the bank. It is a fine gesture and also . . . a sound investment. With an eloquently patriotic gesture he deposits the fruits of his thrift on the counter and then, brandishing his bond like a resounding victory, he departs, dreaming of the next victory . . . *On les aura* . . . Oh happy civilian. (*Aux 100,000 articles*, 26 February 1916)

Civilians were not merely egotists; they were also cowards. As proof the troops put forward the exodus from Paris, evoked here with humour at the time of the final German offensives in the summer of 1918:

> The battle continued fierce at the Gare de Lyon and the Quai d'Orsay. After a violent struggle . . . a detachment of quitters managed to take the train . . . The civilians pursued their strategic retreat . . . They withdrew to positions prepared in advance further to the south, at Biarritz, Nice and Monte Carlo. Their morale is excellent. (*Sans tabac*, August 1918)

And further, not content with running no risks, did not certain civilians tend towards cynicism and provocation? So wrote *Le Diable au cor*, giving this type of argument to a 'shirker' who, having managed to keep himself safe, did not hesitate to express his open satisfaction and his scorn:

> Oh, we don't worry here, you see . . . We have sacrificed those who have gone. That is part of the principles we have adopted, we at the rear. It is always the same ones who let themselves get killed. It's only the b—fools who mount guard. Don't give a damn, and know it. (*Le Diable au cor*, 9 December 1915)

On the whole, civilians were exposed to the opprobrium of never being in danger and they were discredited by this fundamental inequality between the two categories of citizen:

> The civilian holds on. In fact no one knows what this stupid phrase

means, for whether he holds on or not, provided the front line holds on, it makes no difference. The civilian holds on to his skin; he also holds on to his job and holds his feet to the warmth. (*Le Pépère*, 15 October–1 November 1916)

In a few stinging words, this shows that what the civilian population is reproached for is not fighting. But the worst ordeal for the soldiers was that of not being understood: one can be resigned to inequality between combatants and the rest, one can put up with the pettiness of the rear, its carelessness, its moral mediocrity, but only on condition that it expresses its gratitude and recognition to those who sacrifice themselves for its benefit and on condition that it understands the meaning of this daily sacrifice. This was far from being the case; the incomprehension and ignorance of the rear, of everything that was tragic in front-line life, were immense. The attitude of the public in a cinema showing news films is very revealing on this point:

There was an announcement: 'Views of the war'. Most of the civilians got up and left, grumbling, 'The war again, what a bore' . . . While (on the screen) the soldiers mastered the dreadful 'pig's snout' [gas-mask], the audience doubled up with laughter. Perhaps they would not have found the exercise so funny if they had but once had to do it in feverish haste with bells ringing in the trenches to announce the arrival of the dreadful clouds of death . . . The final film unrolled before us: 'The battle-fields of the Marne' . . . the public seemed disappointed that such a terrible battle had left so little trace, and beside me a little old lady, bored with such tranquil scenery, declared with a gentle little pout: 'That's boring: there aren't even any bodies.' (*Le Crapouillot*, August 1917)

However painful such insensitivity might be, it was at least less nauseating than the veiled reproaches:

There are civilians who cannot approach a man on leave without asking him *why aren't you advancing*. Why can we not make use of this ardour of civilians greedy for offensives? We could take them into the front-line trenches and urge them to advance. We bet that anyone returning from such an expedition would no longer enquire why one does not advance. (*L'Echo des tranchées*, 10 May 1917)

If the question put to men on leave appeared both unfair and cruel, it is because by implication it questions the courage of the combatants. Similarly, they were indignant at the widespread ignorance of the mental and physical hardships endured in the front line; their papers drew up lists of comments made to men on leave that are highly indicative of the total ignorance at the rear:

> *Little Phrases Heard by the Man on Leave*
> – But how well you look!
> – You see, you've got away with it!
> – I heard you'd been killed!
> – What does a Boche look like?
> – How many Boches have you killed?
> – A bayonet charge must be magnificent!
> – I heard they were installing heaters in the trenches this winter?
> – How many times have you been in a battle?
> – The worst thing is the rain, isn't it?
> – Oh, it will turn out all right, you'll see!
> – What's this about morale?
> – I read this morning in my paper that . . .
> – It appears that their shells are useless.
> – You can't imagine our sufferings and anguish.
>
> (*Le Bochofage*, 21 October 1916)

Phrases perhaps invented or exaggerated; phrases perhaps not common in reality – but that is not the point: genuine or not, these phrases helped to shape the combatants' image of a civilian population thoroughly ill-informed about the horror of battles, the harshness of their living conditions and the intensity of their distress.

Soldiers were no better, moreover, at tolerating those who displayed an excessive interest in the war and the hazards of the front; nothing seemed more ill-placed than the high-flown patriotism of those who risked nothing. This target was shot down in a sarcastic 'citation':

> Civilian of high moral standards. Sings the Marseillaise twelve times a day and weeps on reading a communiqué. (*Le Plus que torial*, 31 May 1917)

Further, were not certain among them – not content with displaying a surface patriotism – convinced that they were themselves really 'living' the war, and even contributing to the final victory?

The civilian does not fight, but it is he who wins ... and he gains something too. Such-and-such a setback would not have occurred if they had listened to him, and when a victory is announced 'he told us so'. When the war is over we will all go back to Paris, we will watch from the windows of the avenue de la Grande-Armée and the civilians will parade beneath the Arc de Triomphe ... for it is thanks to them that the Boches will have been defeated. (*Bellica*, 5 June 1916)

By such arguments the soldiers devalued the national war effort; they forgot the anxiety of French families over the risks suffered by those of their members who were at the front, and they ignored the patriotism of the majority of the population. They never acknowledged the endurance of the Home Front – without which their own would not have been possible – and this harshness was frequently very unjust.

This is not to deny that the systematic denigration of the civilian population reveals clearly the great gulf gradually appearing between the front and the home front, and the accumulated resentment of soldiers over civilian attitudes. Although applied to virtually the entire non-combatant population, this hostility was aimed more specifically at certain categories, such as the politicians, a target for virulent attack:

You see, my poor friend, you can truly say that a [parliamentary] Deputy is stronger and braver than us! Yes, when you get a bullet you bellow like an ox, but a Deputy can easily stand up to fifteen thousand bullets without flinching. (*Le Canard du biffin*, January 1918)

A combatant also complained in very severe terms about a citation presented to a mobilised Deputy:

I was overwhelmed with pleasure when I read, in one of the latest issues of [the *Journal officiel*], the citation for the *Croix de Guerre* recently won by one of our honourable parliamentarians who was not afraid to abandon his comfortable armchair in the Palais Bourbon ... for a more rustic seat in the quartermaster's offices, for having 'directed with efficiency the provisioning of an army corps in particularly dangerous conditions'. Well! It makes you shiver to think of the funds of energy, gallantry and courage that this hero must have expended. (*L'Echo de la mitraille*, 15 August 1917)

N° 2. JANVIER 1916.   PRIX : **50** Centimes

BELLICA

Composé

sur

LE FRONT

Magazine héroïco-gai paraissant tous les mois o o o o

Ce journal ne peut être crié — ni décrié. — Tous les manuscrits vont au feu.

ADMINISTRAT ON DIRECTION, RÉDACTION, CÈBE & MORELLET — Secteur 140

3 *Bellica*
The front page of *Bellica*. Trench newspapers were not always immune to the temptation of praising warrior heroism, but the caption was not without its humour. Carica-
ture by Abel Faivre.

This looks like a reappearance of the anti-parliament feelings of
pre-war days, with the help of a somewhat complaisant censorship.
But it must be remembered that this hostility to parliamentarians

was hardly diminished by the inquiries undertaken in the combat zone by certain Deputies. According to the soldiers, a fair number of these 'visitors' were ridiculed by troops overwhelmed by such condescension.

Another group very soon detested with equal violence was that of the 'war profiteers':

> And then there is the sad category of profiteers. They do not sound gloomy, and they are certainly smiling, I can assure you. They willingly adopt a heroic stance as craftsmen of the nation's defence, selling for fabulous prices essentials that have grown in the earth, been fished from the sea, or manufactured, under conditions very little different from those of normal times. This is the class of the new rich. They do not, however, wish to appear too obviously joyful, so they adopt an air of overwork, of poor creatures staggering beneath the heroic task which has fallen to them. It is wise to observe the movements of these vampires carefully and the 'high cost of living' can only be avoided by rigorous sanctions. (*L'Echo de tranchées-villes*, 18 November 1915)

With less subtlety but more humour, *Hurl'obus* put the following words into the mouth of one such 'profiteer':

> Business? flourishing . . . [It] goes on growing daily, naturally the profits do the same. Besides, that is what accounts for the extensions to my house and our well-being, and the prime luxury of a holiday in Nice. Economies? of course, despite all these expenses I still make economies. Provided the war goes on for another few months I will have, I calculate, my little place in the country. As you say . . . it's magnificent. But shouldn't one make the best of everything? (*Hurl'obus*, March 1917)

This summary and moralising form of anti-capitalism, buttressed by the notion that it is immoral for some to profit while others are killed, accompanies a somewhat superficial analysis of the nation's economic and social realities. But how can one reproach such attitudes among men deprived of everything?

This feeling of injustice explains why the workers were scarcely more popular than the industrialists. That as 'factory-mobilised men' many workers of combatant age were exempt from going to the front, and that they earned a reasonable living, were causes of bitterness among the soldiers.

There is only this matter which he does not understand: why he, mobilised, far from home and risking his skin, earns five *sous* per day, while the metal-worker, also mobilised, working at his craft close to his wife and far from danger, earns twelve francs for a ten-hour day. (*Le Pépère*, 25 November 1916)

The form of the analysis may sometimes be more subtle but the judgement remains fundamentally severe:

Men in factories deserve esteem; they have no rights either to sympathy or to admiration, *or even to gratitude*. There is an abyss between the sacrifice, the simple risk of one's life, and the fatigue of work, however wearisome it may be. This can neither be evaluated nor compared. (*Le Filon*, August 1917)

Mobilised men sent to risk-free posts formed a distinctly separate category. On the boundary between the rear and the front, half-soldier and half-civilian, they were truly detested. In the front ranks of these 'shirkers' and 'dodgers' the fighting soldier placed quartermasters, doctors, medical orderlies, drivers, stores clerks, staff officers, and all 'service' support soldiers. And when certain among them dared to put on a *brisque* (long-service badge), this was seen as particularly sickening:

It is said that the wearing of long-service badges will be regulated under the following conditions: only men in the temperate . . . zones of the rear, extending more or less all the way along the front . . . in depth can wear long-service badges. As for the fighting men, the real unadulterated men, they will be authorised to appear with mud up to their stomachs, and weary eyes. This will achieve the proper distinction between the two species. (*Le 120 court*, 19 June 1916)

Nor did the soldiers' bitterness spare the policemen and the traders who depended on their military clientèle, the two categories of non-combatants with whom they were most frequently in contact behind the front lines. Concerning the police, the trench newspapers display a certain ferocity:

When they see him as they return to the trenches the *poilus* say to each other 'Ah! Good! Now we are safe!' presumably because by preventing them from drinking too much wine he protects them from the dangers of alcohol. He wears light blue, like everyone else, and that annoys him a bit because he may be mistaken for a soldier. He is not a soldier, he is a policeman. (*Bellica*, April–May 1916)

Sometimes, in barely veiled terms, there is a call for reprisals:

Last week I even treated a policeman: he told me that he had fought bravely against the enemy, but the other wounded men told me quietly that for the policeman, the enemy was not the Boche but the little foot-slogger, and that no doubt it was through an excess of zeal, misunderstood by the soldiers, that he had suffered this bayonet thrust in the arm . . . Habits acquired by some [soldiers] from the Boches with whom they were in contact on the days of attack might procure for a policeman a few days' rest in a good hospital bed. (*L'Echo des dunes*, April 1917)

As for the war profiteers, the traders who pullulated round the rest zones behind the front lines, the soldiers were soon violently hostile to them. Profiting from the fact that they lacked everything on coming down from the front line, did they not abuse the situation shamefully?

The race [of front-line exploiters] swarmed about, the extreme avant-garde of the profiteers at the rear who enriched themselves there in the shadows, without danger. We made known . . . some of the prices demanded for the most essential food supplies such as cheese, vegetables, wine, fruit . . . We are not talking about necessaries for grooming or the table [*sic*] of the *poilu*, such as towels, combs, braces, knives, plates, mugs, etc. Such objects usually cost three or four times the usual prices before the war. (*L'Echo du boyau*, 15 November 1916)

So the rear was thoroughly discredited, and the fact that the reproaches addressed to it were sometimes contradictory should not disguise their substance. Finally, the hostility of the soldiers was linked less to civilian attitudes as such than to the open rift in the national fabric created by forced and prolonged separation between two worlds: that of the rear and that of the front. It made communication very difficult between two communities too distant from each other for easy comprehension.

This difficulty of communication was further aggravated by the conviction that the separation between one sheltered population and another exposed to danger concealed a fundamental injustice. It explains the profound and misplaced satisfaction of the soldiers at the announcement of government measures designed to dispatch certain rather too well protected mobilised men to the front:

> You have read in the newspapers that our Ministry of War has sworn first to eliminate shirkers and then to arrange a little tour along the front for all those who have not yet been there. You cannot imagine, my friend, what a relief it is to know that everyone is going to have a little taste of it! It is good for everyone, even those who go there, because for most of the time it was they who thought the war was not progressing fast enough ... Like this, when they are in the trenches, they will try to do better. (*L'Echo du grand couronné*, January 1916)

It was also in the name of this egalitarianism that the soldiers displayed a certain contentment at hearing of the bombardment of Paris in 1918:

> The civilians are beginning to understand war, through experience. Communication with the troops has abruptly been achieved by a few nights of terror for civilians who, concerned for their own sensitivity, had never tried to comprehend the terrible calvary of the *poilu* at the front. This sudden equality in the face of death, this terrible feeling of powerlessness under the rain of fire, will have made certain full-blown stick-it-to-the-very-end people appreciate much more accurately the unspoken merit of those soldiers whose resistance has not been crushed by the engines of terror, after 1,300 days of battle. (*Le Crapouillot*, March 1918)

'Understand', 'communication', 'equality': three decisive words in one text. This need for understanding, for sharing and for equality has its source in a veritable obsession with forgetting. At the front the soldiers felt as if they were on the furthest island of the continent, and the contents of their newspapers expressed their revulsion at their isolation.

The discredit of the press and the population at large could not fail to affect the way in which the soldiers perceived national events. Their reactions rarely reveal any genuine interest in what was happening in their own country. This does not mean that it is impossible to find items of current affairs in their papers: certain governmental changes and also various political scandals, such as the arrest of Caillaux in 1918,[1] appear in their columns. Measures to regulate prices, or concerning rents and indemnities for mobilisation, can be found there. Restrictions on consumption were also mentioned, together with a few references to women's work and fashions, and sometimes even to strikes. But this selection of news items served above all as fodder for the soldiers' continual recriminations against the remainder of the population.

Such mentions included restrictions affecting civilians, which were in truth not harsh, but which only served as a good excuse to make fun of them:

> While the public news-sheets tell us every day about the difficulty of life and the high prices of food at the rear, how can one fail to cry out that there is more than one *poilu* who would welcome the opportunity to buy his food in the same conditions from the hucksters at the front? It's only funerals that are cheaper [at the rear than at the front] . . . My belief, based on definitive observations, is that the civilians will hold on. (*Bellica*, April–May 1916)

Almost everything that happened at the rear was thus held against it, and the nation's way of life was only evoked in order to sustain the flood of sarcastic comments aimed at the civilian population. News items as such were almost ignored: the war at the rear had no place in the press of the front lines. By disregarding the role of civilians in the war effort in this way the troops assumed exclusive rights themselves.

The generosity of censorship towards their occasionally subversive writings should not really be surprising. From the point of view of the military authorities, there were advantages in letting the men treat the rear with contempt: after all, did this not raise the prestige of the forward positions to a corresponding degree? Did it not add to the prestige of the troops in their own eyes, and reinforce a very

---

1. The arrest of Joseph Caillaux, former *Président du Conseil* and leader of the Radical Party, was part of Clemenceau's large-scale offensive, following his arrival in power in November 1917, against matters of 'treason'. Favouring a negotiated peace, Joseph Caillaux had developed contacts with various people in neutral and allied nations. Arrested in January 1918, he appeared before the Senate, sitting as the High Court, and in 1920 was condemned to three years' imprisonment.

natural feeling of superiority? Overall, the virulence of certain attacks against the rear was only apparent, and they were primarily effective in reinforcing cohesion within the military community. Further, did not the fact that some of the soldiers' bitterness was turned against the non-combatants actually deflect it from other targets such as discipline or the leaders of the whole military hierarchy? It was particularly convenient to render the rear responsible for failures of war management, and certain professional officers did not hesitate to take resounding revenge on civilian society:

> And who said: I want military service to last for two years, one year, six months? You did! And who talked about brutes with commissions? You did! And who was responsible for our lack of preparation? You were! And who has been wearing out the doormats of influential personages to withdraw their sons from military service? You have! And who now wants to be defended? You do! (*L'Echo de tranchées-ville*, 19 August 1915)

It is true that after the frustrations and humiliations of the two preceding decades, the war satisfied the pride of various officers who had long suffered from lack of it. But we should not think of such officers as 'manipulating' the trench press: the high command simply abstained from attaching too many restrictions to the expression of a very genuine resentment, which occasionally overflowed into a wholehearted thirst for revenge.

The Temptation of Revenge

The fighting troops were thus deeply disappointed by the rear, but as the end of the war approached they none the less had to consider their return to civilian life. This approach of post-war life caused some lively apprehension, particularly when Allied victories in the summer of 1918 hinted at a return to peace.

Even at the outset of the war, however, the trench press never lost sight of what the end of the war might mean to combatants in practical terms, and it knew how to give voice to their muffled uncertainties:

> It is reasonable to look ahead and see that when we go home again we shall have to struggle to earn our living, more specifically but no less

bitterly! We will find that our interests, our businesses, however modest, have been affected by the extended neglect they have suffered. We will have to face up to competitors and rivals who have profited from circumstances. (*Le 120 court*, 10 April 1916)

The troops were thus under no illusion as to what would await them after demobilisation, and some did not conceal their indignation:

To those who said in quivering tones: After the war we will think of you, our brave soldiers – how would they reply to this letter, received by one of my friends who, having asked his former boss now working for the government what he expected to be doing after the war, received the following reply: 'I do not know what I can say, and currently I cannot plan any decisions nor can I undertake any commitments.' Go to war and lose your job! Was that the reward we expected? Poor humanity! I have often thought that it would turn out like this, and I know well which side of the front line the fools are on. (*On progresse*, 1 April 1917)

Despite this diffuse despair over the post-war years, the trench newspapers only rarely made specific demands, at least not until victory was clearly approaching:

[This soldier is] an unhappy man who suffers, languishes and weeps over the present and the future in gloomy solitude, in wretched spirits . . . To help the soldier cope with his wretchedness, we would like . . . to bestow on him without further ado the certainty that he (or his family) will be materially rewarded for the terrible sacrifice he has made. (*Le Tordboyau*, September 1917)

Although the word 'reward' was uttered, the extent of the claim remained extremely vague. The demands became more precise as victory approached, but the combatants' anxiety, far from diminishing, tended rather to increase:

[The soldier in the ranks] is particularly depressed because he is well aware that he will return too late and too old, diminished and poorly regarded in tomorrow's world. (*La Fourragère*, October 1918)

Their pessimism was augmented by the attitude of the press, which they considered too silent regarding the fate reserved for them after the war:

> It can be stated that the other press, the 'nationals', leaves us comprehensively in the gutter. The powerful papers . . . conspire towards a deathly silence over the only material question of interest to the troops: the question of their fate once the war is over. (*Le Tord-boyau*, August 1918)

There was no greater reassurance to be had from parliament or the politicians:

> Alas, I lost my illusions many moons ago over parliamentary projects in general and human gratitude – national or otherwise – in particular – or lack of it. (*La Première ligne*, October 1918)

Disquiet in the army as a whole a few weeks before the armistice was thus significant, and merited serious attention; proposals on how to express the nation's gratitude to its soldiers were unlikely to reduce this disquiet:

> Our enthusiasm at solemn glorification, processions, marble plaques, celebratory pillars and triumphal arches is extremely moderate . . . We are too strongly aware of a wish to evade the obligation to recompense the troops that is one of the unavoidable consequences of such a war, and that at the same time people are trying to conceal, by means of some kind of dazzlement, an immense national ingratitude . . . We are kept going with gratuities and temporary allowances, with clothing supplied by the quartermaster, with resoled shoes, everything depressingly like the administrative good works of some kind of patronage towards guilty or morally unsatisfactory young people . . . It would be better to make soldiers understand that they are the unfortunate victims of the war and can count on no one but themselves. (*Le Tord-boyau*, January 1919)

Symbolic rewards and the modest material provision planned were judged both derisory and humiliating, for the soldiers considered that they had rights and demanded their just dues:

> It is a matter of our future, that is of the circumstances into which we will be thrown back in civilian life when our wartime mission is done . . . We

must start working now for our return, to obtain the rights and advantages which are due to us. These are not favours that we are seeking, but formal claims that we are stating. (*Le Bochofage*, September–October 1918)

At the end of the war, therefore, the trench newspapers adopted a demanding attitude. They prepared to defend a new social group, the veterans, and saw themselves as their spokesmen. But they did not stop there; they also demanded that when they returned from the trenches the soldiers should occupy a dominant position in the world of the future:

France will find among us men tested by war, soldiers who, having learned how to die, will know how to live and who *will break with the past*. The future is ours. We must seize it from the cowards, from the faint-hearts, from the traitors and shirkers, from people who don't know what war means. (*Le Filon*, August 1918)

The soldiers felt that such demands were justified because in their eyes the home front had discredited itself during the war. To them it seemed that they must put the country back on the rails and that by accepting fundamental responsibilities they must pursue an undertaking of moral reconstitution. Women, for example, should return to their proper path:

Coming home victorious . . . will it be fair to return to a deserted hearth where our authority, so hard-won, will no longer be recognised? Will he be told on his return that the civil status of Man and Woman no longer exist, that instead there are two human beings with equal rights, two social units? Pushed out of his age-old role as protector at the moment when he has just qualified once more for the title, will he have to put up with sharing civil and political struggles with women? With finding women his rivals everywhere, competing for the work he seeks, and where they already have a head-start? . . . Bring the women back home, keep them out of political struggles, surely that is the plan we should follow, if we do not want to have hundreds of thousands fewer Frenchmen in twenty years' time? (*L'Horizon*, December 1918)

As for the rest of the population, it was their work which was nonetheless to constitute their *raison d'être*:

Work is the only way to achieve the dreamed-of goal, France's pros-
perity, the only way too to sustain morale at the high level attained
through self-denial and love of duty by the soldier in the trenches. (*La
Mitraille*, January–February 1918)

The notion of the return to the land was sometimes the final
objective of this combative moralising:

You must give your children a taste for the free country life, for healthy
work in the fields . . . for the new France to be healed more rapidly of the
deep wounds in her land. (*Le Petit Echo du 18e territorial*, 1 July 1917)

Many themes of Pétainist ideology were germinating in this way by
1918, although they would not bloom fully until the aftermath of
the defeat of May–June 1940. This moral attitude was hindered in its
development in 1918 by the French victory: if the nation had found
within itself sufficient strength to surmount the ordeal of the war,
was not that evidence of its fundamental good health? The ground
was not ready for the development of a collective wish for expia-
tion, but two decades later defeat would achieve what victory had
prevented in 1918.

The deep disappointment caused by civilian behaviour explains
this desire to lead the nation in new directions. To this end, many
combatants vowed purely and simply to replace those who had
acted reprehensibly:

Be silent! For the sake of the nation we endured the most dreadful
ordeals which men have ever had to endure, while you, you wretched
parasites, were betraying us! And when you claim to have played a part
in the great drama of which we were the anonymous stars, you are lying.
Your stupid lies, your absurd distortion of the truth, could not sustain
either the morale of the fighting men in the trenches who sneer at your
idiotic nonsense and who, in order to do more than their duty, did not
need to be driven to the carnage by shirkers or whores, or the morale of
those people at the rear with someone dear to them at the front, who
were ignorant of none of the horrors of war . . . Foolish optimism has
never achieved anything except to discourage initiatives, delay improvements and hide mistakes. Your role was negative, if not harmful, for your
lies served only to create between front-line France and the French at the
rear a malaise which could have had heavy consequences! . . . Now we

are back again and once again we 'heroes', *we are the relief force.* As for you, vampires who have lived off our blood and sold false heroism to silly fools, you have only one more thing to do: disappear! (*Le Crapouillot*, June 1917)

Many believed that this 'relief' which they were determined to carry out would be quite vigorous:

After they have liberated the land, the *poilus* will not have finished their labours: they will still have to conquer the rear and lay down the law there. (*Tacatacteufteuf*, 1 June 1917)

The result was an imperceptible slide towards reprisals. The following anecdote reveals this wish for violence against the civilian population:

Two days ago in the metro, on the 'Nation' line, a civilian had the unfortunate idea of finding fault with a *poilu* who was rolling a cigarette. The cost: the hat of the said civilian knocked out of shape, and three kicks in his backside. The *poilu* was a '*joyeux*',* thus a fellow without fear, a real *poilu* in fact; the civilian would have done better to keep quiet or hide himself . . . It is not the rear's turn to speak. (*La Revue poilusienne*, January 1918)

The war profiteers were threatened with execution:

[The high cost of living] is the fault of the monopolists and the profiteers at the rear! We should shoot a few; that would give the others something to think about. (*L'Echo de tranchées-ville*, 4 November 1915)

Similar measures of repression were also promised to the shirkers:

Look at that shirker over there. Aren't you coming with us? Pass me my rifle, I'll bring him down. (*La Marmite*, May 1916)

---

* Translator's note: a '*joyeux*' was the ironic term for a soldier in the punitive 'disciplinary' squad operating in France's North African territories, to which troublesome or potentially rebellious soldiers were posted.

Sometimes the threats were aimed indiscriminately at the whole civilian population:

> Give me a grenade . . . I want one that's big enough to blow up the whole of the rear. (*Le Tacatac du moulin*, 20 July 1917)

> Prepare your rifles and count your ammunition. (*La Musette*, March 1918)

Civilians were thus threatened with a vast settling of accounts on demobilisation day, and some soldiers became anxious:

> Let us hope that the war between France and Germany will not be the preliminary to a war between *poilus* and civilians . . . and that the standing down and troop relief will pass without incident on the first day of peace. (*Le Crapouillot*, January 1918)

Should this promise of purging deserve to be taken seriously? There was in reality a vast gap between words and deeds, and this fear of some kind of incipient civil war had no genuine basis. The threats mouthed by the troops were above all demands for compensation, the dreams of men who had lived too long under severe tension. Further, indignation was not universally so intense. It was certainly very obvious among combatants of urban origin, while to the countrymen among them the rear appeared more as the modest community they had left behind and with which they had retained a sense of solidarity. The brutal head-on confrontation between the rear and the front conceived by some soldiers could not therefore happen. It is undoubtedly true that the ties between civilians and combatants became progressively slacker as the war continued: the consequence was profound exasperation, turning here and there to open hatred and thirst for vengeance. But the bonds between front and home front were never truly broken, and so the menace to national cohesion threatened by the resentment of its defenders was real, but essentially superficial.

~5~

The Fascination of the Home Front

Wife and Family

The thoughts of soldiers alone in the depths of their trenches quickly turned to their wives and families; by 1915 this is the second most frequent topic discussed in their newspapers. Its importance grew ever greater as time passed, so that during the final months of the war the combatants appeared to concentrate more than ever on those from whom they were separated and whom they hoped – in the end with certainty – to see again.

This exclusively masculine community naturally suffered severe frustrations, both physical and emotional. The complete lack of any feminine presence was however largely 'forgotten' in the writings of veterans, who kept almost total silence on the subject, although nothing indicates its importance more than certain articles about the rare meetings with women that occurred behind the front lines:

> After four months in the trenches the regiment is going for a rest . . .
> Here is a new sight: civilians! Better still, there are women, and some are young and pretty. What gentleness after such efforts! A pretty nape of the neck under beautiful golden hair, a slender waist, a curving leg seen passing, and at once there appears the distant image of the loved one, and the face of love. Those who have not felt this deprivation of everything that brings charm into one's life will never know how cruel it is . . . and what gratitude they owe to those who, for them, accept the sacrifice of it.
> (*Le Poilu du 35*, May 1918)

The adjective used to describe this interminable separation was 'cruel'. This helps to explain why simply seeing a woman pass through a rest-camp could be an overwhelming experience for any squad which happened to meet her:

> We had the exquisite impression of being free men once more, that the war was over, the land cleansed of all the spilt blood, and that there were only carefree hearts, ardent young people dreaming of peace and love. (*L'Horizon*, July 1917)

This same enthusiasm, blended with emotion, inspired one soldier when he described what women meant to his friends :

> For these good fellows who were long used to living out in the rain and the shells [woman] was a whole element of the past, of the dear past which was being reborn, an evocation of happiness, shops, dancing, the reawakening of a forgotten ideal, Life with a capital L. And also the tender memory of past loves. (*Aux 100,000 articles*, 19 February 1916)

In their writings the soldiers give an impression of woman as the very principle of life itself; she symbolised simultaneously peace, pre-war life and freedom, offering the soldiers a moment of gentleness and beauty in the ugliness of their daily lives. She was the obverse image of war, and therein lay her strength.

Meetings with women remained so rare that they were a great surprise every time they occurred:

> There was a general to-do this morning when the news came round in a flash that there was a woman in the area, a real woman, not in disguise, flesh and blood, a young local girl who wanted to see if the German shells had spared her home. (*L'Echo des marmites*, 20 November 1916)

With bitter sarcasm the same astonishment appears here:

> This morning on the road a *poilu* met . . . a woman! Is this the final specimen of a race we thought extinct? (*Le Poilu*, 10 March 1915)

Sometimes the woman was a note of joy in the desolate life at the front. But her prolonged absence more often meant deep distress, sometimes admitted:

All your thoughts are of those women who are forbidden you. Your whole being quivers at the very thought and to your physical sufferings is added the sinister mental suffering of *le cafard*. (*Le Sourire de l'escouade*, 12 September 1916)

This evocation also exudes diffuse suffering:

Those girls from the mining villages were attractive to look at! Tall and slim, with dark eyes! They offered us hospitality: a table in a corner, chairs, a lamp for the evenings . . . And then a little love here and there, a snatched kiss, a brief embrace . . . sometimes more . . . You went off to the trenches and you thought about them, at night, in the dug-out, under the shelling. (*Le Midi au front*, 25 May 1916)

The titillating photographs that circulated freely in the trenches were a poor substitute. But they sharpened the piercing pains of unquenched desire:

Illustrated papers . . . are everywhere and all-conquering; they go right up to the front line, trail about in the dug-outs, stick on to the sides and . . . catch the *poilu* in his lonely sadness. (*Tacatacteufteuf*, March 1918)

There are other cases where the sexual frustration of this entire community of men is sharply evoked:

Soldiers on campaign for fourteen months end by feeling the need to relax. They find they have persistent drives, particularly in the mornings. (*L'Echo des tranchées*, 10 October 1915)

To conclude this article the author bluntly demanded the introduction of BMCs (*bordels militaires de campagne*, military campaign brothels). Others, it is true, would have preferred to see an elaborate system arranged for wives to travel to see their husbands at the front:

Why, in certain circumstances, should women not be allowed to come and see their husbands, to distract them and keep them up to date with family matters of interest to them? Put aside the question of physical pleasure. Can one believe that nearly two years of war do not have an effect on what is a fairly short existence, in fact, since the average marriage lasts for between twenty-five and thirty years together? Obviously one could raise objections, as has happened over granting leave, but they would be no more valid in the one case than they were in the other and if accepted it would be easy to make everyone happy – the *poilus* and their wives. (*Face aux boches*, May 1916)

This prolonged abstinence on the part of the soldiers explains the not-infrequent presence of a certain vulgarity in their papers, the point of contact between the desires of men too long restricted and traditional military licentiousness. More prevalent, however, is a sentimentality of great vacuity; a whole literature of compensation trying to provide a few dreams in the form of insipid love stories where war 'godmothers'[1] and nurses took the leading part. But none of this could conceal the soldier's distress at the thought of being betrayed or abandoned by the girl he had left behind him:

Your imaginings depict your wife in the arms of another man. (*Le Camouflet*, 1 June 1916)

Further evidence of their persistent suspicions can be seen in the astonishment of soldiers from rural backgrounds at the changes in women's fashions in the countryside. How to explain them except by the presence of men who stayed far from the front and courted the women left behind in the villages?

At last he reaches the village . . . He meets some country women. Oh, but how they've changed! No more clogs, no more apron: smart polished boots, jewellery! As the *poilu* says to himself: Are there still men at the rear, to pay for all these fine things? (*Le Cri du boyau*, September–October 1916)

---

1. The expression 'war godmothers' (*marraines de guerre*) refers to women who offered to correspond with particularly lonely or friendless front-line soldiers. They also sent parcels, and met the men on leave. In theory the motive behind such links was essentially patriotic, designed to sustain soldiers' morale. However, the very strong emotional force of these long-distance links often expanded into a relationship of genuine love between the 'godmothers' and their 'godsons'.

It is true that a certain 'luxurious' style of clothing spread into rural areas, but it was the military allowances and the price of farm produce that made it attainable, and it was due more to a move to compensate for the low standard of living among rural populations than to peasant women's idle frivolity.[2] This did not prevent the soldiers from displaying their anger and their fears with a degree of emphasis which does not disguise the unmistakable note of sincerity in their protestations:

> How cowardly they seem to me, those men who are comfortably settled at the rear and who try to profit from the current difficult circumstances by disturbing the noble and dignified solitude of women deprived of their loved ones and their support. I cannot think of any more basely vile or odious crime than that! While others, out there, are getting shot or lie bleeding in a hospital bed, those men whose privileged position should impose on them at least a polite reserve roam like wolves round homes where the head of the household is absent. Yes, there are roaming wolves. (*La Gazette du créneau*, November 1918)

The soldiers' anxiety was genuine, and their appearance in uniform could only aggravate it:

> As the war drags on the favour with which women once regarded the *poilus'* poverty of clothing seems to have diminished sadly. After the 'labyrinth' [the defensive system built by the Germans near Arras, taken by the French in May–June 1915 during the battle of Artois], a woman threw herself at a hairy and lice-ridden *poilu*, calling him 'my hero'; after the Argonne, she received him kindly, pitying him with all her heart; now, the gentleman who arrives in his trench outfit hears only 'Whew! How dirty they are!' (*L'Argonnaute*, June 1917)

The men complained occasionally that the women effectively preferred the more sophisticated turn-out of the non-combatant troops:

> Our elegant Parisiennes admire the muddy rags of real soldiers more especially in literature – in real life they find the silky gaberdine of their

2. Jean-Jacques Becker, *Les Français dans la Grande Guerre*; Pierre Barral, 'La Paysannerie française à l'arrière' in Becker and Audoin-Rouzeau, *Les Sociétés européennes et la guerre de 1914-1918*, pp.237-43.

chosen warriors rather more pleasing . . . and how!!! (*Notre rire*, March 1918)

It would be wrong to underestimate the import of such arguments. They reveal the deep distress of the fighting men and their jealousy of less exposed men who are more fortunate at rest or on leave. As for the virulence with which their bitterness is expressed, it only confirms the importance of women in their thinking and their fear of being less appreciated by them than they feel they deserve. For this reason the articles fall easily into moralising:

Women have committed certain faults of frivolity, of carelessness, [and] the skirts of 1916 look a little too much as though they have no cares in the world. Women have not always raised their souls as far as an understanding of heroism, and I have met some on leave who, with an angelic and dismissive smile, remarked with reference to night attacks: 'That must be fun!' Others could not bear the word *poilu*, and went into raptures at the stiff upper lips of the English. All this was upsetting for the soldiers, who developed a certain scornful pity for the women. *There were many exceptions*, I hasten to add; but they only served to prove the rule. (*La Marmite*, March 1916)

Such harsh treatment was highly unusual, however, for the image of femininity most often meant that of the wife in the family household which gravitated round her. Once again the topic was approached with great delicacy, so great was the soldiers' anguish at the thought of their families:

Although in order not to exacerbate the distress affecting our families we write that they should not feel too sorry for us, they should not deduce that we are living 'the high life', and that the trenches were a garden of Eden. We can put up with having our feet in the water, one can slide over the mud, one learns better every day how to avoid the Boche 'iron-mongery' but . . . you cannot understand how much one can suffer from being far from our loved ones when at any instant one may be lost to them for ever. (*Le Ver luisant*, January 1916)

The same painful nostalgia colours this text of 1918 on the landscapes that the soldiers like to see as they go down the lines to rest:

The countryside made him feel sick. He preferred to see human dwellings . . . in the form of little towns or villages. The regularity of their setting round the church, the tidiness of their red tiles and white walls, the windows discreetly ajar on family happenings, the smoke rising slowly over the rooftops, the peaceful activity of domestic tasks, everything, in the ordinariness of such humble matters, spoke to his wandering weariness of what he had left behind, of what he yearned impatiently to return to: a quiet and stable existence, well-being and the warm feelings of his home. (*Le Bulletin désarmé*, 1 April 1918)

For married soldiers with family ties, their home was a permanent preoccupation. Many of the trench newspapers are illustrated with naïve drawings of families grouped round the hearth, parents holding children in their arms. Not all had children; but their significance for their fathers can be seen in this account of a squad's few days of rest when a young child shared the soldiers' life:

Joseph! A little scrap of a plump and dimpled boy . . . This little chap was a whole chapter of delight and idleness for us, eight days of home life in three years of wandering. And his name, to which such happy memories are attached, recalls a series of red-letter days in our quiet lives. Joseph? . . . It means rest, well-being, a table and a bed; and when we have forgotten all this . . . Joseph will slip back into our minds to remind us that we did have a few hours of peace in our life at war! (*L'Echo du boqueteau*, 11 May 1917)

It is interesting to note the close similarity between the image of the child and that of the wife. Like her, the child is a symbol of life and peace.

The strength of the family's attraction for the soldier is clearly visible, as well as the fact that it also blurred his perception of the rear in general. Seen individually and isolated from the society in which they were living, the non-combatants were the object of a genuine fascination. Women, children, parents, friends, all those whom one held dear, were classed separately and seen differently from the rest of the population. The dichotomy was complete between 'people' – civilians in general – and 'one's own people' in particular. All the ambiguity of the image of the rear is here: from a wholly despised population the fighting men exempted those who 'belonged' to them, to whom they addressed all their thoughts and who alone were important to them. This paradox was rarely noticed by the men themselves, but it certainly helped to avoid a complete break between the rear and the front. Through those close to their hearts the men remained linked – and in all their being – to a world which they claimed to scorn, without managing to take their eyes off it.

Bridges between the Front and the Home Front

This link was sustained ever more strongly by the continual communication and interchange between the men at the front and their families. In effect these permanent or occasional bridges – the letters, packages and leave – materially and emotionally linked the front with the rest of the country.

Because these letters and parcels were not sent regularly from the rear until after the war of movement, and because home leave was not introduced until July 1915, these links were formed only gradually in the soldiers' world; it was not until after the middle of 1915 that the topic became a substantial element in trench newspapers. On the other hand, as the end of the war approached and with it the moment of return to civilian life, these many threads woven between the rear and the front were to lose part of their power of seduction.

Before that, however, leave was a source of the deepest delight:

> The six days, how profoundly we blessed those who first had the happy notion of this reward! and who could dare to claim that it would tend to sap the courage of the *poilus* on their return here? Leave was something sacred. Six days of paradise after long months of hell. (*Le Ver luisant*, February 1916)

Some tried to go further, to define more precisely the importance and meaning of these brief intervals:

> *Leave!* you dream of it while you are on guard duty, or during the rest periods whose relative pleasures can never entirely satisfy the *poilu*. You think about it when the sector is calm, because you are bored; and when the sector is in turmoil, because suddenly the past becomes more precious and life more desirable . . . Leave: the *poilu*'s war aim . . . I don't

want to dwell on a discussion of whether the war could have been continued without these occasional periods of relaxation. I dare not state that the thought of such periods alone brought about a light-hearted acceptance of all wretchedness and all sufferings. Nor do I know if they are the corner-stone of this edifice which has come to be known as 'troop morale'. Going into the trenches, you leave everything behind . . . A single challenge remains: Death . . . This, very simply, is why we think so much about our leave. It is a tie between the past and the future . . . A pink dot on the *i* in the verb 'to die'. (*Le Périscope*, August–September 1917)

A glimmer of hope in a universe of death, leave became a definite fixture in soldiers' lives as the war dragged on. This indeed was the only means of the vital reunion with families left at home:

Your children cried out, 'Here's papa', from the depths of her heart your wife called you by your first name, your father and your aged mother embraced you with their simple and heartfelt 'Well, here you are', followed by a long look – when all this has happened, remember that you have had the best of your leave. (*Sans tabac*, June 1918)

The best way to benefit from this reunion with domestic life was to make it as calm and ordinary as possible:

Six days! Six whole days to spend at home! Time to pick up old habits; coffee drunk in the morning from a cup and not an old mug. Meals taken in comfort, slippers, bed . . . He feels that this should all last for ever, and ignores his inescapable impending departure, back 'up there'. (*Le Canard du boyau*, August–September 1916)

In the soldiers' eyes there was nothing boring about this protected and well-regulated life – quite the contrary: after the servitude of trench life it represented freedom. Leaving such warmth again was extremely difficult, and men on leave were filled with genuine despair when the time came to go back up the line:

Now it's the sad evening of departure! His head hangs as he walks up the to the station. He would really like to cut short this terrible moment. He would have preferred her not to accompany him to the train . . . A few hours later, in the forward post to which he has been sent, the man back from leave will recall during his night's watch a little house and a table where sad and silent people eat with their gaze fixed on an empty place. (*Le Canard du boyau*, September–October 1916)

This wrenching departure was such an ordeal that sometimes it would spoil the few days of freedom and relaxation in advance:

Three times a year we go home for a week's leave. Even during these days, the happiest of our soldiering lives, we cannot fully appreciate such hard-won happiness! You cannot know the despair of leaving, the agony of saying goodbye, the painful sadness of a kiss which may be the last. (*Le Filon*, June 1917)

Both the joy and the heartbreak of leave clearly lay in returning to one's family and then leaving them again. Occasionally such feelings might extend beyond the purely domestic setting and encompass the whole civilian population:

The only memory we all retain of our first leave is of marvellous happiness. It was so unexpected, a trip back home! It was a foretaste of what the real final return would be . . . a sort of dress rehearsal, but more intimate . . . Truly the only memory we all retain is of dazzling joy. We had just escaped from great danger, we arrived clothed in glory. Everyone looked after us. The little boys touched the mud on our capes like a relic, the women turned to look at us, men stopped us in the street to hear our descriptions of the war. (*Le Pépère*, 15 June 1916)

And it was not only their own loved ones that these soldiers were sad to leave at the end of their leave:

We felt that we were leaving the civilised world behind, the world of happiness and hope, the world of civilians. (*Sans tabac*, February 1918)

Once again we should emphasise the ambivalence of the soldiers' attitude towards the rear. It was after all an unadulterated delight to return to this scorned and disparaged set of people, and leaving them again was truly heart-rending. The isolation of life at the front led to an accumulation of resentment: on contact with ordinary civilians, it faded away.

As he returned to the rear, the soldier stepped across the barrier separating him from the rest of the nation and whose two sides now seemed to him less sharply divided than he had thought. Ties between the two communities could be recreated when they came together, proof that the soldiers' resentment was, if not superficial, at least only temporary. The breach was more apparent than real, the cohesion genuine.

Leave was however too infrequent to play more than an occasional role. The value of *rapprochements* created by letter, sometimes daily, was of a different order of importance. Letters were not, moreover, the only factor, for newspapers from home were some-times also awaited with keen impatience:

> The arrival of the national daily papers was another of the day's import-ant moments. Each squad had a set of papers from the liaison officer . . . The men were quick to go through a paper and spot everything in it, so that any news of interest was known at once. (*L'Echo des marmites*, 20 November 1915)

Impatience at this early stage in the war, before the full weari-some effect of 'eye-wash' was felt? Appreciably later, however, other soldiers confessed to this taste for the Paris papers among the combatants, despite their very marked scepticism:

> [The arrival of the newspapers is greeted] with sighs of satisfaction, by 'Ah! Here are the papers!' . . . The *poilus* stretch out on their limp beds made of scanty chopped straw, perhaps an inch thick, and read slowly. There is not a single news item between the first word of the first article and the last word of the last advertisement that is not read attentively and commented on by them. It is in this light that one should imagine the astonishment of these unsophisticated men . . . when they realise from the column dedicated to 'military affairs' that some stay-at-home back at the rear digs trenches, sets up entanglements, launches battles and achieves victories, pierces the German front and through a skilful wheel-ing movement is on his way to set his tricolour flag beyond the Rhine! And all this in a single day! (*Le Camouflet*, 15 March 1917)

The soldiers' view of the press is an intricate blend of contempt and attraction, and this ambiguity is underlined by *Le Crapouillot* with its usual lucidity:

Men almost come to blows to get hold of the newspapers – and I have seen men attack them physically, so stupid does their 'eye-wash' appear to those in the know . . . There is laughter. Are the readers mentally retarded new-born babes, or senile old men? 'Situation stabilised'. Boche attacks which 'fail miserably' . . . The men complain about the papers but read them avidly. Well, well! At the front we are keen to know the line that is being fed to folks back home . . . And we read them because when you are overcome with reality it is a blessing to acquire two *sous*' worth of dreams. (*Le Crapouillot*, April 1918)

The explanation for this paradoxical behaviour lies in the fascination exercised by the civilian world and the combatants' need for escape. It may be that when this article was written the thirst for news was probably intensified by the developing German offensive. Other front-line newspapers noted similar drawing-power during less dramatic periods:

The soldier buys a paper. At the first page he says, 'There's nothing!' At the second page he exclaims, 'Ah! They're telling stories!' At the third he asserts, 'This is disgusting!' And swears never to buy a paper ever again. But there he is next day, waiting for the cyclist to bring them. (*Le Pépère*, 15 November 1916)

Even where the press is concerned, therefore, the gap between the rear and the front does not appear insuperable. The newspapers are hated but at the same time many of the soldiers cannot imagine giving up reading them – which explains why the papers were read in the trenches despite their mediocrity. However exasperating their contents, they formed a link between the national community and the soldiers, and this was sufficient to make them indispensable.

Deliveries of parcels, though infrequent, contributed equally to strengthening bonds between the front and the rear. Getting a parcel in the trench was a pleasure of the greatest intensity:

Parcels are awaited with no less impatience than letters: for they contain precious provisions, and they have been assembled with love by those who sent them. Opening them brings the same joy as that of children opening their Christmas presents. (*L'Echo des marmites*, 20 November 1915)

Parcels represented much more than simply material support, however. The food they contained was also a breath of pre-war life, a taste or scent from home, a morsel of family life left behind. And their contents placed them at the centre of a whole military sociability with a value of its own:

> The arrival of a parcel never goes unnoticed. It is a happy event and more than any other, it sets off public rumour. Everyone knew very quickly that Sergeant Sullerot was getting a parcel . . . Everyone was curious, they wanted to see it . . . His closest friends were already counting on tasty sampling sessions. (*Le 120 court*, February 1918)

But naturally it was the far more regular arrival of letters that created the permanent and vital bond between the rear and the front; hence the extreme significance of the moment of their distribution:

> The distribution [of the letters] is accompanied by shouts and childish jokes. It is the best moment of the day. (*La Saucisse*, April 1916)

> Above all, at around 4 o'clock, as if to break into the oppressive hour of the sleepy afternoon, there was the emotional moment of distributing letters. How intently they were gazed at, with envious and covetous eyes, as they dropped like treasure into the tail-end of our day. (*L'Echo du boyau*, 1 August 1916)

Letters were so important that the slightest delay in their arrival brought immediate complaints, the soldiers feeling suddenly plunged into total isolation:

> To the gentlemen of the censorship: letters take two days or two weeks to reach their destination . . . when they arrive . . . Just consider a little, gentlemen, that these are the only arrivals that give us pleasure. (*Le Vide-boche*, 1 June 1918)

Letters were more than an essential and almost daily link between the rear and the front. They also reunited soldiers with their former lives, restoring to them day after day the pattern of their existence before the trenches:

The post orderly was our link between our current existence and our previous life, our good old way of life as civilians who could never have dreamed of making war for four years! (*L'Echo du boqueteau*, 3 September 1918)

Unaided, letters created both this continual interchange with civilian life and an existence separate from reality. Reading or writing them made it possible to escape briefly from the miseries of the front line:

Your delivery obliterates the misery of the trenches, the unending deprivation, the muddy hell and the stinking charnel-houses. (*Le Filon*, 1918)

Letters were unquestionably semi-magical objects. Navigating intruments for a voyage through time and space, they succeeded in effacing the very consciousness of the present.

Life carried on by correspondence is a separate life, distinct from everything one does or says or thinks with one's friends. It is a way of life that is complete, which has no need of the sustenance of events. *You write*, you isolate yourself, you no longer hear the noise all round you, the guns recede and the teasing of your friends no longer gets through to you. *You write*, and you become what you once were, you forget something of what you have become, you no longer talk about the war . . . *You write*, you reply to the most recent letter, you answer what was in it, you remember, you hope, you create dreams that will be shared. *You write*, you are jealous, yes, for you can be jealous at a distance. A single word is enough to make the *poilu* tremble . . . one little word can mean as much as twelve pages in response . . . And after a clumsy phrase there are scenes: tears at home, *le cafard* in the trenches . . . One cannot know the intensity of a feeling that is born and sustained by correspondence. How many women will have been loved at a distance during this war, more than they will ever be loved . . . close to! . . . The *poilus* already make me welcome, knowing that the post orderly is a god, that letters are a gift of Providence and that the 'war godmothers' are a blessing. (*Bellica*, May–June 1916)

This magic of letters resulted in letters written in the worst of material conditions:

I guarantee that if those to whom we write could see the conditions in which men often settle down to write to them, it would bring tears to their eyes. I have seen men writing home in the most tragic circumstances, and often in settings totally devoid of any comfort. Tables are rare on campaign and in the front lines the writing-desk is often the fire-step or the haversack. Many are even brave enough to scribble a postcard in a shell-hole where the smallest burst may be fatal, or in a damp and poorly lit sap where the water oozes through and drips steadily on to the paper. In a billet near Verdun where the troops were crowded on top of each other the cemetery became a writing-room, and it was an emotional sight to see men scarcely out of the harsh days of Verdun writing to the living from the grave-stones. (*L'Echo des marmites*, 20 November 1915)

Letter-writing tended to be limited in exposed front line sectors where the soldiers were in constant danger, though it never ceased entirely. To make up for this, letter-writing was resumed after leaving the line of fire with the frenzy of putting pen to paper that this text suggests.

The importance of letters, parcels, newspapers and leave is proof of the regularity, the value and the strength of ties between the rear and the front after the first few months of the war. All these bridges built between civilians and soldiers, between life and death – between the past, the present and the future – succeeded from time to time in breaking the pattern of everyday hardship. The significance attached to such bridges by the soldiers proves that the civilian world on which they sometimes sought revenge was ultimately what they valued most highly. Through those whom they loved they remained linked with the universe of the home front, its attractions counterbalancing resentment accumulated against the population as a whole. If the resentment was undeniable, it never completely and irretrievably dispelled the fascination:

We are bound to take up our pre-war lives again. In fact the front has never completely broken all ties with the rear. There is leave . . . We try hard, by every possible means, to keep in touch with civilised life . . . [Letters are] a manifestation of this individual effort to revive our former turn of mind, which we inevitably miss. (*Tacatacteufteuf*, 1 June 1917)

With somewhat unusual lucidity this text challenges the image of the fighting men's insularity. Ultimately the front was more of a peninsula than an island, its defenders were literally still *part* of French society as a whole. These defenders felt wholly cut off from the rear, but at no moment were they every truly cut off (the only exception, at a strictly material level, being the first months of the war and periods of major offensives which interrupted the delivery of letters and the leave system). The fighting men were thus never totally banished, and whatever they may have said, they were not excluded from the nation as a whole. France's capacity to hold on for more than four years despite her clear military inferiority until the summer of 1918 was partly influenced by this underlying cohesion.

Desire for Recognition

The combatants' feeling of being distanced no doubt concealed primarily a profound desire for recognition from those they had left behind and whom they hoped to see again one day. This need for recognition sprang from the fighting man's feeling of superiority, their pride in themselves strengthened by evidence of civilian inferiority. In fact, a feeling of aristocratic preeminence:

> You rage at feeling so lonely, so overwhelmed, so ill-defined in the distorted imagination of people back there. But, conscious of your superiority in terms of fatigue, pain, misery, you derive a clear-sighted pride from it. True, you stand alone in your experience of the worst and least-known aspects of war ... You are engaged in the real war, the awful war, in your hunger, your vermin and your night-watches. The war in which you are engaged is not the war seen on book jackets and cinema posters. It is a sad and dreary war, full of weariness and unnoticed labour. For you it is a trade, with no more prestige or panache than any other. After your short periods of so-called rest spent in muddy valleys, if the odd grenade or shell bursts at the bend in the trench as you go back up to the trenches, you march faster and someone removes the wounded man or the body. That's all: an industrial accident. As an infantryman who consents to live such a life, you are a very great man; people should take their hats off when they talk to you. (*Sans tabac*, January 1917)

The final lines of this text are revealing: they express the conviction that the war has transformed the combatants into human beings of a different kind. Two characteristic words, 'pride' and 'grandeur', keep reappearing. They sum up perfectly the soldiers' image of themselves.

> Here in the silence of the night, a man like you is frozen to the marrow and shivering. His feet, stuck in the ground, are freezing too. These unseen men are greater than you. (*Le Filon*, 1918)

> In a word, 'shirkers', all those who for one reason or another will never reach the lines, will never know the dangers to be met with there ... There are bound to be some, he tells himself, but then his pride grows, for when he gets home and he hears them talking about the events of the war, he will have a crushing superiority over them: he will know what it means, he will have seen it close at hand, what he says will not simply be hearsay, and his prestige will be the greater. (*Face aux boches*, February 1916)

The same words, the same certainties. The inferiority of the rear is such that the entire glory of this great ordeal must belong exclusively to the combatants alone. The others,

> it is they of whom it will be said later that they were not at the Marne, nor at the Yser, that they were not in Champagne or at Verdun nor on the Somme. (*Le Crocodile*, December 1916)

Sometimes this conviction of crushing superiority over the rear encouraged a certain nostalgia for the 'purity' of life at the front and the relationships formed there between the men:

> You breathe more easily there ... And I recalled a long underground corridor, full of smoke from pipes and cigarettes. There were men pressed up against each other on narrow benches. And well-intentioned songsters sang I don't really know what, but almost in a whisper and without choruses for everyone to join in, because the Boches were not far away. (*Le Filon*, August 1917)

This feeling of belonging to a sort of elite of courage and the wish to be distinguished from the mass explains the psychological importance of decorations:

> The ease with which the *Croix de Guerre* was handed out in certain rear

formations took away all the original intended symbolic value which it
should have retained . . . The easiest solution: to ordain that every *Croix
de Guerre* won under fire – *and no others* – should carry a bar with the
word 'combat'. In this way the combatant's cross would be truly a 'cross
of war'. It would be distinct from all the others! This would be the first
step towards a privileged status for the combatant, something which
must certainly be established one day. (*On les aura*, 31 March 1918)

To men so thoroughly convinced of their moral superiority acquired through trial, there is something intolerable in the feeling of
being unrecognised, ignored, or misunderstood:

People do not know us properly. Dammitall, there is no pleasure in living
among us, and it is only there that you could learn to know us. People
prefer to describe us as they would like us to be. That is easier, and it
spares the ordinary ego from thinking about the miseries of our life . . .
Basically, we are furious at being so little understood. (*L'Argonnaute*,
August 1917)

Further, the soldiers were convinced that this lack of recognition
often turned to unadulterated scorn:

The shirkers are all alike in their scorn for the poor *poilu* on leave.
(*L'Echo des bleuets*, February 1917)

The reason for their distress at the looks which they thought they
discerned at the rear, was that the desire for recognition is one of the
keys to their vision of others and of themselves. In exchange for their
daily sacrifice the fighting men expected respect and gratitude from
those whom they were defending, and what exasperated them was not
to find it, or to find it too infrequently. To be noticed, thanked,
respected – such aspirations were expressed by all the front-line newspapers:

The man who has risked his life a thousand times to defend the family
well-being should meet with recognition and respect from his contem-
poraries whose rights and freedom he will, in the great majority of cases,
have protected and preserved. (*Le Bulletin désarmé*, 15 July 1918)

This right to be respected was claimed many times over:

> It is accepted that nothing of what we did was in order for people to be grateful to us and thank us. But we do have a right not to be pushed about. I assure you that we are both very proud and very humble – and the two do not cancel each other out. We do not want people to fall down and kiss our feet. But we would be happy, when we return for a few days' contact with civilian life, to meet with civility. (*Le Filon*, August 1917)

Disdaining such modesty mixed with pride, other soldiers did not shrink from greater claims:

> No man on leave wants to see France weeping. But the nation should be serious, the French people must remember, must always remember, that about 100 kilometres away there is suffering and death. The civilians should read communiqués as they would read a report on the health of someone very dear to them, like a report on the health of France. As soon as he is away from the front the man on leave should feel truly *loved*. Railway employees should not treat him like a parcel which makes a noise and which is pushed down to the end of the platform. The young man in his field-service tunic who is in charge of the station rubber stamp should be alert, extremely polite, friendly. The cab-driver or the café waiter should refuse the tip he offers; women should look lovingly at him. (*Le Pépère*, 15 June 1916)

Now it is no longer a matter of recognition but of love, the writer not hesitating to emphasise the word. But such expectations were inevitably disappointed, because none of the ordeals endured by these men had been witnessed by anyone except themselves:

> The remains of the battalion have returned. They are getting their breath back . . . Civilians, you men of the towns and the countryside . . . who have been saved by him, who have never seen him fighting, sacrificing himself, active in the fires of hell . . . you have seen nothing! . . . You have not seen the death of those who die so that you may live, and that you may live in your own homes! And if one day you meet survivors in the street . . . you will go on your way without noticing them! You have seen nothing! What you should do, to make certain, you see, would be to go out always with your head bowed. (*Les Poilus de la 9e*, 25 April 1918)

Such emphases and lyricism are linked to the tragic circumstances in which the battalion was decimated during the previous month. Affected by this traumatic episode, the writer of the article expresses perfectly the pride of the survivors, simultaneously anxious to see their sacrifices acknowledged and convinced at heart that such recognition is impossible. Not even after the armistice:

> There is a total – or very nearly total – absence of recognition for these *poilus* . . . We claim, if not respect, then at least a modicum of confidence on the part of those among whom we are required to live, and we know that we deserve it, in large measure. (*La Gazette du créneau* 15 April 1919)

The fighting men were thus repeatedly wounded in their self-esteem and their pride. This deep dissatisfaction explains why they frequently colluded in a travesty of truth when they came to describe their lives to civilians. Faced with indifference and ignorance everywhere, was it not tempting to distort facts to obtain a little admiration?

> Fearing to appear cowardly before such judges, many comrades invent all kinds of amazing anecdotes and prodigious feats of arms, they give currency to an inaccurate version better suited to satisfy the demands of non-combatant imaginations misled by a certain school of literature. (*Le Rire aux éclats*, February–March 1917)

The combatants' scorned pride and unassuaged desire for recognition contributed to their image of the rear. Their resentment is disappointed love. One cannot interpret in any other way the somewhat childish satisfaction of so many editors of trench newspapers when they received a word of encouragement from a well-known personality or when a major Paris paper acknowledged the existence of their efforts and published a few extracts:

> We address our warmest thanks to our larger sister publications: *Journal des débats, Le Figaro, L'Echo de Paris, L'Excelsior, Le Cri de Paris, L'Intransigeant, La Presse, La Patrie*, who have acclaimed the birth of our modest broadsheet with such kind praise, and have published extracts from it. (*L'Echo des marmites*, 1 January 1915)

Our thanks to our friendly colleagues of the national press who have kindly quoted *Le Bochofage* in recent weeks: *Excelsior*, *L'Intransigeant*, *La France illustrée*, *Le Journal de Berck*, *Le Courrier de l'armée belge*, *La Presse*, etc., not forgetting *Le Canard enchaîné*. (*Le Bochofage*, 26 March 1917)

This taste for respectability only confirms their concern for the soldiers' proper dignity. Those who cannot find words hard enough for the national press are suddenly disarmed when a journalist appears to treat them with respect and recognise their hardships. This is why an article in a Toulouse daily paper had the honour of being quoted in full in a front-line newspaper:

The infantry is disinherited. And these poor bloody foot-sloggers laugh and make jokes. They offer witticisms as if in a salon. They are patient, charming. The bread brought to them may be covered in mud. No matter. The coffee is cold and has more earth in it than sugar: it has come through the trenches. Bah! We have to take the rough with the smooth! They are truly brave fellows. When I saw a regiment of these mud-stained heroes come out of the trenches I would have knelt down before them, had I dared. How could one fail to be moved by these soldiers whose lives are worse than those of convicted criminals, laughing and joking . . . Despite their uniforms each one has his own individuality, his own rhythm. One is draped in oil-cloth, another has a sheepskin, there's someone hidden in a Balaclava helmet, there's a cape, someone else in clogs, they are dog-tired and glowing with strength, grumbling and disciplined, magnificent. They are not a herd. They do not march in a rabble. They are good workmen, and we can never offer them adequate admiration. The infantry deserve the salutes of all other army corps. When they return to the trenches, laden like mules, they say nothing. They remember the brief moments of joy that they have just snatched. They think of what is to come, of the days of anguish and pain that they will live through. (*Le Périscope*, February 1916)

The satisfaction revealed by *Le Périscope* is the more surprising in that the content of this article is highly insidious. The accent on the cheerfulness and determination of the men of this regiment show it to be a perfect example of 'eye-wash'. Certain expressions are a sure indication: 'These poor bloody foot-sloggers laugh and make jokes.' 'They are patient, charming.' 'They are truly brave fellows.' 'They offer witticisms as if in a salon.' 'They say nothing.' 'They are dog-tired and glowing with strength, grumbling and disciplined, magnificent', etc. If such ineptitudes do not arouse the usual indignation, it is because the writer praises beyond everything the dignity of the soldiers, to the point that he asserts he thought of kneeling as they passed by. Little was needed, in effect, for certain misunderstandings between civilians and soldiers to be blurred over, as seen in this anecdote:

Quick! Just time to jump into the metro! Luckily the lady whose job it is to punch the tickets had guessed from my outfit that I was on my way back to the front. She was quick to share my haste and then, handing back my punched ticket: 'Off you go, my friend!' That was a year ago. The simple tenderness of her voice still moves me. (*L'Horizon*, April 1918)

There was civilian compassion, at least occasionally. Similarly, behind the front lines or at rest camps, soldiers were sometimes taken aback by the welcome they received:

The friendliness of the inhabitants, their warm welcome, are ample compensation for the weariness of bad roads; we will all remember the buttered bread, the jugs of beer, the little glasses of gin so generously handed out by the people. The first platoon settled into a guard billet in the girls' school; the thoughtful teachers had lit the fire and prepared hot coffee. (*L'Echo du groupe cycliste*, 20 May 1917)

The men were particularly receptive to these simple gestures because such attentions were evidently all too rare; the fact that they were mentioned in such heartfelt tones indicates this rarity. It seemed to the soldiers that they met with such solicitude only when the civilian population had felt itself genuinely threatened:

The *poilu* who has no particular liking for bombardments has none the less a marked predilection for billets that are shelled from time to time. This is not only because inspection drill is more difficult there – and consequently less frequent – and the police more conciliatory. It is also because the civilians in such places are 'nicer' to the *poilu*. Shells have a curious effect on civilian psychology. (*L'Echo des marmites*, 1 January 1917)

A certain promiscuity, shared distress, a strongly felt need for protection against an enemy near at hand, these sometimes brought non-combatants close to their protectors. Such anecdotes, however, are no proof that fraternity between those at the rear and those from the front was the general rule – far from it. They merely underline the ease with which certain rapprochements could develop when circumstances allowed. This account of a regiment crossing Paris on its way back to Artois illustrated these occasions of extraordinary communion between rear and front:

We were hailed from the windows of the houses, from café doorways, from pavements, from trams going down the avenues, we were acclaimed and cheered. The *poilus*, much moved, forgot the tedium of their labour, the terrors of yesterday and the anxietes of tomorrow and the dragging length of the terrible ordeal, and enjoyed this precious reward with wholehearted delight: the cheers of a nation which is under an obligation to us. A strange pride swells our chest⁓ as we think that it is thanks to our efforts and our long Calvary that these women, these children, these old people, can stroll about in complete tranquillity on Sundays in the sunlit streets. The thrill at being admired, of having a 'public', dispelled a certain bitterness and distaste from our hearts, together with the scorn of the fighting man for those who remain outside the conflict. Yesterday, in the mud and under mortar fire, the *poilus* sneered bitterly at the easy optimism of people at the rear who would never understand the hardships at the front – today these same men, disarmed by the plaudits, denied their revolt, they were keen to display themselves to the spectators in legendary style, as light-hearted and cheerfully heroic *poilus*! Suddenly, as a train glides slowly into a station packed with travellers, without a command, singing burst out from one end of the procession to another and rose to the skies: 'The Republic calls us! We must conquer or we must die!' With tears in our eyes, overwhelmed, we sing at the tops of our voices, drunk with the applause, proud of our muddy capes, insanely proud of a glory so painfully won and sincerely prepared for any sacrifice . . . We feel that it is Paris that we are setting out to defend out there, under the grey skies of Artois. (*Le Crapouillot*, January 1917)

These men's ability to forget is immediately striking: forgetful of their *cafard*, their weariness, their bitterness, even forgetful of the war. All this is possible only because the miracle of recognition is operating. The rear is showing its obligation to the troops. In those cheers it submits, it makes an act of allegiance, it surrenders and gives in. This homage is so overwhelming that it operates almost instantaneously on the men, who respond with total communion with the nation: civilians and fighting men, all are on a level footing in an atmosphere of patriotic fervour as extraordinary as it is unexpected.

There are other such accounts; a procession was described in similar terms the previous year:

> It seemed to me that in those moments I could genuinely feel the heart of the crowd beating with my own heart . . . I admit it, every soldier felt that this welcome from the nation rewarded him generously for his pains, both past and future. It is good, surely, to be honoured thus after the tragic days of Verdun and the Somme? I have been thinking . . . of the miserable processions that left the trenches in Belgium nearly two years ago, those slow, muddy, dreary processions with no witnesses but the mutilated trees beside a main road distorted by the rain, and I was happy and proud to see that we were cheered because we had known how to suffer. (*Le Poilu du 6–9*, 1 October 1916)

This too was the mechanism of mass exaltation, a phenomenon of crowd mentality. In contrast, in the zone recovered after the German retreat in February 1917, it was one old woman on her own who provoked a similar reaction among the men of the 25th infantry Regiment as they marched past:

> A little old woman sitting in a corner watched them pass and, very quietly, murmured: '*Vive la France! Vive la France!*' That was all she could give us, but we felt she was giving us kisses or roses. (*L'Argonaute*, March 1917)

The breach between the rear and the front line was thus far from total: and its nature and meaning have frequently been misinterpreted. If so little was needed for a resurgence of feelings of solidarity between civilians and soldiers, it was because the misunderstanding separating them was nourished by disappointed expectations more than by genuine hostility. True, the combatants were convinced that the ties binding them to the rest of the nation had almost completely disappeared; but apart from the physical separation between the front and the rear, the profound cohesion within French society as a whole cannot be challenged. Whatever the men in the trenches said or thought, they never genuinely formed a separate class, for the bonds between them and the society from which they sprang did

L'ECHO des GOURBIS

JOURNAL ANTI PÉRIODIQUE

CAMPAGNE 1914-1915

DES TRANCHÉES ET BOYAUX / ORGANE DES TROGLODYTES DU FRONT

ABONNEMENTS :

France, un an.... 5 fr.
Étranger un an... 10 fr.

S'adresser à l'*Écho des Gourbis*
131e Territorial de Campagne
SECTEUR POSTAL 38

N° 4 ❖ JUIN 1915

Le Numéro 5 c.

Directeur Général : PIERRE CALEL | Directeur Artistique : FRANC MALZAC | Directeur Administratif : JEAN CAZES

UNE CARTE DU PRÉSIDENT DE LA RÉPUBLIQUE
UNE LETTRE DE MADAME POINCARÉ
aux Soldats, à leurs Familles, à l'Écho des Gourbis

CARTE

du

PRÉSIDENT DE LA RÉPUBLIQUE

Président de la République

à Rédacteur de l'Écho des Gourbis :

« Mes remerciements à l'Écho des Gourbis

et mes meilleurs vœux au 131e territorial. »

RAYMOND POINCARÉ

Président de la République

LETTRE
de
MADAME POINCARÉ

PALAIS DE L'ÉLYSÉE

Messieurs,

Je vous remercie de votre lettre. Elle évoque en moi des heures inoubliables.

Vous voulez bien me rappeler que j'ai parcouru, il y a tantôt deux ans, la belle province du Quercy où se recrute le 131e Territorial.

Soyez convaincus que je me souviendrai toujours du magnifique accueil que, dans vos communes en fête, vous, vos femmes et vos enfants, vous avez fait au Président de la République.

Aujourd'hui bien des deuils sont venus attrister vos foyers, alors si joyeux. Mais rien n'ébranle votre courage ni celui des vôtres.

Tandis que vous, sur le front, vous combattez bravement, vos femmes, comme toutes les Françaises, donnent l'exemple d'une sainte résignation. Elles sont vaillantes, parce qu'elles veulent être dignes de vous. Elles

assurent les travaux des champs, elles tricotent pour les soldats, elles soignent les blessés, elles vous suivent constamment du cœur et de la pensée, elles parlent à vos enfants du père absent et appellent avec eux la victoire de tous leurs vœux.

La France entière vit ainsi dans une même espérance.

Vous pouvez être fiers de défendre un aussi noble pays ; nous autres femmes, nous sommes fières de ceux qui la défendent.

Recevez, je vous prie, avec mes remerciements pour votre aimable souvenir, mes souhaits les plus émus, auxquels le Président me charge de joindre tous les siens.

HENRIETTE POINCARÉ.

Nous remercions Monsieur le Président de la République et Madame Poincaré qui ont bien voulu, au moment où va se décider le sort du Monde, dire aux soldats, à leurs familles et au petit journal du front les mots émouvants que l'on vient de lire. Ces mots rendront plus facile la grande victoire française prochaine. Ils touchent, font, nous en sommes sûrs, tous les cœurs français comme ils ont touché le cœur des soldats du front qui ont reconnu en eux la voix immortelle, noble et affectueuse, de la France elle-même, toujours plus digne d'être aimée.

4 *L'Echo des gourbis*

Madame Poincaré's homage to the men of the 131st reservist regiment was greeted with emotion and pride by *L'Echo des gourbis*

not give way. That being so, why should the lack of confrontation after the armistice be surprising? The fighting men's fascination with the image of a peaceful family life scarcely predisposed them to adventure and action – quite the opposite. Their subsequent retreat into the simple joys of private life was already foreseeable in their attitude to life and its values when in the trenches. As for victory, despite the severe anxieties which it might inspire on the strictly material plane, it had the same effect on the army as a whole as that of the spectators quoted above, acclaiming a regiment passing through Paris a few years earlier. Victory was in effect a redemption, it forced resentment into oblivion. And all this simply because it was an all-pervading delight, both physical and moral:

> To the almost animal joy of the man who celebrates openly having 'come back in one piece' was added the moral satisfaction of total victory. (*Le Crapouillot*, November 1918)

This certainty that one could now carry on living was surely likely to efface everything else.

> The armistice was signed on 11 November 1918, and after eleven o'clock on that day there was no more fighting. What is the point of remarking on this tremendous piece of news, proclaimed everywhere by bugles and bells? The war is over, the dreadful nightmare is fading, life opens out for us again . . . The future is available to those who remain. (*L'Argonnaute*, November 1918)

The armistice was an explosion of joy. One description among so many reads:

> The bells were ringing at full peal everywhere, tricolour flags were flying in the wind, the soldiers were overwhelmed with delirium, they laughed, sang, wept, organised torch parades, set off fireworks, sang *La Marseillaise*, and appeared to have gone mad. (*La Fourragère*, December 1918, January 1919)

Even before 11 November, just at the glimpse of approaching victory, a change of tone was already perceptible in the front-line newspapers, and particularly among those which had hitherto been the most critical and incisive:

> For the soldier who has experienced the monotonous and dreary trench life inside its horizon of barbed wire, interrupted from time to time by those terrible and deceptive offensives of which the modest results could

never efface the great sacrifices made, for all the good men who for four years tramped between double walls of earth, what satisfaction, finally, to advance! . . . Although this is victory there is still the mud and the blood, the wounded who suffer and die, and yet, in every heart, the war has changed its appearance. The war without end, without distraction and often without hope, has been succeeded by a war that is equally painful but full of the unexpected, of new landscapes and new sights: the *poilus* have the pleasure of seeing their superiority confirmed, for the enemy is retreating day by day. They make triumphal entries into reconquered cities, they are acclaimed by cheering crowds who never despaired of their courage. All feel that so much suffering and so many sacrifices will not have been in vain because they have served to seize peace from the enemy, just as they have seized victory from him. (*Le Crapouillot*, October 1918)

As if its *raison-d'être* had vanished, the mordant tone disappeared from the columns of *Le Crapouillot* after October 1918, giving way to an entirely new patriotic cheerfulness. In such an atmosphere, how could carrying out the promised settling of accounts retain any meaning? With the end of the war, and well before their demobilisation, the soldiers were once more mentally reintegrated with the nation as a whole. And then the difficulties inherent in their return to ordinary life were reduced because it was long-drawn-out, with the men trickling back into civilian society in driblets throughout the slow demobilisation of 1919. The attitudes of mind acquired in the isolation of the trenches could not survive the return of the individual soldier to the civilian life to which he had always felt attached, which he had never entirely abandoned, and which he had never despaired of rediscovering. From November 1918 the misunderstandings of the four preceding years inevitably began to fade away.

The gap which developed between the rear and the front during the war created a substantial split at the heart of the nation, but because of the fascination exercised by civilians over soldiers, and because of the bridges maintained between them, the breach was not irrevocable; more than denial, more than contempt, the resentment of the fighting men was a demand and a hope.

A complete break would have seriously damaged the determination of French society to continue the war. This did not happen: the ties between the front and the rest of the population were seriously strained, but never reached the breaking-point which would have put the unity of the nation at risk and jeopardised its capacity for endurance.

~6~

National Sentiment

Soldiers' Indifference

The question of national feeling is one of the key matters concerning France at war, involving the whole of the nation: the men in the ranks could not have endured successfully without the endurance of the civilians left at the rear. As far as the combatants are concerned, the explanation for their four years of tenacity should be sought in the neglected domain of their psychological world, in a military configuration unfavourable to their own nation until the final but late reversal of fortune in the last months of the war. The troops defended the national community without major lapses from 1914 until 1918: but no statement of this kind can do full justice to the nature, the strength and the development of what may be called, perhaps for want of a better expression, their national feeling.

This topic has already been partially explored. The moment of entering the war has now been definitively clarified by Jean-Jacques Becker; he reveals the lack of enthusiasm among civilians and soldiers – with a few exceptions – at the time of mobilisation, while stressing the patriotic determination, after 1 August, of a nation determined to defend its country under attack. The same author has also emphasised the strength of feeling among the civilian population throughout the whole of the war, even at its worst moments in 1917 and 1918.[1] True, the working classes expressed serious discontent, but except in some very minor cases their actions were never sufficiently grave to make the notion of a national defeat acceptable.

1. Jean-Jacques Becker, *1914: Comment les Français sont entrés dans la guerre*, Paris, Presses de la Fondation Nationale des Sciences Politiques, 1977; Jean-Jacques Becker, *Les Français dans la Grande Guerre*, Jean-Jacques Becker, *La France en guerre, 1914–1918. La Grande mutation*, Paris, Editions Complexe, 1988.

In the final analysis the non-combatants' will to endure was strengthened by this form of resistance.

But what about the soldiers? Antoine Prost has emphasised the pacifist nature of *veteran* combatants' patriotism;[2] but their state of mind during the conflict itself remains somewhat obscure. Propaganda has naturally offered its own version, putting forward the unfailing heroism of the soldiers, their impassioned patriotism and their visceral hatred of the enemy. This image, purveyed by *bourrage de crâne* in all its forms, was very swiftly discredited and in reaction the image of a totally passive herd semi-indifferent to the fate of the nation was often imposed in its place.

It is true that the soldiers' lack of interest in anything resembling war 'news' is very marked. Their newspapers disregarded both national and international news, the soldiers concerning themselves above all with individual and immediate problems. Their attention was seized first by anything affecting their daily life and their survival, and this became increasingly the case as the conflict wore on.

> The *poilu* is a man . . . A prolonged sojourn in water or in mud may leave him with rheumatism or frostbite; he may be prostrated with fatigue, and, since his sense of self-preservation has not been eliminated, he suffers from the weakness of wanting to save his own skin . . . He may curse himself, and even quarrel with his companions under arms, and everyone knows that the distribution of any extra wine in a squad is rarely a peaceable occasion. He eats his bully-beef with caution and mutters when there is a shortage of food. He does not sing as he goes into attack, preferring not to waste his breath. He suffers from *le cafard* when he thinks of his family and his life before the war . . . As for what is Right, for Civilisation and Humanity, the *poilu* does not think about them much. It would indeed be quite easy to count up the number of *poilus* who have a clear idea of such abstractions. The poilu thinks quite simply about his house, his bit of land, the retrospective delights of his pre-war life. (*Le Périscope*, 1916)

It would be hard to put forward a more effective challenge to the image of the soldier as spread by propaganda, nor to illustrate more effectively his indifference to all collective values, equalled only by his fascination with domestic life. Indeed it must be admitted that the soldiers took little interest in the general evolution of the war

2. Antoine Prost, *Les Anciens Combattants et la société française, 1914–1939*.

and events being played out on their own soil. A few items of news were occasionally mentioned briefly, but often much later, while most were simply ignored. At the very beginning of the war the earliest front-line newspapers tried to keep their readers informed of current operations, to make up for the lack of news from the rear. This wish to inform disappeared completely in 1915, however, although references to current affairs increased slightly at moments of great tension.

The only event to which the trench press made greater reference was the battle of Verdun. The response this time was relatively rapid, with some papers even reporting the beginning of the battle before the end of February (most only mentioned it during the subsequent two months, and some even later than that). Despite the fact that Verdun was the best and most rapidly 'covered' event of the trench newspapers, one searches their columns in vain for any precise detail. This paper restricts itself to vague allusions and an extremely summary analysis:

Even incomplete, even if it holds some painful surprises for us, the battle of Verdun now unfolding constitutes an enormous moral success for France. Alone, without the support of her Allies, France has checked the most powerful army in the world, has inflicted on the enemy army corps the most resounding losses, which nothing can restore. The Germans may announce victories: the slowness of their advance, the breaking off of assaults which appeared designed to carry all before them, have revealed all too clearly that they are far from being invincible, and no one needs to believe in their victory. France will be victorious, *poilus*, in a future no longer distant. (*Le Mouchoir*, 26 March 1916)

The trench press is here essentially restricted to an assertion of the French moral victory and to faith in the outcome of the battle: there is no reasoned comment on its significance, what is at stake, or even its progress. Such detachment is the more surprising because the 'replacement' system threw all units in turn into the furnace of Verdun and the great majority of the army therefore had direct knowledge of what was happening on the field of battle. But there was something perhaps even more striking: despite nine months of extraordinary tension, the end of the great confrontation of 1916 passed practically unremarked in the front-line press.

The lack of interest in other major events was even more marked. This applies to the United States' entry into the war in April 1917: a substantial minority of the newspapers did not even refer to it, and the remainder not until much later. The significance of this decisive piece of news, despite its potential capacity to restore the very low morale, was generally not perceived until several months later. Most soldiers were so ignorant about the American intervention that they saw it purely as a formality. Some newspaper editors, however, better informed or more aware than their colleagues, felt obliged to combat this general attitude of scepticism:

> The American nation declares its respectful admiration for France, and its unlimited affection. The war has become a sacred duty for them. They do not enter into this duty lightly but with a stubborn will to win . . . It is wrong to make fun of the Americans in France, and it will not be long before this is realised. (*L'Echo de la mitraille*, 1 January 1918)

Accused before 1917 of being indifferent to the fate of the Allies, the United States did not always enjoy a favourable image in the soldiers' newspapers, even after its entry into the war. Although some expressed satisfaction at the intervention, others did not hide their persistent scorn, as seen in this warning:

> Ah! The Americans! . . . They wrong us *poilus*! . . . Pretty 'godmothers', don't forget that these gentlemen know nothing of three years of war, or of wounds . . . None of this would matter if our 'Aces' back at home did not squawk in unison: 'Be patient! . . . The Americans are coming and with their inventive minds, they will soon bring the war to an end!' Steady! oh noble pen-pushers, and remember that we still exist. (*Brise d'entonnoirs*, 1 November 1917)

In fact the front often felt that the rear made too much of transatlantic troops. The Americans were not, however, the only ones to be unpopular in the trenches: the British were not spared either. The notion that the fate of the war rested on their shoulders alone was so firmly rooted in French soldiers' minds that they were quick to take offence at the prestige of the Allied armies in civilian eyes.

Other events were even more generally ignored than the American intervention, notably the Russian revolution: its outbreak was mentioned by only a minority of papers, and only after considerable delay. When its consequences were considered, it was only from the point of view of the potential military disaster that might ensue for the Allies, but ignorance or indifference were such that the peace of Brest-Litovsk in March 1918 passed virtually unnoticed. Censorship and self-censorship may lie at the origin of this silence – it was not thought desirable for readers to be weighed down under an avalanche of bad news at this very difficult period. But in this case how should one explain the similar – though less marked – detachment concerning a better item of news, such as the United States' entry into the war? In reality the soldiers in the ranks, and to a lesser degree the editors of their newspapers, took very little interest in the unfolding of the war as a whole. If the episode of Verdun occupied more space it was because it occurred earlier, because it took place on French soil, and because it had immediate repercussions for the troops; more distant events, with less directly perceptible consequences, aroused only widespread indifference. The range of war news in the trench press therefore remained narrow, with few items breaking down the wall of indifference that the combatants raised against them.

If national as well as international news clearly lay outside their preoccupations it was also because the soldiers neither received nor wished to receive more than a faint echo of the main events:

> For us, the *poilus*, the desire to know does not exist. All our aspirations lie in the present. Accustomed to this day-to-day and hour-by-hour life, we leave to others the task of sending patrols into the future. (*Le 120 court*, 1 September 1916)

This type of indifference was in truth simply a gap between the individual and everything outside his dialogue with death. Life at the front engendered a completely different perception of time and space and profoundly redefined the relative importance of all matters. Everything comes down to the present moment, to the 'here and now', and the soldiers' indifference was a direct consequence.

> You know that we become aware of events many months later! As for foreseeing . . . It's already quite enough to know in the morning where one will be in the evening. (*Bellica*, 1 December 1915)

Such ignorance was doubtless virtually inevitable. At the front, how could one fail to feel incapable of appreciating or understanding?

He [the soldier] does not himself seek understanding as an ordinary civilian does. He knows that the pattern of this war necessarily escapes him, that he lacks information, that he is bound to lack information, that even if he possessed it he would be unqualified to appreciate it. (*L'Echo des marmites*, 25 March 1916)

Such inevitable ignorance was however occasionally justified with a certain degree of affectation:

If you only knew how little it [the news] concerns us and how little we think about it! (*L'Explosif*, 20 March 1917)

Because the national newspapers managed to get through to front lines and were occasionally read by some of the soldiers, current events could not be ignored. But it is less the capacity of knowing than that of being interested that is here under consideration. Reading the national press responded less to a true need for information than to a desire to escape back to pre-war life. The indifference of the combatants was primarily linked to the impossibility of thinking about the future, of looking beyond the question of one's own fate, away from local and immediate concerns and outwards to the exterior world. Despite their more or less extensive reading of national newspapers, the men in the ranks remained psychologically cut off from current affairs because life in the trenches largely deprived them of any wish to know, to be interested, or to understand. Even middle-class townsmen, more cultivated and of broader vision than the countrymen, do not appear to have escaped this attitude.

When they made their own comments on the conflict, which was rare, the combatants limited themselves to asserting their hatred of the war and to defending a fundamentally pacifist ideal. In their eyes – hardly surprisingly – the war was absurd and wholly evil:

Meditation over the ruins confronts you with some startling truths. You suddenly see clearly the enormity and the improbability of the war. Life here is impossible except in deep cellars. Movement is impossible except at night. And you who are carrying on this war and who claim to know it, you ask yourself now how you can do it. (*Le Périscope*, 1917)

This notion of a preposterous state of confusion is expressed again here:

The human mass acts and argues in the midst of the shadows to which pride, hatred or cupidity have brought it. This chaos, this annihilation of things and of individuals, these violent contrasts, this anarchy of deed, thought and feeling, this is war. (*La Bourguignotte*, 1916)

The war is thus an atrocity, the ultimate peak of hideousness, and the soldiers' disgust is firmly emphasised:

I have seen the war with all that it trails in its wake of sadness, tears and heroism. I have seen the enthusiastic departure and the welcome in Belgium, and I have lived through the hour of defeat, marching day and night on an empty stomach but with hope in my heart. I have seen the Marne, the victorious push and the Germans fleeing, then stopping, cornered. I have seen Charleroi, Rheims and Verdun ablaze. I have seen bloody and horrible battles, wounded men dying, dead men trampled under foot! I have seen sufferings without number, men who day and night, in sun or rain, in the snow, marked their man . . . I have seen desolation and ruin everywhere. (*Bombardia*, 30 January 1918)

War was therefore devoid of meaning – or justification – unless it was to lead to peace. From the first outbreak of hostilities the theme of the 'war on war' is solidly established:

When tomorrow . . . you go home again, after these visions of horror and terror, you will remember that you have another duty to accomplish, equally noble and equally great! This duty is to prevent such carnage ever happening again. You would not wish that tomorrow those for whom you sacrifice yourselves might be exposed to the same ordeals again. Therefore everyone must concentrate on fighting wholeheartedly, according to his ability and without weakening. And in the end we will establish a peace which nothing will break. (*Le Poilu*, 10 March 1915)

There is no break between this pacifism of 1915 and that expressed after the victory:

We fought, above all, so that future generations might be spared the horrors of war . . . It is up to us, as war veterans, to create a clearly pacifist movement of opinion as soon as we return home. (*Le Bochofage*, December 1918)

Denial of war. Deep-seated pacifism. Yet the pacifism that gained ground as the war stretched on was not, except in a few cases, of a political nature. It did not develop into an ideological challenge, and the Zimmerwald and Kienthal conferences had virtually no repercussions. The combatants rejected all verbal heroics, to the extent of depicting themselves occasionally in a very sombre, even deliberately pessimistic, light:

> Mud, blood, the death of friends, suffering in every way: fatigue, hunger, thirst, wounds, illness. Do *you* like the sound of that? (*Le Tuyau de la roulante*, May 1916)

Thus many soldiers insisted on the wretched aspect of the human being stuck in the ground and facing danger:

> In the mêlée there are no handsome young leading men who mouth fine words and stick out their chests . . . as the shells rain down, there are only weak beings flattened on the ground by their instinct for self-preservation because the ability to utter fine phrases has never been needed as a prerequisite for dying. (*Grenadia*, 23 April 1917)

This open breach in traditional imagery was exploited in turn by *L'Argonnaute* in 1917:

> And people will say, they were heroes! Alas! We are only poor devils and are not always brave enough for the harsh and lengthy job of killing. (*L'Argonnaute*, May 1917)

> Poor wretches who have been struggling for three years, deprived of most poor human pleasures, struggling all the same so that so much pain should not be wasted, hoping still for some miraculous return, when it may be a smashed head – that is what we are. (*L'Argonnaute*, August 1917)

Resisting the heroic image, all stressed the human banality of the men in the trenches:

> The *poilu* is not, as described by the stay-at-homes of the two-penny papers, a muddy hero who scratches himself and jokes as he attacks. No, I swear it. The *poilu* is something simpler: he is a man. (*La Mitraille*, January–February 1918)

Indifference as to what was happening in their own country; lack of interest in the progress of the war; hatred of the war, and fundamental pacifism; rejection of all heroic imagery; stress on their appalling wretchedness. How could one resist the temptation in all this to deny all national feeling among the men in the trenches? Their submission and their passivity have sometimes been emphasised, together with their supposed indifference to the fate of their nation. If the soldier in the ranks held on, as for example Louis Mairet wrote in his memoirs, it was because 'he fought out of integrity, habit and force. He fought because he could not do otherwise'.[3] This somewhat gloomy image of the combatants, with purely negative reasons for holding on and moreover totally lacking any true hostility towards the enemy, is the version often given by soldiers' writings. Many of the elements of the trench press would support this interpretation. But if it were true that front-line experience succeeded in destroying national feeling at the beginning of the war, how can we explain the extraordinary endurance of the army during these four years in the worst of physical and psychological conditions endured by the men in the ranks?

Hostility towards the Enemy

The image of the adversary is decisive, for there are close links between perceptions of the enemy and national feeling, to the extent that they are one of its fundamental roots. Many veterans vigorously resisted any notion of hostility towards their former opponents, and on certain points the trench press supports them. German militarism and the civil or military leaders of Germany were thus more severely denounced than the German nation itself, seen as being primarily swept along by the upper classes:

> The emperors ordained an onslaught in which, alas, the dead pile up in hecatombs, to preserve the crown and to preserve their prestige, and it is the people stirred into fanaticism who willy-nilly suffer the cost. The nation must truly have been blind, or blinded, and if they know, they should remain silent . . . In this land of *Kultur*, human life is prized as highly as that of a cockroach in the barracks or the life of a rat in the trenches. (*Le P'tit pépère*, 9 December 1917)

3. Louis Mairet, *Carnets d'un combattant*, p.172.

It mattered little whether the German nation was reduced to silence or to insanity: it was the leaders who bore the responsibility, in particular the military aristocracy and the businessmen of the middle classes. The fact that the German people were occasionally called upon to revolt indicates that they were not considered responsible for the war, and there were occasional traces in the front-line press of a quite marked indulgence towards the opposing forces:

> For some time now little conversations have been taking place between the lads in the German and the French front lines, between two bitter-sweet brackets, exchanging a few salty phrases which come close to expressing sympathy. (*Marmita*, 10 January 1915)

It is worth noting the date, January 1915: it shows that a certain rapprochement between soldiers in the two opposing camps did not wait until the wearing-down of 1917 to become apparent, the feeling of proximity being necessarily encouraged by the actual lay-out of the trenches. But, as may be imagined, censorship did not allow the appearance of many texts of this kind. On the other hand, and without any risk of describing it as 'fraternisation' in the strict sense of the term, censors 'passed' some accounts of these brief encounters between adversaries:

> It happened in a quiet sector. A thick mist blurred everything that morning. It was impossible to see two paces in front of your face. We had set up an outpost in front of our lines. It was cold and drizzling; suddenly a Boche patrol appeared out of the mist ahead. They were walking quietly, hands in pockets, rifles slung at their shoulders and smoking cigarettes. Dumbstruck, our men hesitated for a moment. That was when the Boche n.c.o. suggested in a mournful voice, 'Sad war, gentlemen! Sad war!' Then they disappeared back into the mist. (*La Saucisse*, June 1916)

Such gestures were naturally encouraged by the atmosphere surrounding the armistice:

> Military bands suddenly struck up loudly and Boches jumped up from the German trench like jack-in-the-boxes, hands high, and came towards

us shouting '*Kamarads*, the war is over!' They sang, their faces were full of joy. Goodness, they looked happier than we did, these conquered men. But I looked at these faces bending towards us with expressions, like our own, illuminated with release. After all, we all share the same idea now, we are the same, men finally delivered . . . In the middle of the night another Boche appeared at our post. He said, 'You have won the game. We are quits. Goodbye!' And he disappeared into the shadows without another word. (*L'Argonnaute*, November 1918)

The feeling of proximity sometimes turned into compassion – a soldier offering food and drink to the prisoners he was leading to the rear, or a battalion of light infantrymen handing out cigarettes to the captured Germans marching in front of them. Or again, friendly talk between a wounded enemy soldier and the stretcher-bearer looking after him. With their identical daily lives, it was surely logical that sometimes the enemy seemed to be part of the same humanity.

At one of the entrances to tunnel B—, in one of the enormous excavations made by our 400s, two elderly Germans, probably pioneers, supported a dying friend. These three men must have been great friends. The two without wounds had their eyes full of tears and as the wounded man died, one of them leaned slowly across to his brother in distress and embraced him lengthily. Impressed by such misery, and despite the urgency of the moment, the *poilus* stopped, moved. (*Poil et plume* October 1917)

The respect felt by soldiers for their enemies is beyond question, but there were links other than the feeling of common identity between human beings of two opposing camps. The enemy was respected equally for his strength and courage, and the danger he represented. Three years after the beginning of the war a soldier described in the following terms the shock he felt when he met men who had already fought the Germans:

As we approached the lines, identified by the confused grumbling of the angry artillery, we met combatants, real ones, 'who had seen them', who had encountered the terrible efficiency of their machine-guns and had developed from the experience a simple, incoherent and familiar insolence. They swore at us, mocked us, and we could not tell if they were heroes or devils. They teased us on our healthy petit-bourgeois looks, sparkling, fully equipped, wearing new uniforms. And they faced us with their insulting rags. They invited us, with broad sarcastic grins, to go and have a little look, to see if the Boches were easy, and you could feel in their words an accurate appreciation of the redoubtable enemy, a sort of respect. (*L'Echo du boyau*, July 1917)

This respect, forged in battles from the beginning of the war, was sustained to the very end. Certain trench newspapers did not even shrink from outright praise of the enemy:

Up to the very last moment the enemy displayed admirable courage and coolness. We have seen a Boche officer operating his machine gun wearing white gloves, and not surrendering until after the last of his ammunition was gone. We have seen appallingly cruel hand-to-hand fighting. We have had to surround groups of the enemy to overcome them and we have taken small strongpoints with cold steel. (*Le Filon*, April 1917)

Here again, only a local anecdote; but on occasions there would be expressions of true admiration for the whole German army:

Yes, they are strong. It would be childish to deny it, and moreover this is no revelation except for some who no doubt believed that it would be easy to finish them off. They are strong, that is obvious, but have we not been strong for nearly four years, and are we not still strong? (*Face aux Boches*, 1918)

These texts should, however, be interpreted with care, for there is a danger of reading more into them than is appropriate. True, episodes of fraternisation revealed that feelings of proximity existed between men in the two camps – but to draw definitive conclusions from these encounters would be to forget a little too quickly that such moments of rapprochement could only be exceptional. Had they been the rule and not the exception there would simply have been no trench war, and that they occurred from time to time does not prove the existence of any kind of permanent feeling of fraternity across the barbed wire barriers. In fact such anecdotes can easily be read in two ways, for having mentioned the enemy with praise or indulgence it was not unusual for these same trench newspapers to undergo a brusque change of tone. Such is the case in *Poil et plume* after its account quoted above of the two Germans supporting their mortally wounded comrade:

> X— [in the 3rd battalion] was quietly watching the search of the '*Kamarads*'. A Prussian officer, still self-assured and who still wished to play the part of the petty seigneur, held out his cigarette case and offered a cigarette to a *poilu*. The Frenchman was indignant. He seized the case from the German: 'Not those, do you understand, you won't smoke any more of them!' And the *poilu* put the case in his pocket. A healthy response to the cheek of this thick-skinned man trying to preserve command after he had surrendered. Did he forget that the least of these soldiers was his superior, both in his national culture and in his personal merits? (*Poil et plume*, October 1917)

Having stressed the 'courage' and the 'coolness' of the enemy, *Le Filon* also turned to his despicable characteristics:

> Following the fashion, the Boches surrendered to the leading waves then, after the light infantry had passed them, fired at their backs. What does it matter! The reinforcements will put the villains behind bars. (*Le Filon*, April 1917)

There is another example of ambivalence in the following account of the display of the bodies of two German airmen brought down over the French lines:

> The bodies of two airmen were brought here and put in the German cemetery. I deplore this public exhibition. That everyone can come and joke and look at the disfigured faces and mutilated bodies without respect shows a lack of tact that shocks me, a Frenchman. Death should be respected. These were two German officers killed on duty. They were brave, energetic, bold. We should recognise that and salute them. (*On progresse*, 1 November 1917)

There can be no doubting this writer's respect for the enemy and his courage in battle; but does not such protest reveal that his own attitude was clearly a minority view? For undoubtedly there were public displays of bodies, a practice apparently to the liking of some since they came to 'joke without respect' over the corpses of their victims. This article therefore has the effect of a recall to order directed against companions who do not seem to have distinguished themselves by the nobility of their minds. It was a characteristic of this feeling of 'proximity' that it was strictly limited in extent; for example, the hostility of the least well-educated soldiers appears to have been more marked than that of their better-educated fellow rankers. Was not this a significant observation of Norman peasants in March 1917 as they crossed the front-line area abandoned by the Germans?

> The Normans, of whom there are many among us, cried out long and loud in anger: 'Oh the wretches! They have cut down all the apple trees.' They could never forgive the Boches for that. (*L'Argonnaute*, March 1917)

It is striking to note that the writer of this account, although expressing equal indignation, stresses this hostile reaction with a trace of condescension, as if he found such a strongly marked display of rancour somewhat ridiculous. In any case, the columns of the front-line newspapers reveal far fewer signs of understanding of the enemy than displays of hostility, which sometimes take on imaginative forms:

> And we'll get the most out of it, by a trial of strength, which is what the sauerkraut-eaters understand best. (*Le Vide-boche*, 1 June 1918)

And to underline the argument further, France is shown in an allegory gutting a pig hung up by its feet.

Occasionally, it is true, denunciation of the enemy appeared in a more 'reasoned' way:

> They have burgled houses to send souvenirs to their women;
> They have burnt churches with women and children hiding inside;
> They have murdered old people and the sick without reason;
> They have shot nuns and doctors caring for the wounded;
> They have cut the hands off little children who begged them for mercy;
> They have perfected the most barbaric and cowardly tortures;
> Faced with such horror, civilised people have to resign themselves and exclaim 'Oh, the monsters!' (*On les aura*, 1 December 1916)

The purpose of such anti-German propaganda, which did not trouble itself over subtleties of meaning, was obviously to discredit the enemy by any means available and incite the soldiers to hatred. But does this ridicule prove that hostility did not exist beforehand in the great mass of the army? Certainly, the image of the adversary improved steadily in the trench press between 1914 and 1918. The papers appeared much less harsh at the end of the war than at the beginning, but despite this moderation it was a negative image of the enemy that prevailed until the end of the conflict.

What conclusion should be drawn from so many apparently contradictory indications? First, that several different views of the enemy could very well co-exist or be superimposed one on another, according to times and individuals. For example, it is noticeable that sharp little outbursts of animosity appear in the newspapers of units which had just taken part in a particularly murderous encounter, but later, in rest periods or calm sectors, such hostility tended to diminish or disappear. The image of the enemy was doubtless never simple or unequivocal; but it remained negative in the minds of the majority of the soldiers. That their hostility, at first very marked, later softened into a more objective view or a certain indifference, can hardly be doubted, but the animosity never disappeared entirely. The lengthy duration of the ordeal and the similarity of life and attitudes on either side of the barbed wire brought the adversaries together, but it did not blend them into a sort of community which could have overcome the difference in uniform.

One can however agree with the veterans when they deny the existence of any extreme or unshakeable hatred of the enemy. The open hatred sometimes apparent behind the front lines was not part of front-line life, as is suggested by this iconoclastic question:

Why do shirkers show themselves more arrogant than *poilus* towards the prisoners? (*L'Echo des marmites*, 25 May 1916)

The soldiers assessed their comrades and their leaders by the yardstick of their courage under fire, and they judged the enemy by the same criterion: it was this which forbade the latter to be denigrated. Self-respect and respect for the enemy were inseparable, but did that of itself exclude hostility?

The newspapers are right to persist in reminding us of the Boche crimes and atrocities! The long duration of the ordeal should not dissipate hatred. It has been proved that the Boche is a villain. But is the most cruel of villains necessarily a coward? ... It has been proved that the Boche totally lacks the keenness of the French soldier in the ranks. It is beyond question that thousands of men surrendered on the Somme, stupefied by the terrible pounding of our artillery. But have you never read communiqués referring to: 'desperate battles', 'terrible hand-to-hand fighting', 'furious counter-attacks'? In these human clusters where each soldier exists only as part of the unit, do you think that the deliberate submerging of the individual in the mass is not a form of courage? Even if they are only brave as a result of their discipline, why deny it? In recognising the worth of your adversary on the battlefield, are you afraid of making him appear sympathetic? Is he not already too vile elsewhere for us ever to be tempted to esteem him? *It is not the cause of the Boche that I am pleading, but that of the* poilu *who is appalled by the systematic disparaging of the enemy.* (*Le Crapouillot*, September 1916)

Le Crapouillot rejected the habit of disparaging the enemy, but this time the Germans were not treated lightly. In this it agreed with very widespread accusations of German cruelty, blind discipline and inferior determination in battle, but varied the tone by recalling their 'valour' as a group. Respect and hostility are thus closely blended, and it was no doubt as part of this average blend that most soldiers recognised themselves. In this connexion, the following article in 1918 appears very much to the point:

It may be said that the soldier does not hate; that if he happens to talk about the Boche, it is in tones that exclude the existence of any deep hostility. This is worth looking at closely ... He therefore possesses only a minimum of hatred, the minimum amount necessary to pursue the war. But it exists, and that is sufficient. We all have this indestructible kernel, but we do not consider it necessary to dress it up in the grand words dear to the propagandists and braggarts. Without it the front could not exist: it would fade away like the Russian front. If they did not hate the Boche and all the barbarity that he incarnates ... how would the soldiers have stuck it out for four years, enduring what they endure? The soldiers' hatred is not an external and spoken hatred, but let no one suppose for that reason that it does not exist ... In battle the soldier who fires his rifle or the artilleryman who aims his gun at a group and sees the effectiveness of his fire both feel they are carrying out a useful bit of work, without any bloodthirsty instinct. They congratulate each other with delight on the death of any of the enemy, because they are driven by

a legitimate hatred. It is this hatred which sustains them . . . the intimate
and sometimes unrecognised hatred which animates everyone. (*Le Tord-
boyau*, June–July 1918)

Note that the term 'hatred' appears unsuitable to designate the state
of mind that the writer seeks to evoke, with the expressions 'hostility' or 'animosity' appearing distinctly more appropriate.
Hostility goes without saying, unrecognised or half-recognised, not
to be talked about, which cannot be properly expressed either. This
ambiguity remains however perceptible in the writings of the combatants, for those who read them with care.

Several of the front-line papers published certain extracts from a
book by Pierre Chaine[4] which seemed to them to describe with
accuracy the relationship established between the adversaries:

In no way did he display continually overwhelming hatred for the Boche,
and one day as he watched the enemy from a loophole, without any
thought of firing at him, he thought that that tiny silhouette was a soldier
like himself, carrying out the same service but wearing a different uniform. Both ran the same dangers, suffered the same bad weather,
laboured at the same fatigues. Although the same actions were devoted to
opposing causes, they constituted in fact a community of life and concerns that was sufficient to create a point of contact from which arose,
despite the surrounding hostility, an obscure sympathy. (Pierre Chaine,
Les Mémoires d'un rat, extract quoted in *Le Crapouillot*, August 1917)

'Obscure sympathy' . . . these two words may seem surprising, and
appear to contradict our own interpretation. But they should be
looked at closely: it may be admitted that a form of sympathy could
develop from awareness of a shared fate, but the text states clearly
that it is not a matter here of anything except a particular selected
instant, of a thought that 'one day' came into the mind of the hero
of this novel. The author refutes the artificial and extreme hatred
distilled by propaganda, but without rejecting the reality of a 'surrounding hostility' which seems clearly dominant. Such a text thus
only apparently undermines discipline.

What remains to be understood is the nature of this latent hostility between the combatants, doubtless linked to a feeling of

4. Pierre Chaine, *Mémoires d'un rat*, Paris, A L'Oeuvre, 1921, pp.65–6.

difference which persisted despite the adversaries' proximity to each other. In this context, the following encounter in 1918 between a demobilised Alsatian and two Frenchmen billeted in Alsace appears very significant:

> He had been in the war too, and served as an officer in a regiment of field artillery ... but on the other side of the barricades. The guns that he aimed were 77s. *Krieg ist Krieg*! He spoke of villages where he had fought, first in Lorraine and then at Verdun, and on the Somme. My friend and I looked at him. We knew the names of these villages, and not only because we had read about them in communiqués. We needed details, dates. Chance is a great master. The man in front of us had gone right through the war against us, and now here he was on the other side of this table with its flowered table-cloth, in this sleepy little bar, with a little glass of spirits like the ones we were drinking. He spoke with politeness and we kept our distance. It is difficult to express in everyday terms the feelings that arise from such an encounter, and conversation languished. He is Alsatian, but why beneath his tricolour cockade has he retained the black and white ribbon of his Iron Cross? We parted without shaking hands. (*Le Crapouillot*, December 1918)

No hatred, certainly, particularly because the man in question was from Alsace. Neither his cirumstances nor his behaviour would allow the slightest hostile thought, but there was certainly embarrassment. They and he had after all not fought on the same side, and that Iron Cross helped to revive a feeling of separation which was ultimately indestructible.

Two years earlier, there was a very similar reaction when a convoy of prisoners passed by:

> They marched in fours, in good order, n.c.o.s at the front, between lines of immobile and silent fellows. No a murmur, not a shout. Great coldness. The watching men felt strongly and clearly that they were not part of the same race as the men marching past. No arrogant hatred towards the vanquished, for the *poilus* knew from experience the terrible distress they had endured under the pounding: but a hint of scorn for this interminable column of soldiers who had surrendered their weapons and let themselves be led by a few hussars with bare swords, like a herd of cattle. (*Le Crapouillot*, October 1916)

What separated the French from these Germans marching past

them? Was it not the impression – unspoken and inexpressible – of not being of the same blood? Between the former and the latter there appeared to be an impassable mental barrier – or passable only with difficulty. The complete absence of hostility and of all feeling of difference was no doubt only available to a small number of the elite, for it required a breadth of vision which was not shared by the mass of the men. But it was this elite that was to take up the pen between the wars, retaining from experience only that which had been of advantage to all: breadth of mind being more morally praiseworthy than hatred, to have conquered without individual hostility for the enemy gave a more elevated feeling to the accomplishments of those four years. The deliberate pacifism of the veterans thus contributed to a genuine distortion of memory. Moreover, the final issues of the front-line newspapers were to indicate clearly that such a change was necessary to the cause of peace:

> Banish hatred from your heart and show the beaten enemy at your feet that if the sons of France can be insanely brave in battle, they can also be insanely great, good and humane in victory. Hatred never produced anything but hatred . . . What makes France truly immortal is that she has always been able to show herself fraternal and generous towards all, even her defeated enemies. (*La Mitraille*, January–February 1919)

If hostility, or at least a feeling of difference, was genuinely part of the combatants' mental universe, most of them wished afterwards to be rid of its memory; but even if the soldiers of the two sides did not really regard each other as enemies in the full sense of the term, they were never friends. From beginning to end, they were above all adversaries.

Soldiers' Patriotism

The French victory was never genuinely doubted by the fighting men from the beginning of the war until its end: it was obvious; it needed no discussion. The contents of the front-line papers indicate that despite a brief lowering of confidence in May 1918, which was rapidly overcome, the conviction of a victorious end to the conflict was never more than very slightly undermined throughout the four years of combat. Such constancy is remarkable in view of the war's evolution, the living conditions and the length of the ordeal. The majority of the combatants confidently believed that their nation could not lose the war. It was one more reason why the passing events of the conflict aroused no more than very moderate interest: was not the final outcome already an established fact? And could peace be associated with anything but victory?

> Tomorrow! This is the new year of definitive reparation and victory; of the crushing of the odious German tyranny, the era of universal peace won at the cost of such sacrifices! (*Le Poilu*, 1 January 1915)

This unsophisticated certainty at the start of the war was not immediately lost. A year later came the luxury of making ironic comment on those who feared that the war might not finish within a year:

> On this question of leave, the funniest thing is that someone has calcu-lated that, with the percentage on leave, they will not get back home before Easter of next year. That's really a joke because by then . . . the Allies will have done enough to ensure that we can all go back home to our own little corner without having to come back and take our place in the trench. (*L'Echo du grand couronné*, December 1915)

A year later, confidence appeared unbroken:

> We hope that the year 1917 will bring all our friends and readers good health, safety amid danger and . . . VICTORY . . . Courage then, soon our sufferings will be over, soon success will reward our efforts and our unbelievable sacrifices, soon we will go back home to our peaceful labours, soon we will embrace our mothers, our dear wives, and our grandchildren with the kiss of victory. (*Le Mouchoir*, 1 January 1917)

None the less the terrible setbacks of 1917 ended by instilling doubt and creating a breach in this fine optimism. Henceforward perception of the length of the war was to be modified:

> So when will the war be over? A question posed all too often. But people respond less frequently than they used to. No one dares . . . Even the

most well-informed just nod their heads. The truth is, no one knows . . . Hostilities may end next month or in two years. The best solution is to be patient and to wait. (*La Saucisse*, 1918)

'Next month or in two years . . .' Truly, the tone has changed, but there must be no mistake: even much longer and more cruel than anticipated, the interminable ordeal cannot end in defeat:

Obviously losses are heavy, both in men and in national wealth, but such losses are balanced to some extent by those of the enemy, so that the two situations, though not identical, may none the less be comparable. So the Boches are strong – we know that – but we have been stronger: thanks to us they have not broken through and in the end we will be stronger than them because they will not overcome us and we will overcome them. (*Face aux Boches*, 1918)

A certain discouragement surfaced at the beginning of 1918, but the hope of victory was never the less not lost:

It is because the hour is serious that we must hope. In four years of war we have seen it in all its aspects and we have learned to measure the extent of our hopes through the strength of our nerves . . . That is why we must hope, at this most emotional time. Be calm, you who put your hope in us. We shall conquer, for we have the strength to suffer for the famous fifteen minutes longer . . . and even longer. (*L'Argonnaute*, April 1918)

Strong in this belief, the combatants do not appear to have been particularly surprised by the realisation of their hopes. After all, was not victory their due?

We were fighting for what was Right, and does not victory go morally to those who hold the Right? It was an inevitable outcome. Impossible to think of a Boche victory. So . . . what is the point of shouting 'bravo' for something that could not turn out otherwise? (*Sans tabac*, October–November 1918)

It would be wrong to see such arguments as contrived. According to what the soldiers wrote, their faith in the success of their nation was never truly questioned, despite immense weariness. Partial successes hastened victory; setbacks delayed it, but never did more than delay it. This notion that victory was ultimately no more than a simple matter of time was one of the strongest foundations of the soldier's patriotism.

But fear of falling into the style of the Paris press engendered a certain reserve when their papers referred to this patriotism. The front-line press also appeared to falter markedly in the spring of 1918, but over the four years of the war patriotism remains in general unfailingly evident. This constancy is in itself a powerfully significant indicator: in effect, if the patriotic determination of August 1914 had fallen away in the face of the realities of war, there is no doubt that the soldiers' newspapers would have shown evidence of this development. But this did not happen, and it is reasonable to think that these four years of daily hardship did not result in any serious or lasting breach in patriotic conviction.

There were occasional doubts, however. One such moment followed the setback of the Nivelle offensive in April 1917, which set off the surge of mutinies in May and June of that year. The crisis in morale affected nearly the whole of the army at that time, but Guy Pedroncini has shown that the number of mutineers never exceeded 40,000, five divisions being particularly affected.[5] Censorship meant that the mutinies could not be mentioned in the front-line press, although signs of depression there are unmistakable. But however serious the mutinies of May–June 1917, it cannot be maintained that the army's malaise constituted any kind of genuine crisis in national feeling. This wavering at the heart of the army was matched in the civilian population. One cannot then totally exclude the possibility that the military edifice was close to breaking-point; but this lapse seems to have been of short duration.

Overall, everything seems to indicate that national feeling held up well. It was deeply rooted in the republican patriotism of pre-war days, of which the trench press sometimes picked up the main themes: land of the Revolution, of the Rights of Man, France was the incarnation of liberty, justice, law and peace, and its defence was thus identified with that of civilisation, of the whole of humanity. But references to the idea of 'revenge' and the recovery of the 'lost provinces' were only very discreet, confirming the disaffection from which these two topics suffered in pre-1914 France. Even if the trench press made explicit reference to the *idées-forces* of pre-war

5. Guy Pedroncini, *Les mutineries de 1917*, Paris, PUF, 1967.

patriotism, they may have been too general or too abstract to provide long-term nourishment for the national feeling of the great majority of soldiers. That patriotism was profoundly rooted in each one of these men, moulded by their primary education, but it did not mean that patriotism would be capable of acting indefinitely as their line of mental resistance during their unending torture. On the other hand, in the daily experience of the war, their patriotism developed new roots that gave a certain focus to the fighting man's national feeling. Defence of their soil, of the land with which they felt in almost physical communion, was a factor which gave meaning to the sufferings endured:

We were entering conquered territory! Poor French soil, of which every mound had been turned over, crushed, ground down by steel. (*Sans tabac*, 1 November 1916)

Born with the soldiers' burial in the trenches, this relationship with the soil remained closely linked to the role of the colossal cemetery that was the front line:

Every fragment [of this land is] soaked with the blood of our brothers, is a sort of sacred clay ... Who can forget reliefs through the crumbling communication trenches, over bodies melting in the sun, through the frozen wreckage of bits of upturned ground which settles slowly, retaining the imprint of merciless struggles? (*L'Argonnaute*, 15 March 1916)

The imprint. The imprint of dead men, of spilt blood, of every man's sufferings and struggles; this bond between the dead men and the earth where they fell is emphasised sometimes with tragic force:

This soil [which the soldier] sifts with his hands, which he defends with his life, this soil is impregnated with the blood of his friends: every metre seized from the enemy has cost the life of a man. There, close to him, there are many cemeteries which bear witness to this. (*Marmita*, 21 February 1915)

The feeling of attachment to a terrain nourished with corpses and the sight of comrades' improvised tombs played an important though paradoxical role in the tenacity of the survivors. This bond between the will to hold on and respect for the earth-tomb is clearly evident in this desperate account of the French retreat in the spring of 1918:

> We had other bitter feelings. We had to leave all the graves of our dead pals . . . all these funeral plots enriched by the war, in enemy hands. To lose one's dead who believed that at the cost of their lives they had won the right to sleep within the breast of their motherland – that is profoundly bitter. (*L'Argonnaute*, April 1918)

Fidelity to the memory of those who have been killed, fidelity to the ground in which they are buried: these are two determinant elements in the combatants' patriotism, for this double allegiance created personal obligations for each man. It may perhaps have been a resurgence of certain nationalist themes from before 1914, but it demonstrates supremely the sense of a personal lesson, intimate, the result of daily experience of death striking at one's side and the charnel-house vision of the field of battle.

Defence of the soil was therefore perceived as an obligation which could not be ignored. And each time that they had to give up great stretches of terrain to the enemy, a profound anxiety seized the fighting men:

> I have only to recall our violent wish to read the paper recently. I have only to recall the avid curiosity with which we devoured the communiqués concerning the Kolossal offensive. I have only to recall the vivid flame which burned in our eyes when we knew that we had held them, even sometimes driven them back. I have only to recall, finally, our expressions in those moments of anguish, our heartfelt cries: 'Oh, good God! They shall not pass! Our men are there! There are no more like them! But some of them must die!' And such words were spoken with clenched fists and the heart full of rage! (*Le Poilu marmité*, 20 April 1918)

Fear of retreat was expressed, and the inexpressible fear of a defeat pure and simple, at the worst moment of the war since the battle of the Marne. The word was never written, for it was a taboo which could not be transgressed. But, sometimes, the distress of such an event appeared:

> *30 May*. Our thoughts are not cheerful. We gather bits of information along the way. The Boches are said to be at Château-Thierry: we cannot

believe it, but we feel that things are not going well. The pessimists consider it definite that they have crossed the Marne: so . . . our throats feel tight, as if we are going to weep. (*Le Crapouillot*, June 1918)

On the other hand, any gain of terrain provoked a delight that was often disproportionate. At the very beginning of the war, this happened to an inexperienced troop:

18 August 1914. The company gathered in the shade of a field of fruit trees. The lieutenant, who wore a policeman's cap, read out loud the *Bulletin des Armées de la République* . . . The news of the war is excellent . . . Such victories cheer us on! The lieutenant interrupted his reading, he was so excited! Finally, he said joyfully, this is revenge! With tears in our eyes we felt the bitter delight of living through heroic times and, impatient to receive the baptism of fire, we were burning with the desire to win glory in our turn. (*Le Crapouillot*, September 1916)

No false heroics here, the writer inevitably going on to laugh next at the naïve satisfaction of these neophytes who will quickly be restored to reason by their first battle. But the men were never indifferent to the prospect of a 'forward march'. Thus in March 1917, following the Germans' retreat to shorten their front line:

Splendid day . . . almost the last of the winter . . . cheerful rumours are circulating . . . they claim that the front is broken. Bapaume has been retaken . . . Péronne is finally French once more . . . but we are waiting for communiqués. All at once the cyclist arrives with a paper, all the good news is confirmed, and I can still see the air of triumph of the brave fellow repeating: 'And they say that the English cavalry is on the heels of the Boches.' Our dreams of last summer have become living reality, and the trench war is over for this part of the front. (*Le Plus que torial*, 31 March 1917)

Once again the sequence of events soon refuted this fine enthusiasm. But it reappeared with the Allies' final advance:

And now, now we shall follow their retreat and go back, in the opposite direction, along the road where we were two months ago. This time the way will be more agreeable, of course, and this march northwards cheers us up. (*L'Argonnaute*, September 1918)

If this particular extract is moderate in tone, it was not always thus:

[We have known] the emotion of advancing where three months earlier we had to hold on, the thrill of liberating our old trenches ourselves. And then, the threshold of the drama, the second leap forward to Roye . . . Sacrifices, a cruel day, more bloody sacrifices, another day . . . and already the first onset of a weariness which one does not wish to acknowledge, of dust and mud, and this treacherous influenza that makes inroads into our ranks . . . and the pestilence from the corpses along the roads; the gas which seizes the active man by the throat . . . And then the third burst for Nesles, the skilful marches, the distrust of everything one passes, of the smallest twig, the least thread of copper wire; and the thirst too, at polluted water, and always the influenza, and the weariness which weighs on your feet like lead . . . But the hour came for the fourth departure . . . This was a starlit march by a skeletal battalion desperate to finish with dying, but running out of breath at its last gasp . . . They came in threes this time against the battalion: the enemy, the flu, fatigue. And twelve days after beating them, the battalion went up to the sector. Vive la France! (*Les Poilus de la 9e*, 25 September 1918)

One could hardly put this text in the category of propaganda articles. Down to its precipitate and almost frantic style, it displays a collective exaltation enhanced by the extreme fatigue of the moment, and highly characteristic of the deep patriotism of the final weeks of the war.

This is very far from the picture of soldiers little concerned with defeat or victory. They were in no way indifferent to the loss of ground, or its recapture, and their ignorance of the ups and downs of war did not prevent the strengthening of the bonds between these men and the terrain which it was their mission to defend. Such attitudes also corresponded well with the state of mind of peasant-soldiers; but it seems to have extended beyond the limits of this social group to include the whole army.

To this attachment should be linked the instinctive reflex of defence of 'one's own'. Whatever the civilians may have thought, the soldiers were strongly conscious of the need to protect them, in an almost primitive reaction of defence of their 'clan':

We meet the wretched procession of refugees from the area . . . These people do not weep, but one can feel them prey to immense distress, and they move like poor beasts turned out of their lair, without really knowing where they will be able to stop . . . And so 'we' have not been able to prevent this: I feel it like a kind of shame. (*Le Crapouillot*, June 1918)

Such guilt is the more painful because it is linked to a feeling of collective responsibility, even though no one could reproach himself personally for any failure of duty. It is somewhat comparable to the state of mind in this description of the recently liberated Ardennes population:

If the poor civilians meet us twenty times over in a day, they raise their hats to us twenty times. 'Good morning my fine soldier. Ah! We knew you would come in the end!' Shame on me! They were always confident, these poor wretches! I was afraid they might perceive how recent my own *real* certainty was. (*L'Horizon*, January 1919)

The feeling of obligation concerning the defence of civilians illuminates the effect of expressions of gratitude, the source of a secret pride:

Confidence grew as we went north, behind this front line, as we appeared in our blue uniforms. You were proud of that *whatever you say*. When the civilians said to you, 'Ah! we aren't afraid of anything now you have come', you felt it, you are different from other men. And during this triumphal procession by car through the wretched villages that you have recaptured you felt flattered by the confidence and the esteem of your fellow citizens. (*Le Filon*, May–June 1918)

Another soldier expresses with lucidity the strongly felt moral obligation to defend his country and its inhabitants:

We fought because we could not do otherwise . . . We were forced to make war and to fight by all the social ties which bind us: by the dependence and the subjection in which the individual exists in relation to the State within modern societies; by the thousand threads which attach him to the soil, to the very atmosphere of his land, and which form morally binding attitudes more powerful than any physical shackles. (*Le Tord-boyau*, August 1917)

This text exudes an impression of semi-despair. In every phrase it expresses constraint: the impossibility of not fighting 'because we could not do otherwise' 'forced to make war', 'the social ties which bind', 'the . . . threads which attach', 'dependence', 'subjection', 'morally binding attitudes', 'shackles', etc. There is nothing rational, he implies, in the significance of fighting to the soldiers: this meaning springs from an intuitive perception of what links them to the national community, but which cannot be explained, which can neither be rationalised nor denied. More or less consciously, the soldiers appear firmly *forced* into national feeling: this feeling obtrudes on them at the death of their comrades, the acclaim of the local people, at a front-line advance or retreat, and they are ultimately unable either to escape it or to resist it. It is in this sense that the concept of duty should be understood.

Far from being a meaningless military formula, this concept appears to be laden with significance and it resurfaces in an almost obsessional manner:

Each one knows the state of mind, the strength of purpose and of character, the great patriotism of doing his duty as a Frenchman needed to plunge bravely back into the turmoil (with which all are already familiar), determined to do his duty once again, with every likelihood of not coming back this time, or of getting a less 'useful' wound than previous ones. (*Nos tanks*, February 1918)

This feeling of duty accepted day after day is evoked again here:

Meanwhile, you carry on with your little bit of duty, without grand gestures, without making a lot of noise, like Papa, because it has to be done. There are days when you bring back a seriously or slightly wounded comrade, other times when you stand to attention for one of us who has paid for his share of idealism with his life. Then everything returns to the usual self-effacement . . . That's war. (*L'Explosif*, 20 March 1917)

It's duty because it's duty: this assertion is one of the poles of national feeling, even if it lies beyond words. J. Galtier-Boissière attempts none the less to describe its principal aspects in two profoundly moving articles, with a year between them:

In the trenches [the soldier] stands guard at the look-out point, spends the night at the listening-post like everyone else, takes part in patrols when so instructed. He complains when the sergeant-major puts him on fatigue duty two days running but he does it all the same; he prefers digging to doing weapons drill, because 'digging, that's something he knows about'; he knows how to be wary of shells and if he is killed it will not be his fault. He has got into the habit of living underground before being dead, and does his jobs conscientiously, like a good workman who earns his money honestly. He talks little and does not read the papers; when an attack is announced he does not clap his hands but, after the grog distribution, when the squad gathers round one of those little ladders that the *poilus* have christened 'the scaffold', when the whistle blows, he is there when it is his turn to go over the top. (*Le Crapouillot*, September 1916)

The poor beggar, alone in a shell-hole, in the middle of the unrestrained elements, has a feeling for 'what must be done' and for 'what need not be done' . . . Detached from all the big resounding phrases, the feeling of duty . . . comes down to the pride, personal and collective, of excellent war workers. It's the ordinary feeling of the conscientious fellow who earns his pay honestly, who, knowing that he *has* to make war, prefers work that is 'well done' to work botched up, and who . . . finds intense personal satisfaction in the very accomplishment of his demanding labour. (*Le Crapouillot*, December 1917)

'What must be done'. Here is the key concept which gives structure to national feeling. To hold on daily, to go into the attack, these are so many necessities that are beyond questioning. You submit to them as to something inevitable, the inevitability of the war against which it would be pointless to struggle and of which the acceptance corresponded very closely to the mentality of a peasant army. And so, when one reads that the soldiers made war because they could not 'do otherwise', there should be no misunderstanding: it does not mean that that they had no reason to fight and to hold on, but precisely the opposite. The reasons for fighting, for continuing to hold on despite everything, were on the contrary so imperious that soldiers were obliged to submit without any possibility of escape. This submission to the war experienced as a 'trade' not freely chosen, far from indicating an absence of national feeling, is on the contrary proof of such feeling: indeed it constitutes its very heart.

This national feeling was built round a few simple ideas, voiced to a greater or lesser degree. But its very simplicity undoubtedly made it stronger and more unanimously shared. Without being highly exteriorised, it constituted a line of mental endurance on which the soldiers sustained themselves from the beginning of the war to its end, and if it appears not to have broken, it is because the fighting men always sensed, somewhat incoherently, why they could not do other than continue to hold the trenches. And so, even in the war's worst moments, the impossibility of causing the defeat of their own nation by collective weakness constituted a psychological barrier that nothing could overcome.

Conclusion

The image of the soldiers of the Great War was slow to acquire its final form in the French collective memory. During the conflict both press and literature presented the soldiers in a heroic light. The armistice of 11 November did not immediately mean the end of this style of depicting the men in the trenches, but the disappearance of 'eye-wash' and the troops' return home dealt it a perceptible blow. However, a version of the war which claimed to be 'realistic', of which Henri Barbusse's *Under Fire* is the most famous example, had already appeared during the course of the war.[1] This version ultimately engendered the now dominant image of the soldier of 1914–18. The fighting man of earlier legend, happy to mount an assault against a hated enemy and light-heartedly consenting to die for his country, was replaced in some accounts by someone who retreated hastily from his initial patriotism, indifferent to victory as to defeat, sometimes less hostile to the enemy than to his own officers, and finally wanting one thing only: to see the nightmare ended as quickly as possible, no matter what the cost. Both these versions of the soldier in the trenches should be discarded in favour of a more credible and more subtle image.

The soldiers' lack of interest in the day-to-day progress of the war is one of their more striking psychological traits. The progress of the war often remained outside their knowledge, particularly when its implications appeared less urgent or less directly linked to the vagaries of the French front. National life was also largely ignored, the war effort of the whole nation never being appreciated at its proper value. Little given to reflection on the war itself or on its consequences, the soldiers retained from these facts only those

---

1. Henri Barbusse, *Le Feu*, Paris, Flammarion, 1916; English edition, *Under Fire*, tr. W. Fitzwater Wray, London and Melbourne, Dent (Everyman Library), 1926, reprinted 1988.

which discredited a civilian population poisoned by the information it received. These factors help us understand the way soldiers plunged into the turmoil of war but remained indifferent both to its development and to its consequences; how soldiers were concerned exclusively with their own immediate world and the present moment.

Everyday life in particular held their attention, to the point that it became the trench newspapers' favourite topic. Descriptions of everyday existence concealing nothing of its harshness meant the recovery of undermined dignity and the avoidance of topics that were even more painful. These men lived in a perpetual distress which found an outlet in fascinated complacency regarding death and suffering, evoked sometimes with an irony that sought to contain danger, avert risk and overcome fear. This explains the value of moments of relaxation and the true worth of the bridges enabling soldiers to remain in communication with those whom they had to leave at home. Submitting to the ordeal of a prolonged separation, endlessly exposed to death, the combatants lived with their eyes turned towards their families for more than four years.

This did not prevent them from being exasperated by the attitude of the civilian population. Conscious of living in inhumane conditions, the soldiers felt justified in reproaching the non-combatants with their cowardice, their ignorance, their facile patriotism, their light-heartedness based on egotism and blindness. The combatants' reaction of rejection deepened as the war dragged on, and fed on the discredit with which the national press was viewed. Accused of misrepresenting the realities of the war and of lying about the troops' life as well as their state of mind, the distortions of the national press assaulted both their dignity and their future image. However, thanks to the ties created and sustained between the soldiers and their families, the trauma of separation between the rear and the front had only limited consequences.

The trench press highlighted the gap between what was felt during the ordeal and what was recalled afterwards. The importance of the rear in the eyes of the soldiers and their fascination with it, mixed with resentment, were largely concealed in accounts written later. Victory, the joy at returning alive and returning to civilian society, pushed into the background a resentment which was expressed forcefully at the time. The mechanism of an 'edifying' reconstruction was in operation, just as it was to operate in the discovery of that 'fraternity of the trenches' which the soldiers in fact encountered only quite rarely. As for the description of battle and its atrocities, there were many veterans who accorded it considerable importance because it gave them an opportunity to denounce the horror of war itself. The morbidity of the troops assumed a different significance, however: it had the power of exorcism in the face of unbearable fear. On many points there is thus a visible blurring between what the soldiers felt and expressed immediately and what they said about it later, although historiography has generally only retained the later accounts.

The analysis of the feeling of being part of the nation demands more important revisions. The soldiers' behaviour constantly reveals a sharpened sense of their dignity, of not having been the 'beasts of burden' sometimes described. A powerful assertion of identity has always been evident, together with very deep aspirations to comprehension and recognition. That the civilian population should be able to appreciate the sacrifices suffered for its sake was one of their most deeply rooted desires, and it is to this wish that the ambivalence of their perception of the rear relates. The civilian population stood accused, but it was this same group which was most highly valued by the men in the ranks. Their chagrin was nothing more than a reaction of resentment: resentment at not being written about, understood or appreciated on a scale matching their hardships, resentment at not meeting with the recognition which they regarded as their due. Such longings were never satisfied, could not be satisfied; but the resulting frustration was not sufficient to detach the soldiers from the rest of the national community, the links maintained with their families preventing any irreparable breach. The soldiers' aspirations betrayed above all their distress at being cut off from the nation to which they continued to be linked with powerful bonds. Cohesion was thus stronger than the destructive elements.

The strength of feeling of attachment to the nation as a whole, the need to defend it: the two matters are closely linked. The first entailed the second, and this is why the obligation to defend their nation was never seriously challenged by the soldiers. Among many other elements, hostility towards the enemy made its contribution: a measured hostility which did not exclude either respect for the adversary or the 'accommodations' of the front lines, but which was founded on a feeling of irreducible otherness. Except for a few very small minorities, the enemy never ceased to be an adversary to conquer.

To conquer: a key word. Until the very end, victory was an act of faith. The most serious military setbacks could never do more than defer the conclusion, without putting it fundamentally in question. This inward and irrational certainty was all the more securely rooted, in that defeat would have meant abandoning a defenceless nation and ground rendered more precious because comrades were buried in it. Those were unacceptable possibilities which set up a mental barrier of moral interdiction. The strongly felt obligation to 'do one's duty' and to do it 'to the very end' expressed the interiorisation of a simple but imperious necessity, that of defending one's threatened nation.

It is therefore impossible to understand the fighting men of 1914–18 without reference to national feeling. This formed the solid foundation of their mental world, and herein lies the explanation of their resistance over more than four years. More resolute than enthusiastic when they set out in August 1914, they were able to preserve a large part of their resolution until the end of the war. This does not mean that their determination was unassailable. The terrible realities of the front line, the Allied setbacks, the prolongation of the conflict, everything conspired to wear down the determination of their departure in 1914. But this determination diminished only slowly, and was never permanently breached. One cannot deny that the army sometimes came close to breaking-point during those final two years of war, but it is also true that that threshold was never crossed. National feeling constituted an indestructible barrier against the discouragement aroused by the trials of endless war. In this respect the attitude of the soldiers of 1914–18 was the test of the truth of national feeling, crowned with tragic success, for the entire French nation.

Bibliography

In the context of this study it is not our intention to offer an exhaustive bibliography of the First World War, or even of all aspects of the French army. Although it does not omit works of general interest, or those dealing with the background against which the soldiers operated, this bibliography concentrates on the fighting man himself, and above all on his psychological world.

I General Works on the War

Some studies of purely military aspects of the war are useful as working aids:

General F. GAMBIEZ and Colonel M. SUIRE, *Histoire de la première guerre mondiale 1914–1918*, Paris, Fayard, 1968, 2 vols
General L. KOELTZ, *La Guerre de 1914–1918, les opérations militaires*, Paris, Sirey, 1966
Service Historique des Armées, *Les Armées françaises dans la grande guerre*, Paris, Imprimerie Nationale, 1922–37, 10 vols
General Jean-Etienne VALLUY, *La Première Guerre mondiale (1914–1918)*, Paris, Larousse, 1968, 2 vols

Some classic general works:

Georges BONNEFOUS, *La Grande Guerre (1914–1918)*, Paris, PUF, 1957, vol.12
Jacques CHASTENET, *Histoire de la troisième République, vol.4: Jours inquiets et jours sanglants (1906–1918)*, Paris, Hachette, 1957
Pierre RENOUVIN, *La Crise européenne et la grande guerre (1904–1918)*, Paris, PUF, 'Peuples et civilisations' series, vol.19, 1962

(These three books have very little on the soldiers.)

Jean-Baptiste DUROSELLE, *La France et les Français, 1914–1920*, Paris, Editions Richelieu, 1972 (little on the fighting men but a few particularly pertinent lines on their innermost motivation)

Written in a very different tone, a work by three men who fought in the war, characteristic of the thinking of veterans:

André DUCASSE, Jacques MEYER, Gabriel PERREUX, *Vie et mort des Français, 1914–1918*, Paris, Hachette, 1959

Three works of synthesis illustrating the development of historiography since the inter-war period:

Henry BIDOU, *Histoire de la Grande Guerre*, Paris, Gallimard, 1939 (with virtually no mention of the fighting troops)

Marc FERRO, *La Grande Guerre (1914–1918)*, Paris, Gallimard, 'Idées' series, 1969. (The soldiers are dealt with here at some length. There is brief mention of the trench newspapers, with a few illustrative quotations.)

Pierre MIQUEL, *La Grande Guerre*, Paris, Fayard, 1983. (This work includes recent confirmation of historiography relevant to the outbreak of war and civilian experience during the war. The troops figure in it with particular reference to the 1917 mutinies, but without any fresh material.)

Five more recent publications provide extensive analysis of the combatant troops:

Jean-Jacques BECKER and Serge BERSTEIN, *Victoire et frustrations 1914–1929*, Paris, Seuil, 1990

Jay M. WINTER, *The Experience of World War One*, London, Macmillan, 1988

Les Sociétés européennes et la guerre de 1914–1918, published under the direction of Jean-Jacques Becker and Stéphane Audoin-Rouzeau, Centre d'Histoire de la France contemporaine, Université de Paris X–Nanterre, 1990

14–18: Mourir pour la Patrie, L'Histoire, no.107 (special number), 1988

II   Trench Newspapers

Despite their specific nature, the trench newspapers cannot be studied without reference to the national press of the period, if only because the former appeared, at least in part, in reaction against it. On the press during the Third Republic, the essential work is:

Claude BELLANGER, Jacques GODECHOT, Pierre GUIRAL, Fernand TERROU, *Histoire générale de la presse française, 3 vols, 1871–1940*, Paris, PUF, 1972 (with only a brief mention of the trench press, on p.439)

There is, however, a patriotic and eulogistic chapter by General Weygand in:

René de LIVOIS, *Histoire de la presse française, vol.2 (de 1881 à nos jours)*, Paris, Société Française du Livre, 1965, 2 vols.

Works devoted to the trench press are rare. Two collections of 'selected extracts' should be noted, both concentrating principally on the front-line papers' qualities of energy and patriotism:

Pierre CHAPELLE et Jean Germain DROUILLY, *Tous les journaux du front*, Paris, Berger-Levrault, 1915
Les Ecrivains de la tranchée, 1914–1918 (extraits des journaux du front), Paris, Berger-Levrault, 1920

For comparison:

F. BERTRAND, *La Presse francophone de tranchée au front belge 1914–1918*, Brussels, 1971

A German study of the French trench newspapers:

Entz WERNER, *Die französischen Feld und Schützenbrabenzeitungen während des Weltkrieges*, Frankfurt, Diesterweg, 1937 (a list of the principal titles with a few pages of comment)

A fundamental work on the British trench press:

John G. FULLER, *Troop Morale and Popular Culture in the British and Dominion Armies, 1914–1918*, Oxford, Clarendon Press, 1991

The most important study, in 1935, of the French trench press:

André CHARPENTIER, *Le livre d'or des journaux du front 1914–1918, feuilles bleu-horizon*, Paris, Editions des Journaux du Front, 1935. (This is above all a book in praise of the front-line press, identifying each newspaper and its editors. A pioneering work, it continues to be a very useful working tool despite its outdated perspective.)

Two short studies:

Marcel JEANJEAN, 'Les Journaux du front de 1914–1918', *Revue historique de l'Armée*, no.2, 1971, pp.110–20 (a revealing account of the higher command's intentions regarding the trench press)

Georges THURIOT-FRANCHI, *Les Journaux de tranchées*, Nevers, Imprimerie de la Nièvre, 1921 (illustrating both the qualities and limitations of the trench press, conditions of production, and content; very succinct)

III The Soldier's Surroundings: the Background
Civilians

The French soldiers cannot be studied in isolation. Still less can the home front be ignored, in view of its significance in the minds of the troops. However, only the most important works on this topic are listed:

Jean-Jacques BECKER, *Les Français dans la Grande guerre*, Paris, Laffont, 1980; English edition, *The Great War and the French People*, tr. Arnold Pomerans, Leamington Spa, Berg, 1986 (the essential work on the topic, particularly on national feeling in the civilian population)

——, La France en guerre, 1914–1918. La grande mutation, Paris, Editions Complexe, 1988

Alain JACOBZONE, *En Anjou, loin du front*, Maine et Loire, Davy, 1988 (a well-used local study)

Annie KRIEGEL, *Aux origines du communisme français (1914–1920), contribution à l'histoire du mouvement ouvrier français*, Paris, Mouton, 1964, 2 vols. (Sections 1 and 2 of Part I are indispensable in the study of the home front and the French worker movement during the war.)

Gabriel PERREUX, *La Vie quotidienne des civils en France pendant la Grande Guerre*, Paris, Hachette, 'La Vie quotidienne' series, 1966. (superficial, but with useful information on certain practical details)

Pierre RENOUVIN, 'L'Opinion publique en France pendant la guerre de 1914–1918', *Revue d'histoire diplomatique*, October–December 1970, pp.289–336 (an article of fundamental importance, extending beyond the setting of the civilian population to pose the question of the soldiers)

Françoise THÉBAUD, *La Femme au temps de la guerre de 14*, Paris, Stock, 1986

R. WALL and J. WINTER (eds), *The Upheaval of War. Family, Work and*

Welfare in Europe, 1914–1918, Cambridge, Cambridge University Press, 1988 (with several fundamental articles on French circumstances)
1914–1918 – l'autre front, studies collected by Patrick Fridenson, *Cahier du mouvement social no.2*, Les Editions Ouvrières, 1977

Two fundamental works on civilian attitudes at the outbreak of war:

Jean-Jacques BECKER, *1914: Comment les Français sont entrés dans la guerre*, Paris, Presses de la Fondation Nationale des Sciences Politiques, 1977 (see also below, section V)
Jean-Jacques BECKER and Annie KRIEGEL, *1914, la guerre et le mouvement ouvrier français*, Paris, Armand Colin, 'Kiosque' series, 1964

Command

Guy PEDRONCINI, *Pétain, général en chef (1917– 1918)*, Paris, PUF, 1974 (the basic work on problems of command in the last two years of the war)
——, *Pétain, le soldat et la gloire*, Paris, Perrin, 1989
——, 'Remarques sur la décision militaire en France pendant la guerre', *Revue d'histoire moderne et contemporaine*, vol.20, January–March 1973, pp.139–52 (very important for information on the general conditions experienced by the troops)

For placing command in a broader context:

William SERMAN, *Les Officiers français dans la nation (1848–1914)*, Paris, Aubier, 1982. (This study ends in 1914, but is very useful in defining the thinking of active service officers, of which certain traces can be seen in the trench press.)

IV Soldiers, in their own words
Combatants' Accounts

These are particularly numerous. The list given here is selective, noting only the most useful titles and including as many accounts as possible by soldiers from working-class backgrounds:

ALAIN (pseud. for Emile-Auguste CHARTIER), *Souvenirs de guerre*, Paris, Bartmann, 1937

——, *Mars ou la guerre jugée*, Paris, NRF, 1921

Jacques d'ARNOUX, *Paroles d'un revenant*, Paris, Plon, 1925

Henri BARBUSSE, *Le Feu*, Paris, Flammarion, 1916; English edition, *Under Fire*, tr. W. Fitzwater Wray, London and Melbourne, Dent (Everyman Library), 1926, reprinted 1988

Lucien BAROU, 'La Guerre de 1914–1918 à travers les témoignages de paysans foréziens', *Bulletin du Centre d'Histoire Régionale, Université de Saint-Etienne*, no.2, 1976, pp.13–36 (interesting for the social origins of the narrators, but with a distorted overall view)

Louis BARTHAS, *Carnets de guerre de Louis Barthas, tonnelier (1914–1918)*, Paris, Maspero, 'La Mémoire du peuple', 1978. (The author has rewritten his 'war notebooks' from diary notes written during the war. The audience addressed by the book now seems to have largely disappeared: Louis Barthas's anti-militarism takes the distortion of recall to extremes.)

Jean BERNIER, *La Percée*, Paris, Albin Michel, 1920

Marc BLOCH, *Souvenirs de guerre 1914–1915*, Cahiers des Annales, no.26, Paris, Armand Colin, 1969 (remarkable despite its brevity, particularly on certain aspects of the soldiers' mental attitudes)

Georges BONNET, *L'Ame du soldat*, Paris, Payot, 1917

Roger BOUTEFEU, *Les Camarades. Soldats français et allemands au combat 1914–1918*, Paris, Fayard, 1966. (Extracts from 600 unpublished accounts collected by the author, the outstanding work in this respect. However, as indicated by the picture of fraternisation on the cover, the overall perspective is often distorted.)

André BRIDOUX, *Souvenirs du temps des morts*, Paris, Albin Michel, 1930

Max BUTEAU, *Tenir. Récits de la vie des tranchées*, Paris, Plon, 1918

Paul CAZIN, *L'Humaniste à la guerre – Hauts de Meuse 1915*, Paris, Plon, 1920

Blaise CENDRARS, *La Main coupée*, Paris, Denoel, 1946. (As far as I know, this does not appear in any other bibliography; yet it is a remarkable account, even though set on the borders of dreams and reality. It evokes the setting of volunteers posted to the legion: fascinating on all aspects of national feeling.)

Pierre CHAINE, *Les Mémoires d'un rat*, Paris, A l'Oeuvre, 1917

Gabriel CHEVALLIER, *La Peur*, Paris, Stock, 1930

Maurice CONSTANTIN-WEYER, *La Salamandre*, Paris, Les Etincelles, 'Témoignages de combattants français' series, no.3, 1930

Michel DANIEL, *Ier Régiment de marche de zouaves. Un caporal et son escouade. Tous les jours du 20 mars 1916 au 14 juillet 1918*, La Mémoire de 14–18 en Languedoc, FAOL, no place of publication, undated (facsimile reproduction, post-1976, of a war notebook rewritten from daily contemporaneous notes)

Max DEAUVILLE, *Jusqu'à l'Yser*, Paris, Calmann-Lévy, 1917

——, *La boue des Flandres*, Paris, Valois, 1930

Bibliography

Roland DORGELÈS, *Les Croix de bois*, Paris, Albin Michel, 1919. (Apart from Barbusse, *Le Feu*, this is undoubtedly the best-known work. It has some obvious errors, but various pertinent comments on behaviour and attitudes.)

André DUCASSE, *La Guerre racontée par les combattants. Anthologie des écrivains du front*, Paris, Flammarion, 1932, 2 vols (a well-ordered selection providing contact with the literature of the front line)

Georges DUHAMEL, *Civilisation 1914–1917*, Paris, Mercure de France, 1918
——, *Vie des martyrs 1914–1916*, Paris, Mercure de France, 1917

Jean GALTIER-BOISSIÈRE, *La Fleur au fusil*, Paris, Baudinière, 1928
——, *En rase campagne, 1914. Un hiver à Souchez, 1915–1916*, Paris, Berger-Levrault, 1917
(These books by Galtier-Boissière are remarkable works, from which many extracts – of great value in studying attitudes – appeared in *Le Crapouillot* before being published in book form.)

Marcel GAZON, *Mémoire des deux guerres. Reportage par un engagé volontaire 14–18 au 4e régiment de zouaves et résistant 39–45*, Paris, La Pensée Universelle, 1980 (an account by a soldier of rural background who became a schoolteacher after the war, based on a notebook and letters written during the war)

Maurice GENEVOIX, *Ceux de 1914*, Paris, Flammarion, 1950

André MAGINOT, *Carnets de patrouille*, Paris, Féd. Nle A. Maginot, 1964 (interesting on national sentiment)

Alain PREVOST and Ephraim GRENADOU, *Grenadou, paysan français*, Paris, Seuil, 1966 (the valuable account of a peasant, although written long after the event; only one part on the war period)

Albert JAMET, *La Guerre vue par un paysan*, Paris, Albin Michel, 1931 (a unique work, for the period: a peasant's account of the war, unfortunately 'improved' by the editor)

Journal de guerre d'un ouvrier creusotin, Clamecy, SARL Civry, 'L'Oeil écorché' series, 1980. (The account of a telephonist, later an artillery observer. An untouched text, valuable particularly for the social background of the author, who remains unidentified.)

Raymond JUBERT, *Mars-Avril-Mai 1916. Verdun* (introduction by Gérard Canini), Nancy, Presses Universitaires de Nancy (an interesting reissue of a posthumous work first published in 1918)

Fernand LAPONCE, *Journal de marche d'un artilleur de campagne, 1ère période: la guerre de position 1915–1917; 2ème période: la guerre de mouvement 1918–1919*, Bois Colombes, chez l'auteur, 1971, 2 vols (the diary, rewritten after the war, of an artillery sergeant)

Paul LINTIER, *Avec une batterie de 75. Le tube 1233. Souvenirs d'un chef de pièce (1915–1916)*, Paris, Plon, 1917

Léopold NOÉ, *Nous étions ennemis sans savoir pourquoi ni comment*, no place of publication, La Mémoire de 14–18 en Languedoc, no.3, FAOL,

1980. (Notebook of a vine grower, a soldier in the ranks of the same regiment as Louis Barthas. His notes written on the spot were rewritten after the war and unfortunately 'improved' by the editor.)

Jules ROMAINS, *Prélude à Verdun*, Paris, Flammarion, 1938

——, *Verdun*, Paris, Flammarion, 1938 (a civilian's view, but very accurate)

Fernand TAILHADES, *Ils m'appelaient tout le temps 'camarade'*, no place of publication, La Mémoire de 14–18 en Languedoc, no.2, FAOL, 1980 (account of a soldier in the ranks, a sheepskin worker from Mazamet)

Jean-Louis TALMARD, *Pages de guerre d'un paysan, 1914–1918*, Lyons, Vitte, 1971 (a valuable peasant account written in 1918 from his day-to-day notes)

Jérome and Jean THARAUD, *Une relève*, Paris, Plon, 1924

André THERIVE, *Frères d'armes*, Paris, Les Etincelles, 'Témoignages de combattants français' series, no.1, 1930

Louis THOMAS, *La gloire*, Paris, Les Etincelles, 'Témoignages de combattants français' series, no.4, 1930

Related to combatants' eye-witness accounts

A number of works add to combatants' eye-witness narratives and clarify their specific details:

Jean AUGÉE, *L'Image du combattant dans le roman de guerre français et allemand (1914–1918)*, roneoed university doctoral thesis, Paris, Sorbonne, 1955. (presented as a memoir, but gives little further insight into the soldier in the trenches)

Gérard CANINI (ed.), *Mémoire de la Grande Guerre. Témoins et témoignages*, Nancy, Presses Universitaires de Nancy, 1989 (a series of recent studies)

Geneviève COLIN and Jean-Jacques BECKER, 'Les Ecrivains, la guerre de 1914 et l'opinion publique', *Relations internationales*, no.24, 1980, pp.425–42 (interesting details on writers of the home front as well as the front line, and fresh comments on 'eye-wash')

Jean Norton CRU, *Du témoignage*, Paris, Gallimard, 1930

——, *Témoins. Essai d'analyse et de critique des souvenirs de combattants édités en français de 1915 à 1928*, Paris, Les Etincelles, 1929. (This remains the essential work, with its analysis of 300 titles. Very valuable in seeking out inaccurate reporting; but the author, over-anxious to denounce the war and to establish the notion of a total absence of soldiers' hostility towards the enemy, finally arrives at a dogmatic and simplistic image of the fighting man.)

Antoine PROST (*Les Anciens Combattants et la société française 1914–1939*, Paris, Presses de la Fondation Nationale des Sciences Politiques, 1977, 3 vols. (The beginning of vol.3, *Idéologies*, is essential reading on this topic.)

Bibliography

Maurice RIEUNEAU, *Guerre et révolution dans le roman français de 1919 à 1939*, Paris, Klinksieck, 1974 (very useful on the war writers)

Eye-witness accounts

This list aims to include the greatest possible number of eye-witness accounts, written at the time of the event and not rewritten later. Such narratives are more numerous than might be expected, and are obviously a very valuable source. The principal obstacle, when such accounts have not been published in book form, lies in the difficulty of access to the scattered journals in which they appeared.

Books

André BENOIT, *Trois mois de guerre au jour le jour (1914), Journal d'un fantassin*, Paris, Vuibert, 1967 (the notebook, written up daily, of a platoon commander who was unfortunate in being taken prisoner on 3 November 1914)

Georges BERNANOS, *Correspondance*, Paris, Plon, vol.1 (1904–1934) and vol.3. (Bernanos was a machine-gunner and liaison officer with the 6th Dragoons. The letters written during the war are of some interest, but the extent to which the author was typical is obviously limited.)

Antoine BIEISSE and Paul GARBISSOU, *Plus d'espoir, il faut mourir ici!* no place of publication, La Mémoire de 14–18 en Languedoc, no.5, FAOL, 1982 (the notebooks of two Languedoc soldiers in the ranks, killed in 1914)

Roland CHABERT, *Printemps aux tranchées. Notes de campagne de Joseph Astier, soldat de la grande guerre. 6 mars–1er juillet 1916*, Lyons, Elie Bellier, 1982. (The war notebook of a peasant soldier in the ranks, and therefore of great interest. Unfortunately put into 'correct' French by the editor.)

Henri DESAGNEUX, *Journal de guerre 14–18*, Paris, Denoel, 1971. (The war notebook, unrevised and including contemporary press-cuttings, of an infantry captain. An outstanding eye-witness account by a front-line officer.)

Jean-François KAHN, *Journal de guerre d'un juif patriote (1914–1918)*, Paris, J.C. Simoen, 1978 (the diary of a young barrister of the Jewish bourgeoisie from eastern France, serving with the medical service and therefore little exposed to danger, but interesting for its strength of patriotism and hatred of the enemy)

Maurice LAURENTIN, *Carnets d'un fantassin de 1914*, Paris, Arthaud, 1965. (The author, an infantry lieutenant, architect and designer, wrote two books from his war notebooks; the notebooks are presented here as an integral unit.)

Bibliography

Eugène LEMERCIER, *Lettres d'un soldat, août 1914–avril 1915*, Paris, Chapelot, 1916

Jacques LOVIE, *Poilus savoyards (1913–1918)*, Monmélian, 1981 (a remarkable collection of letters from a Savoy peasant family, presented almost uncut, but unfortunately with very little comment)

Roger MARTIN DU GARD, *Correspondance générale*, vol.2, *1914–1918*, Paris, Gallimard (a very sensitive eye-witness account by a 'service' combatant)

Paul REYBAUT, *Correspondance de guerre d'un rural (1914–1917)*, Paris, Institut d'ethnologie, 1974 (5 microfiches of 60 reproductions). (The letters of François-Victor André, olive-grower in the Alpes-Maritimes, who was soon taken prisoner. A very valuable document.)

Roger SARGOS, *Témoignage 1914–1918 d'un officier forestier*, Bordeaux, 1967, 3 vols (posthumous work of a lieutenant who became a battalion commander, consisting chiefly of letters and extracts from a personal diary written during the war, without any attempt at embellishment)

Two remarkable officers' notebooks, recently discovered:

Pierre PETIT, *Souvenirs de guerre, 1 août 1914–15 octobre 1915*, Paris, Académie Européenne du Livre, 1990, 3 vols

Benjamin SIMONET, *Franchise militaire. De la bataille des frontières aux combats de Champagne, 1914–1918*, Paris, Gallimard, 1986

Pacifist correspondence addressed to the socialist Deputy Brizon in 1916:

Nous crions grâce. 154 lettres pacifistes, juin–novembre 1916, introduction by Thierry Bonzon and Jean-Louis Robert, Paris, Editions Ouvrières, 1989

Periodicals

Periodicals (generally local magazines) sometimes publish noteworthy eye-witness accounts, such as the following:

Clément d'ANDURAIN, 'Carnet de route du début de la Grande Guerre (du 4 août à la fin de l'année 1914) d'un sergent du 142e territorial', *Revue régionaliste des Pyrénées*, no.231–2, 1981, pp.82–95; no.233–4, 1982, pp.67–91 (excellent)

'Août 1914. Lettres anonymes d'un jeune lieutenant rouergat à ses parents', *Revue du Rouergue*, no.71, July–September 1964, pp.271–80 (interesting eye-witness account by a patriotic and active Christian lieutenant)

General J. BLANCHARD, 'Les Dardanelles à la pointe de l'Europe, le débarquement (25–30 Avril 1915). Le journal de marche du lieutenant Marcel

Blanchard', *Revue historique des Armées*, no.2, 1981, pp.129–66 (particularly interesting as a means of comparison with the French front)

Jean-Richard BLOCH, 'Lettres 1914–1918', *Europe*, no.135–6, March–April 1957, pp.178–98; no.137, May 1957, pp.105–29; no.138, June 1957, pp.102–32; no.139–40, July–August 1957, pp.177–98; no.141, September 1957, pp.118–49; no.142–3, October–November 1957, pp.297–320 (letters from Lieutenant Jean-Richard Bloch, writer and socialist, who became a communist after the war)

General F. BUTTNER, 'Les Carnets du commandant Cano (1914–1915)', *Carnet de la Sabretache*, no.52, 1980, pp.47–50 (a personal diary showing that a battalion commander could be closer to his men than generally realised)

Ernest CARAYON, 'Souvenirs de guerre: les premiers combats de 1914. Textes recueillis et annotés par son neveu', *Revue du Tarn*, no.38, 1965, pp.157–72 (the interesting campaign diary of a soldier in the ranks, a tailor by trade)

'Carnets de route d'un officier lorrain, le capitaine Edouard de Warren, dans les combats en Lorraine de l'automne 1914', *Le Pays lorrain*, no.4, 1978, pp.179–93

Elie CHAMARD, 'Carnet de route d'un brancardier du 77e d'infanterie aux gaz asphyxiants de l'Yser (2 avril–4 mai 1915)', *Société des Sciences, Lettres et Beaux-arts de Cholet et de sa Région*, 1967, pp.102–6

Jacques CLÉMENS, 'Le baptême du feu d'un socialiste, Renaud Jean (2 août–13 septembre 1914)', *Les Cahiers du Bazadais*, no.44, 1979, pp.21–41 (a mixture of anti-militarism, verbal anti-patriotism, and distress at defeat)

——'Textes et documents: une lettre d'Henri Barbusse à un poilu agenais en 1916', *Revue de l'Agenais*, no.4, 1971, pp.309–12 (very short, but interesting on the problem of national feeling)

Capitaine DELACROIX, 'La compagnie 7/3 du Génie à Fontenoy-sur-l'Aisne en septembre 1914, extrait du carnet de route du capitaine Delacroix', *Vauban*, no.25, November 1969, pp.24–8

'Extrait du journal de guerre du sergent Paul Gourdant, du 1er au 26 août 1914', *Bulletin de la Société des Amis de Vienne*, no.74, fasc.4, 1979, pp.12–26

René GANDILHON, 'Lettres de soldats écrites pendant la guerre de 1914–1918', *Mémoires de la Société d'Agriculture, Commerce, Sciences et Arts du Département de la Marne*, vol.92, 1977, pp.287–304 (very interesting letters from wards of the National Assistance Board)

Suzanne JOUGUELET, 'Un pacifiste dans la grande guerre – les lettres de Roger Martin du Gard de 1914–1918', *Revue de la Bibliothèque Nationale*, no.2, December 1981, pp.99–106 (very cursory but accurate on the relationship between national feeling and pacifism)

André MARSAT (Monseigneur), 'Les Carnets de guerre (1915-1919) de Mgr

Roserot de Melun', *Bulletin mensuel de la Société d'Agriculture, Sciences et Arts et Belles Lettres du Département de l'Aube*, no.6, June 1969, pp.91–6 (the brief but unusual eye-witness account of a Carthusian priest who was a front-line soldier)

Charles PÉGUY, 'Quelques lettres inédites de guerre', *Amitiés Charles Péguy*, no.80, 1960, pp.5–8 (five very short letters, from 16 to 26 August 1914, of little interest despite the writer's fame)

Gratien RIGAUD, 'Lettre du 2 août 1914', *Revue du Rouergue*, no.91, 1969, pp.325–7. (A long letter from a soldier of rural background, illustrating very clearly Jean-Jacques Becker's theory on the departure to war. Valuable for its national sentiment and sense of duty.)

V   Studies of the Soldier in the Ranks

Methodology

Three methodological articles are particularly valuable for the history of attitudes and the use of sources:

Jean-Noel JEANNENAY, 'Les Archives de la commission de contrôle postal aux armées – 1916–1918, *Revue d'histoire moderne et contemporaine*, vol.15, January–March 1968, pp.209–33 (a valuable source for the contemporary history of opinion and attitudes)

Jean NICOT, 'L'Histoire de la première guerre mondiale: l'apport des archives de l'armée', *Revue d'histoire moderne et contemporaine*, vol.15, July–September 1968, pp.535–42

Pierre RENOUVIN, 'L'Etude historique de l'opinion publique', *Revue des travaux de l'Académie des Sciences Morales et Politiques*, 4th series, 1st session, 1968, pp.123–43

Behaviour and attitudes

Several works offer useful surveys:

Jean-Jacques BECKER, *1914. Comment les français sont entrés dans la guerre*, Paris, Presses de la Fondation Nationale des Sciences Politiques, 1977 (conclusive on soldiers' attitudes in the first days of August 1914)

Louis HUOT and Paul VOIVENEL, *La Psychologie du soldat*, Paris, La Renaissance du livre, 1918 (account by two doctors, not without interest)

Jacques MEYER, *La Vie quotidienne des soldats pendant la Grande Guerre*,

Paris, Hachette, 1967 (a survey full of precise observations, combining personal memoirs and quotations from combatants' writings)

Antoine PROST, *Les Anciens Combattants et la société française*, 3 vols (a very important analysis)

On attitudes at specific moments of the war:

General F. GAMBIEZ, 'Le Combattant de 1918', *Revue historique de l'armée*, no.4, 1968, pp.7–16 (a militaristic tone, but with accurate conclusions)

Jacques MEYER, Vie et mort du soldat de Verdun, in *Verdun 1916, Actes du Colloque International sur la Bataille de Verdun, 1975*, Verdun, 1976, pp.187–95

Jean NICOT, 'Psychologie du combattant français de 1918', *Revue historique de l'armée*, no.2, 1972, pp.61–74. (This confirms the extreme weariness of May, June and, above all, July 1918, without collapse of national feeling.)

On daily life, in conjunction with attitudes at specific moments of the war:

Gérard CANINI, *Combattre à Verdun. Vie et souffrances quotidiennes du soldat, 1916–1917*, Nancy, Presses Universitaires de Nancy, 1988

On the attitudes of particular groups of soldiers:

Roland ANDREANI, *Armée et nation en Languedoc méditerranéen (1905–1914)*, Thèse de 3ème cycle, Montpellier III, 1974 (less closely concerned with our subject, but with some interesting comments on national sentiment in Languedoc at the beginning of the war)

Annick COCHET, 'Les Paysans sur le front en 1916', *Bulletin du Centre d'Histoire de la France Contemporaine*, no.3, 1982, pp.37–48 (the only study of peasants, based on postal censorship archives)

Jules MAURIN, *Armée-Guerre-Société. Soldats languedociens (1889–1919)*, Paris, Sorbonne, 1982. (The final section, based on letters and personal diaries, is the most valuable for the study of attitudes.)

——, 'Le combattant lozérien de la classe 1907 lors de la 1ère guerre mondiale', *Revue d'histoire moderne et contemporaine*, vol.20, January–March 1973, pp.124–38

On Catholics and mobilised members of the church:

Jacques FONTANA, *Les Catholiques français pendant la Grande Guerre*, Paris, Cerf, 1990

On troops from non-metropolitan France:

Bibliography

Gilbert MEYNIER, 'Les Algériens en France 1914–1918', *Revue d'histoire maghrébine*, no.5, 1976, pp.47–58

——, 'Le Problème du loyalisme des Algériens dans l'armée française (1914–1918)', *Bulletin de la Société d'Histoire Moderne*, no.10, 1981, pp.2–8

However, the most important study of troops from non-metropolitan France is:

Marc MICHEL, *L'Appel à l'Afrique. Contributions et réactions à l'effort de guerre en AOF 1914–1919*, Paris, Sorbonne, 1982

More specifically, on problems of morale (also covered in the works cited above):

Annick COCHET, *L'Opinion et le moral des soldats en 1916, d'après les archives du contrôle postal*, doctoral thesis under the supervision of Jean-Jacques Becker, Paris X–Nanterre, 2 vols, 1986 (an essential thesis, based on the postal censorship archives)

J.P. DEVOS and P. WAKSMAN, 'Le Moral à la 3ème armée en 1918 d'après les archives de la justice militaire et du contrôle postal', *Revue internationale d'histoire militaire*, no.37, 1977, pp.89–107 (confirming, despite weariness, hostility to the enemy and the feeling of duty)

David Englander, 'The French Soldier, 1914–18', *French History*, no.1 (1987).

Patrick FACON and Jean NICOT, 'La Crise du moral en 1917 dans l'armée et la nation d'après la commission du contrôle postal de Belfort', in *Actes du 103ème Congrès des Sociétés Savantes, Nancy–Metz, 1978, Section histoire moderne et contemporaine*, Paris, 1979, vol.1, pp.277–93 (making possible a study combining the home front and the front line)

Guy PEDRONCINI, 'Le Moral de l'armée française en 1916', in *Verdun 1916, Actes du Colloque International sur la bataille de Verdun, 1975*, Verdun 1976, pp.159–74. (Important article on individual or collective lapses. Also, thanks to the archives of the postal and military command censorship, it permits an accurate study of attitudes in 1916: it was at the end of that year that the factors behind the crisis of 1917 became established.)

The study of French troop morale in combat outside their own country suggests possible comparisons. There are two significant surveys:

Patrick FACON, *Le 12e corps français en Italie (novembre 1917–novembre 1918). Une étude du moral*, Mémoire de maîtrise, Université de Paris X–Nanterre, 1973

——, 'La Crise du moral en 1917 à l'armée française d'Orient', *Revue historique des armées*, no.4, 1977, pp.93–114

Problems of insubordination:

Guy PEDRONCINI, *Les Mutineries de 1917*, Paris, PUF, 1967 (the essential study)
——, 'Indiscipline et mutineries dans l'armée française en 1917', *Forces armées françaises*, no.11, 1973, pp.56–61
——, 'La Justice militaire et l'affaire des quatre caporaux de Souain (mars 1915–mars 1934)', *Revue historique de l'armée*, no.2, 1973, pp.59–69
——, 'Les Cours martiales pendant la Grande Guerre', *Revue historique*, no.512, October–December 1974, pp.393–408

A point of view diametrically opposed to that of Guy Pedroncini:

Gilbert MEYNIER, 'Pour l'exemple, un sur dix! Les décimations en 1914', *Politique aujourd'hui*, January–February 1976, pp.55–70 (asserting the truth of the decimations and attacking the reliability of military institutional archives)

On the same lines:

P. DURAND, *Vincent Moulia, les pelotons du général Pétain*, Paris, Ramsay, 1978 (the story of a corporal, mistakenly condemned, who escaped; very harsh concerning military justice)

Also worth consulting:

Annie KRIEGEL, *Aux origines du communisme français (1914–1920)*. (Chapter 6 in Part I deals with the mutinies.)

For a fresh overall view of the problem and the questions it raises:

Leonard V. SMITH, *Command Authority in the French Army, 1914–1918. The Case of the 5e Division d'Infanterie*, Doctoral thesis, Columbia University, 1990

From soldiers to ex-soldiers:

Antoine PROST, 'Combattants et politiciens. Le discours mythologique sur la politique entre les deux guerres', *Le Mouvement social*, no.85, October–December 1973, pp.117–54 (particularly important on the methodological approach)

Bibliography

———, *Les Anciens Combattants et la société française 1914–1939*, 3 vols, 1977. (On veterans' history, sociology and ideology. The definitive work on the veterans.)

René RÉMOND, 'Les Anciens Combattants et la politique', *Revue française de science politique*, vol.5, no.2, April–June 1955, pp.267–90

For a brief survey:

Antoine PROST, *Les Anciens Combattants*, Paris, Gallimard/Julliard, 'Archives' series, 1977; English edition, *Veterans of the Great War*, tr. Helen McPhail, Oxford and Providence, Berg, 1992, 'Legacy of the Great War' series

On the cultural impact of front-line experience:

Annette BECKER, *Les Monuments aux morts: mémoire de la Grande Guerre*, Paris, Errance, 1988 (the most sensitive work on French war memorials)

George L. MOSSE, *Fallen Soldiers. Reshaping the Memory of the World Wars*, Oxford, Oxford University Press, 1990 (a particularly stimulating study, equally relevant to French circumstances)

Jean-François SIRINELLI, *Génération intellectuelle. Khâgneux et normaliens dans l'entre-deux-guerres*, Paris, Fayard, 1988, (a fundamental study of pacifism in intellectual circles in the inter-war years)

Index

Books of Related Interest Published by Berg

Jean-Jacques Becker, *The Great War and the French People*

Wilhelm Deist (ed.), *The German Military in the Age of Total War*

John E. Godfrey, *Capitalism at War. Industrial Policy and Bureaucracy in France, 1914–1918*

Jürgen Kocka, *Facing Total War: German Society 1914–1918*

Gerd Krumeich, *Armaments and Politics in France on the Eve of the First World War*

Michael Scriven and Peter Wagstaff (eds), *War and Society in Twentieth-Century France*

Bernard Waites, *A Class Society at War. England 1914–1918*

In the Wake of War

'Les Anciens Combattants' and French Society
1914–1939

Antoine Prost

Eight million Frenchmen served in the Great War. This path-breaking study examines their politics and social situation within French society in the interwar years. The author provides the authoritative account of the veterans and their associations, which spanned the gamut of French politics. Above all he shows conclusively that veterans' patriotism, while profoundly held, was an expression of their commitment to civic rather than military virtues and values. Indeed, the didactic, pacifist intent of much of their commemorative and public work in the interwar period distinguishes their outlook and aspirations from those of most other European veterans' organisations. The author has prepared a new introduction especially for this English edition.

Antoine Prost is Professor of History at the University of Paris I.

July 1992
256pp
0 85496 672 2 (cloth)
0 85496 337 5 (paper)

The French Home Front 1914–1918

Edited by
Patrick Fridenson

Translated by Bruce Little

During the First World War, French citizens accepted national union on the home front as a necessary act of self-defence, but not without a considerable degree of ambivalence. At the political level, this union altered the balance of forces by improving the position of the Right, destroying the identity of the Radical party and creating the means by which the Socialist party first had access to power. However, what makes this study exceptionally important is that beyond the sphere of party politics it also deals with the industrial aspects of French wartime history. Industrial mobilisation was the force behind the *union sacrée*, but it also concealed deep conflicts of interest. While businessmen developed large corporations, new industries and scientific management, and reluctantly cooperated with an ever-expanding state, rank-and-file workers accepted concepts of productivism but rejected the sacrifices imposed on them. Their complaints eventually surfaced in the form of open resistance. The subsequent attempt on the part of management to repress the worker's movement led to a stalemate on the home front at the end of the war.

Patrick Fridenson is at the Centre de reserches historiques, Ecole des hautes études en sciences sociales, Paris.

July 1992
256pp
0 85496 693 5 (cloth)
0 85496 770 2 (paper)